BEYOND THE SOCIOLOGY OF KNOWLEDGE

An Introduction and a Development

Kurt H. Wolff

UNIVERSITY
PRESS OF
AMERICA

LANHAM • NEW YORK • LONDON

Copyright © 1983 by

University Press of America,™ Inc.

4720 Boston Way
Lanham, MD 20706

3 Henrietta Street
London WC2E 8LU England

Copyright © 1974 by
John Wiley & Sons, Inc.
as *TRYING SOCIOLOGY*

Present edition consists of selected revised chapters
from *Trying Sociology* and additional new material.

Library of Congress Cataloging in Publication Data

Wolff, Kurt H., 1912-
    Beyond the sociology of knowledge.

    Previous ed. published as: Trying sociology. 1974.
    Includes bibliographies and index.
    1. Sociology.   2. Sociology of knowledge.
3. Civilization, Modern—1950-   . I. Title.
HM24.W65   1983   301   83-14774
ISBN 0-8191-3506-2 (alk. paper)
ISBN 0-8191-3507-0 (pbk. : alk. paper)

To My Fellow Students

CONTENTS

Foreword

BEYOND
THE SOCIOLOGY
OF KNOWLEDGE
SURRENDER

I. Beyond

Part I goes beyond the sociology of knowledge developed in Part II. It confronts some essential features of this sociology of knowledge: what today it is to be an intellectual; evil; history; a social science informed by man's historicity and dualism.

The central question of the first chapter, "The Intellectual: Between Culture and Politics," is what I can responsibly mean, at this time in our history, by an intellectual. Although most of the specific references are to the United States, this question, as well as other matters discussed or alluded to, applies to contemporary industrialized society in general. Some passages, especially those on anti-intellectualism, are polemical; they debunk sloppiness or hypocrisy, and the sharpest deal with certain colleagues at institutions of higher learning (typified, not personally known colleagues), above all fellow social scientists who accommodate themselves to the inanities and comforts of holding a job, which sometimes is glamorous or even powerful. The chapter, which is dedicated to Herbert Marcuse, polemicizes against his detractors, whose ammunition is usually more ideological than analytical. Finally, it addresses the relation between human and political radicalism, that is, its variant indicated in the title: culture and politics. The paper is an outgrowth of the sixties, whose essential movements—student, black, woman—pervade it far more than explicit references to them indicate. It thus is historical, but of more than historical interest by virtue of the questions it asks, no matter that they arise at a given place and time. Of particular relevance for the overall thrust of this book are the oblique references to "surrender," by which the author understands cognitive love characterized by the most immediate feasible contact with something or somebody, identification with it and with its experience, total involvement in which "everything" is pertinent, and the maximally practicable suspension of received notion: here there is the "advocacy of the maximum suspension of received notions" and of the social scientist's taking "as little for granted as he [she] can manage"; for this is the time in human history in which "we have nothing to begin with but ourselves."

The second chapter, "Sociology and Evil," presents a view of social science, especially sociology, that is critical of extant varieties of both sociology and society. This view sees the inevitable presence of nominalist *and* realist, specifically scientific *and* existential, elements in research, even though the emphasis in less than maximal or optimal research may be on one or the other; and it argues the distinction and the relation between scientific and existential truth. The word "surrender" occurs no more than in the first chapter, but the reference is even more distinct: there is, among other things, the "suspension of the world" as "an extraordinary experience, in which the whole being, not only the cognitive faculty, is at stake."

The second half of the third chapter, "Sociology and History; Theory and Practice," presents the distinction theoretical-practical, which is applied to the very structure of Chapter 4; this distinction is a variant of the scientific-existential dichotomy stressed in the preceding essay on evil. In "Sociology and History," this distinction is connected with different characteristics of historiography and sociology, characteristics which are partly clarified, partly corrected in the next chapter, on man's historicity and dualism: such systematic or theoretical contrasts as theoretical-practical, or nomothetic-idiographic, or others yet, do not coincide with differences among disciplines—between sociology and historiography, for instance—for all of them have those characteristics among their elements; the contrasts are ideal-typical, a matter of emphasis or aim. And indeed, despite the insistence on sociology, in contrast to historiography, as theoretical, the major impetus of the chapter is to drive home its *practical* aspect. The semicolon in the title is to suggest the complexity of aspect and contrast; a colon would have too bluntly, indeed misleadingly, declared sociology theoretical and history (that is, historiography) practical.

Thinking as an example of an atemporal activity points to a quality not only of the extraordinary experience (surrender) of Chapter 2 but to a feature common to all situations in which we forget time because not time but logic, or reason, which applies atemporal standards of judgment, is the judge. This atemporality, which is shared by love, anxiety, solitude (Chapter 4), meditation, creation (Chapter 2), is a feature of the focused attention or absorption common to all these otherwise heterogeneous states or activities.

"Man's Historicity and Dualism," Chapter 4, is, among other things, an attentive reading of Hannah Arendt's *The Human Condition*. Although selective, in part admittedly so, it means to be a meeting with the book, thus with its author, her reader and the reader's world themselves, a meeting which the reader is communicating to the fellow inhabitants of this world. With all its analysis, thus, this essay is predominantly practical, as made explicit in its very structure. Its theme, announced in its title and analyzed in terms of freedom, nonsovereignty, and necessity, anticipates what will later, in the developing conceptualization of "surrender-and-catch," enter as the notion of "man as a mixed phenomenon," a notion (though not yet the term) here shown also in its consequences for conception and practice of the social sciences — the subtitle ("significance for sociology") suggests that this is a major concern. To repeat: despite — better still, *in* — its furious analyzing, this is a rhetorical, practical piece, perhaps weightier than the other critical pieces on sociology found in Part II of this volume, on the sociology of knowledge.

Part I goes beyond the sociology of knowledge by its themes and by the traces of the concept of surrender, found here and there in the four chapters which make it up. This emergence will become more distinct in the later chapters of Part II and be explicitly confronted in III.

II. The Sociology of Knowledge

Part II has a more articulate and articulated place in this book than what precedes and follows it. It is the longest part. It spans the author's work from fairly early to fairly late; only Part III, that is Chapter 11, is (considerably) later. The chapters, written between the early forties and the early seventies, necessarily reflect historical and biographical circumstances and changes — among the latter, notably the author's attitude toward "mainstream" sociology in the United States, from eagerly learning about it to becoming critical. The chapters, incidentally, also present two important contributors to the sociology of knowledge who are less well known than they deserve: Arthur Child (Chapter 7) and Ernst Grünwald (10). The unifying thrust of Part II points to a sociology of knowledge of great affinity to "surrender-and-catch," an affinity which is explicated in the concluding Part III. Readers may want to consider Part III to perceive this thrust more clearly, before they get into II.

The six chapters of Part II are arranged in chronological order (except for Chapter 8 which, though much later than 7, supplements it). The first, "The

Sociology of Knowledge: Emphasis on an Empirical Attitude," shows the influence of both Karl Mannheim, under which the author studied, and the "relatively natural *Weltanschauung*" of American social science: the term "metaphysical" is used if not pejoratively at least residually, without being analyzed even though the whole paper is a plea for an "empirical" attitude, that is, for postponing theoretical closure until the subject matter is investigated more thoroughly than is customary in the "speculative" attitude. It also urges (n. 18) that the use of terms be specified in case of ambiguity, a recommendation developed in the next chapter into the concept of the unique. There also is the recommendation of a subject matter far broader than knowledge itself. The notion of central attitude will be applied in Chapter 6 also to culture, personality, and intellectual product and will develop, much later, into identification as a characteristic of surrender. The distinction between immanent and sociological interpretation will shift emphasis in the next two chapters in favor of both of them as indispensable for maximum understanding. The quotation from Hofmansthal, here used to convey the "artistic attitude" will be used later to analyze surrender.[1]

In the last section of Chapter 5, there is a list of a large number of research complexes as if anticipating what was to become a matter of self-conscious methodology: the postponement of hypotheses until the imagination could extend to a maximum number of possibly pertinent candidates for the study at hand; cf. the considerably later Chapter 2 above.

Like much of the author's work from the beginning, Chapter 6, "The Unique and the General: Toward a Philosophy of Sociology," shows its Mannheimian provenience; it also shows, as do other early pieces, including the preceding chapter, his eagerness to be "properly scientific." The variant of the previously made distinction between immanent (intrinsic) and transcendent (extrinsic) interpretation here leads to the epistemological question of how, given the possibility of experiencing the "unique," understanding the other—somebody or something—can theoretically be accounted for. The received distinction between scientific and epistemological concerns is questioned, which by hindsight can be seen as the beginning of two aspects of "surrender": the suspension of received notions and the conviction that understanding (later the "catch") cannot exhaust experience ("surrender"). The advocacy of "greater scientific concern with the unique" will later be radicalized into the idea of surrender entailing the catch, and efforts to help readers recall experiences of the unique will later be used to help recall surrender. The emphasis on the impossibility of human beings to live continuously in the experience of the unique and on the need for routine will turn, about twenty years later, into the effort to locate surrender in the everyday world.

Cultural relativism is declared incompatible with understanding, and the "fundamental methodological question of the human approach [as the author then called his own, is] how we can investigate unilluminated aspects of man"; here Arthur Child's theory of the categories is drawn on. The affinity—always by hindsight—between the sociology of knowledge and "surrender-and-catch," here clearer than in the preceding chapter, is even more apparent in the next.

Indeed, in Chapter 7, "A Preliminary Inquiry into the Sociology of Knowledge from the Standpoint of the Study of Man" (which replaces the "human-studies" or "human approach" of Chapter 5), the word "surrender" itself occurs for the first time (p. 185) in the chapters on the sociology of knowledge; its (partial) description (pp. 182, 184, 185) may be recalled from the much later but in this book earlier Chapter 2, "Sociology and Evil" (pp. 40-41). The whole chapter exemplifies the author's surrender to Arthur Child's sociology of knowledge, with the results of the inquiry—its "catch" (the word is not yet used here)—the discovery (among others) of "dualism" and "naturalism" as metaphysical premises of the sociology of knowledge and of our "historical situation that must be envisaged to appreciate the specific function of the metaphysical premises of dualism and naturalism in the sociology of knowledge" (p. 186).

That is, here, as in later writings on surrender-and-catch, the connection between this idea and a diagnosis of humanity now is seen as inextricable. Among our characteristics now is (cultural) relativism, a theme which also recurs in later essays on the sociology of knowledge—here most significantly in Chapter 11, "The Sociology of Knowledge and Surrender-and-Catch." In the present chapter, it is through the sociology of knowledge that "man adapts himself to living in one world and through it he transcends cultural relativism toward the view of himself as dual and inexhaustibly challenging his own exploration" (p. 187; end of chapter). Instead of "sociology of knowledge" we may also read "surrender."

We do so a dozen or so years later, in a reassessment of this chapter (the very short).(Chapter 8, "Presuppositions of the Sociology of Knowledge and a Task for It"). It begins by challenging the anonymous asker of the question, "What is the sociology of knowledge?," to come forward (the "asker" includes the author and his audience), rather than hiding behind tradition, in which, in our time, we have at best a problematic trust, and which therefore we ought to suspend as best we can. The chapter ends with a concrete if enormously vast task for the sociology of knowledge, and the contrast between it and the large number of research complexes listed at the end of Chapter 5 of a quarter of a centry earlier is striking. There a diligent and open-minded gatherer collects materials the relevance of which he does not know but is confident of finding. Here instead there is one who is assaulted by myriad evidences of the lives the majority of his fellow men lead. Between writing the two papers, he has come to recognize the human being as a mixed phenomenon, that is, one that has exclusive features and features shared with other contents of the cosmos—and this is a variant of the dualism of Chapters 4 and 7—and thus also human products as mixed phenomena. In surrendering to one of them, the sociology of knowledge, he cannot be concerned only with what is exclusively human but must also do justice to what man shares with other beings and things. He wishes to improve the mixture that human beings are so that the distance from the image of beings capable of surrender-and-catch may be lessened.

"The Sociology of Knowledge and Sociological Theory" (Chapter 9) announces itself as a joint venture of author and readers, as does even more emphatically the next chapter. Indeed, the various essays which deal with existential truth or knowledge appeal, explicityly or implicitly, to the readers for their participation and assessment. For existential knowledge is intersubjective in the dialogical sense, whereas scientific knowledge might better be called "interobjective," inasmuch as its testing is less by interacting than by comparing observations of the "same" object by a number of observers.

The first section, "What Is the Sociology of Knowledge?," has its title in quotation marks to indicate the unanalyzed nature of the question: as in the preceding chapter, whoever has asked it has not come forward; the question thus is indistinct; it is asked by an outsider. The outsider is here contrasted with the insider, exemplified by Karl Mannheim, most poignantly in a letter by him. Unlike the outsider, the insider takes risks (see also n. 49): he surrenders; and the risk of being hurt (in special ways) is another characteristic of surrender.

The question of the basis of the categories is mentioned but is considered of secondary importance in the context in which it comes up ("In the pursuit of understanding it is of secondary importance whether by our 'transcendental selves' we mean a supracultural core or residue, biological or spiritual. . ."). Here again it is the task of the sociology of knowledge to transform a new and shattering experience into a problem; the various premises of the sociology of knowledge developed in Chapter 7 now are even more intimately related to our time.

Beyond the allusions to surrender already remarked on, two others deserve mention. The section "On Our Place and Time" (on the world as underdeveloped) contains the proposition that "we may help reason in its cunning, recognizing in our befuddlement a reminder of objective reason and of the relation of objective to subjective reason." Ten years later, "On the Cunning of Reason in Our Time" (*S&C*, Ch. 20) asks whether talking about the cunning of reason is at all tolerable in the face of Auschwitz or Vietnam—which (once more) leads back to surrender as the highest exercise of reason at this time in our history. And under the heading of "one world and cultural relativism," there is here, in Chapter 9, the claim that "the pursuit of understanding . . . perpetually challenges us to keep the fine line between the belief of being in grace and the sin of pride," which will be said of surrender.

The subtitle of "Ernst Grünwald and the Sociology of Knowledge: A Collective Venture in Interpretation" (Chapter 10) tells what this paper is meant to be: a venture for a reader who opens himself or herself to it and thus might actually experience, "at the very end, a perhaps unexpected climax," better yet, a shock; the worm of a question. This chapter is more constitutionally a surrender paper than any other in this book, far more even that "A Preliminary Inquiry into the Sociology of Knowledge from the Standpoint of the Study of Man" (Chapter 7 — surrender to Child's sociology of knowledge), for it is not a *post-factum* report as the earlier one is but is surrender to (Grünwald's sociology of knowledge) *in actu*, the wording of its process, as it were; and it is so, not despite, but *in* its analyticity.

There is need here to stress only two components of the analysis presented. One is, once more, the distinction between scientific-theoretical and (historical-) practical-existential truth. The other is the nature of the existentiality (Mannheim's *Seinsverbundenheit*, usually mistranslated as "social determination") of knowledge, that is, the question whether existentiality is selective or constitutive. This question has not yet come up here in quite these terms but actually pervades the whole of the sociology of knowledge, notably Mannheim's, Scheler's, and Child's — and indeed much of contemporary Western consciousness. For what it is is a harmless-sounding, esoteric way of asking whether we can be sure that there are objects at all, whether if there are we can know them, whether there is truth other than essentially arbitrary, relative, conditional truth. The analysis of Grünwald (the "documentary Grünwald") shows that for him the answers to all these questions are negative, and the perhaps unexpected climax of the paper is readers' sudden confrontation with these questions, provided that they surrender to them and find themselves on their own, thus falling back on what they share with all human beings. In less haunting terms, the questions concern the nature of subject and object and their relation. We see Grünwald claiming the categories of thought and the laws of formal logic to be oriented exclusively toward the object of knowledge (*objektadäquat*), claiming, that is, that there are at least *some* objects and that these can be truly known. We also see, however, that he draws no conclusions form this, apparently not trusting himself. The matter is left dangling.

III. Surrender

An answer to this question, and to other questions that haunt the sociology of knowledge and that have come up, again and again, is submitted in Part III. This answer is tentative, but here this means relatively absolute. That is to say that it is the result of the author's most careful examination of what to the best of his "consciousness and conscience" he can imagine as relevant to it, and of his searching discussions with others. But tomorrow, even today yet, new considerations, new insights, new questions he has not been able to imagine thus far modify this — never "absolutely absolute" — answer: that it is so is in the nature of thinking and of science.

St. John's, Newfoundland
29.x.82

NOTES

1.   Kurt H. Wolff, *Surrender and Catch: Experience and Inquiry Today* (henceforth *S&C*) (Dordrecht and Boston: D. Reidel, 1976), p. 31, and Ch. 5.

I
BEYOND

1

THE INTELLECTUAL: BETWEEN CULTURE AND POLITICS. 1971, 1963

For Herbert Marcuse

To think about intellectuals without at the same time considering the world we live in strikes me as preposterous. The intellectual as a topic is historical. There is no sense in discussing it independently of the world. In fact, I must start with this world to find out where, if anywhere, intellectuals are; I must constitute both, intellectuals *and* world, if I am to have any hope of attaining either.

So to argue is to be much starker than I found being on either of two previous occasions on which I turned to the topic—much starker because the situation has become starker. Recalling those occasions will help the argument.

I

Ten years ago I wrote a review of *The Academic Mind*, a book on *Social Scientists in a Time of Crisis*, the McCarthy period, by Paul F. Lazarsfeld and Wagner Thielens, Jr. [1], which is a report on the interviews held in

1955 with some 2400 professors of the social sciences in 165 colleges of various types concerning their experiences during "the difficult years." Constructed as central among the characteristics of the professors were the indices of their apprehension (made up of worry and caution) and permissiveness. The apprehension index was derived from the respondent's answers to such questions as whether he wondered if his politics affected his job security, whether he toned down recent writing to avoid controversy or worried about student misinterpretation causing trouble. The permissiveness index was derived from indicators of a permissive orientation (e.g., would not fire a teacher who admittedly is a communist) and of a conservative orientation (e.g., considers a radical teacher a luxury for a college); it ranged from clearly permissive to clearly conservative.

The authors found that permissiveness correlated with the Democratic vote, approval of classroom discussion, high importance given to students' education as contributors to the improvement of society, opposition to teacher oaths, and interest in civil liberties. They found that the more permissive a teacher, the more apprehensive he was and the more he thought that his own academic freedom had been threatened, that he had been reported to higher authorities, and had felt pressure to conform politically. They found that the better a college (as measured by several criteria), the clearer its administration's stand and the higher the proportion of respondents who expected administrative support if accused of leftist leanings. They found patterns of worry and caution to have been reflected in colleagues' behavior, in the respondent's own behavior in the classroom, and in impaired relations with students.

In responding to the book, I recalled Max Weber's lecture on "Science as a Vocation" (1918). I pointed out that the widespread concurrence with Weber's view by American social scientists largely ignored the historical circumstance in which this view had been set forth. Weber's pleas remained impotent. Not much more than a decade later the world witnessed the enthronement, by due process, of the *Führer*, whose destructiveness Weber had not foreseen [2], even though he had a distinct sense of the tragic.

Many social scientists, I suggested, are impatient with terms like tragic— if only because they have no operational definition for it. "The difficult years" could have given them one if they had inquired into their own experiences and found that "tragic" had one of two quite different meanings: either the professors' fight for their right to say, in and out of the classroom, what to their best knowledge and conviction was the case or the conscious acceptance of having lost all interest in this right. I quoted Lionel Trilling [3]:

> I am not asking for heroism. . . . I am only wondering why
> there is no record of some sense of outrage. . . . At no point
> do any of the responses suggest that the pressure in this in-
> stance had been exerted upon a very special group, upon
> scholars, upon men of the mind. Indeed, nothing is more
> striking than the teachers' inability to think of themselves as
> special in any way—as special because they are superior, as
> special because they have a certain relation to ideas, as special
> because they are committed to certain ideas. . . . no respon-
> dent feels that in his person Mind itself has been belittled and
> mocked.

This fear of identification as intellectuals had been noted before, I
recalled, by Melvin Seeman in "The Intellectuals and the Language of
Minorities" [4], a study of professors at a large state university. Seeman
had not asked whether there might be a difference between intellectuals
and professors, and Lazarsfeld and Thielens had not called professors
intellectuals. Trilling apparently had thought they were and had found
them wanting. He had supposed that it was Lazarsfeld-Thielens' desire
for objectivity that had prevented them from expressing their own outrage. I disagreed, insisting that their fear of value judgments had prevented them from being objective and bore witness to

> their alienation from history, from a common tradition, from
> a common world, and from a common sense of what it is to
> be a man in history, in tradition, in the world.

II

My conception of the intellectual and the world did at that time little
more than stress certain elements of the liberal conception: vigilance
against threats to academic freedom and the complaint that intimidation
had been successful and vigilance and academic freedom weakened. There
was no analysis of the world in which this had been made possible, no
hint even at the relevance of such an analysis. This conception was not
idiosyncratic, but not the less shortsighted for it. Its strongest component,
because it was the least history-bound if history-bound at all, was the
moral plea directed at fellow intellectuals to recall their own, our own
experiences, to take them, thus us, more seriously than we had been
"trained" to do and to act and live accordingly.

III

Two or three years later I wrote an essay on anti-intellectualism, "the enemy within" [5]. It belongs here.

In the early fifties, a journal of the social sciences devoted an entire issue to anti-intellectualism. This phenomenon, the editor wrote in his introduction,

> can be described as a fairly broad attitude . . . a negative attitude or prejudice against those who believe that society continually changes, and who favor using scientific and democratic methods to guide and control the changes. . . . Our contributors do not all have the same view of anti-intellectualism, but all of them deplore it to a greater or lesser extent. . . . My own favorite suggestion sounds very conservative: re-emphasis on the fundamental American principles of freedom, and tolerance of dissent. . . . Parents can aid school and community agencies in showing how originality and independence of thought and expression are largely responsible for that which is best in our nation today!

He thus ended with an exclamation point, though not without adding a footnote:

> A parallel is furnished in studies of the best way to answer prejudicial remarks, which showed that an appeal to American principles was most effective.

Anti-intellectualism, a deplorable negative attitude or prejudice, calls for some response, be it ever so humble (my own favorite) and old-fashioned (very conservative), but let us not forget that our attic harbors some downright revolutionary knicknacks—namely, the fundamental American principles of freedom and tolerance of dissent. Parents in particular should remember this, because if they do they can help school and community agencies to show how nice, if not wonderful, originality and independence of thought and expression really are—and this does deserve an exclamation point, for has not an appeal to American principles proved the best and most effective answer to prejudicial remarks, a parallel to anti-intellectualism and, of course, equally deplorable? Studies in this area of our national life, an area as delicate as it is important, appear to tease a tentatively affirmative answer from the data, no matter how difficult it may be to compensate for their slipperiness by neat design and statistical elegance.

My animus is quite impersonal, nor is it in the least directed against the publication in which this sample of editorial merchandise appeared. Examples can be found everywhere, in our newspapers, their editorials, news items, feature stories, and ads, vitiating our newsreels, and at their hottest or coldest in the commercials. Nor, surely, are they altogether absent from our learned or literary periodicals, as my sample suggests. This sample, of course, is especially useful or, to adopt blander language, "not random," for being taken from the introduction to a symposium on anti-intellectualism itself and it suggests that the writer exhibits what he means to analyze. He exhibits one kind of anti-intellectualism, its most pernicious kind, just because it is so customarily engaged in and so little examined: the merchandization of our culture.

1

"Our" is more than American, for the merchandization of culture is indeed not limited to the United States, although different here from what it is elsewhere. The expression "our culture" suggests that the phenomenon is not anything perpetrated by a small malicious band or cultural elite on the rest of us but is in ourselves or, again to use blander language, has been internalized by members of society. This language, which I have euphemistically called blander and of which I have given several examples, both quoting and parodying—is at once the most inconspicuous and the most reliable clue to "merchandization." This term refers to a view of culture as a vast inventory of values that can be bought, sold, advertised, and manipulated and to the cultured man or valuable member of society as duty-bound so to view and treat it. Did not the editor write that

> anti-intellectualism can be described as a . . . negative attitude
> or prejudice against those who believe that society continually
> changes, and who favor using scientific and democratic methods
> to guide and control the change?

Not "anti-intellectualism is," but "can be described as," that is, looked at, displayed, arranged, namely, as a "negative attitude or prejudice"—as if the two were the same. From there he issues a whole string of shoddy merchandise: first intellectuals, a package labeled "those who believe that society continually changes," which tells us far less about its contents than the label on a can of orange juice; then in an abrupt change, he insists that the very same package also contains those "who favor using scientific and democratic methods"—as if they were identical or even always compatible, rather than in an often problematical relation—"to guide and control the change." The editor wants to sell an idea. Some of us may buy it, though others will not. Contrary to the saying, however, ideas are *not* salable.

We see that language itself is afflicted with merchandization and it is the deadliest carrier of the disease. Most of us, most of the time, are only its victims, but we may count on the vigor and continued growth of the plague if only we place our trust in the communications industry, inside and outside the schools. Indeed, communications is being widely researched and even more widely put to practice, but some of us, subversives and deplorably wanting in confidence, cannot manage to forget that it is not the same as language. It follows the means-end scheme, as language does not. It instructs, informs, commands, forbids, warns, insinuates, cajoles, and takes on innumerable other roles, addressing itself to categories of men, men taking on roles, not to people, not to unmistakable individuals. It aims at, aims to, uses means—anything but *is*, no more than the categories *are* which it addresses. When we react to communications, we are not ourselves either. When I speak, on the other hand, I am; I become as I speak; indeed, I reveal myself to others as I speak.

What does it mean to say that this merchandization of our culture, which I have merely illustrated at its core, in language, is a form of anti-intellectualism? Anti-intellectualism, in a broad understanding of the term, refers to two things: hostility or related feelings toward ideas and other intellectual matters and hostility and the like toward kinds of people who in some fashion stand for such matters—intellectuals. Although the two are related, they must also be distinguished. So far I have mentioned only the first and have given examples not so much of hostility toward ideas as of disrespect and uneasiness toward language and so toward culture more generally. But it is men who speak and men who have culture, and disrespect and uneasiness in regard to language and culture are therefore disrespect for human activities and characteristics and uneasiness in relation to them. These human activities and characteristics are, of course, not those of intellectuals alone nor of people other than those who show disrespect and betray uneasiness, for they, too, are human; they too speak and have culture. Thus they are disrespectful and uneasy about their own activities and characteristics and the essential features of both themselves and other men. This suggests that the anti-intellectualism I have referred to as the merchandization of our culture develops psychologically (though in a typical rather than an empirical sense) from the fear or distrust of people, of oneself and others.

Ideas are indeed powerful—wonderful and fearful—recalling, in this power, the age-old ambivalence of the sacred, of the holy and cursed, blessed and damned. Why then should there not be a tendency to attenuate man's encounters with the sacred, whether its forms be God or gods, saints or angels, Satan or devils, or ideas, religious or not? Thus, for instance, in most or all societies special times are set aside for men to approach the sacred, and the approach is further attenuated by that psychological crutch of prescription which is known as ritual. In quite a different, much milder example often what we call relaxation serves to justify our turning away from preoccupation with ideas, from thinking. Hence the surrounding of the sacred with ritual and, in more secularized periods, the intermittent turning away from intellectual matters are both understandable phenomena and by no means exclusive of our time or place. By contrast, the fear of persons, actual people, Unamuno's "men of flesh and bone," the fear that I suggested at the bottom of the merchandization of our culture, *is* a historical, and a recent, phenomenon, and it is a problem for us to understand.

It was caught early by Dostoyevsky. " 'I must make a confession to you,' " says Ivan to his younger brother Alyosha in *The Brothers Karamazov;*

> I never could understand how one can love one's neighbours. In my view, it is one's neighbours that one can't possibly love, but only perhaps these who live far away. . . . To love a man, it's necessary that he should be hidden, for as soon as he shows his face, love is gone. [And a bit later in the same conversation:] Theoretically it is still possible to love one's neighbours, and sometimess even from a distance, but at close quarters almost never.

The fear of persons is involved in a gerat many more things than in the anti-intellectualism under discussion: in all kinds of psychological defenses, in racial and other prejudices, in dogmatism, bigotry, intolerance, fanaticism, in much compulsive behavior, aggressiveness, hate, contempt, infatuation, in hysteria and many other mental disturbances, in more localized fears, such as men's of women or women's of men, adults' of children or teen-agers, in wars, and, most awful of all, in the consideration and use of thermonuclear weapons. We all know some of these fears— though fears being what they are we probably prefer to know them in others rather than in ourselves. Assume them indeed so widespread that there is some justification in calling our time, as Auden has, the age of anxiety, and we see that the anti-intellectualism that draws on such fears is located in an extraordinarily vast landscape that I cannot possibly trace, let alone attempt to show in its evolution, for this would require a broad study of the total recent history of man.

Instead, we must be content to take this scene, this characterization or at least this characteristic, of our time as unproblematic, hoping that it may throw light on the anti-intellectualism I have recalled, the one that is in all of us.

2

I suggest that if this anti-intellectualism is a manifestation of the fear of human beings anti-intellectualism in the second sense of the term, that directed against intellectuals, is a manifestation of the first. Just as focused fear is more tolerable than diffused anxiety and just as scapegoats are easier to handle than reality, so it is a relief to discharge our intellectual discontent on to those who would remind us of it, compared with our having to live with this reminder, and with no end of it in sight. This discontent is a historical phenomenon; it is neither the ahistorical disquietude over injustice and evil, error, constraint, and ugliness nor the discontent Freud claimed to be intrinsic to civilization—although Freud's writing about it when he did *is*, of course, a historical fact symptomatic of our age and related to the discontent referred to, perhaps even an expression of it. *Our* discontent, both the anti-intellectualism in us and that directed against intellectuals, has to do with our attitudes toward tradition.

By traditions I mean group habits—habits of doing, feeling, conceptualizing, judging, and so on; when we use tradition in the singular in such expressions as "the American tradition," "the Western tradition," "the Judeo-Christian tradition," the group, Americans or Westerners, is very large, often the largest the speaker can think of as having a common tradition. In a strict sense there are as many traditions as there are groups, though much of what we say on this will depend on what we mean by group. At any rate, traditions are often in conflict with one another and perhaps more often felt to be in conflict by people to whom one or the other is important. Much of the so-called conflict between science and religion, for instance, can be understood as conflict between traditions. On the other hand, pluralism refers to the coexistence of traditions without conflict.

The question is, which circumstances favor the perception of coexisting traditions as conflicting, as against the perception of them as unproblematic or acceptable? It seems that when the tradition of the group a person identifies with is felt to be threatened by another tradition, in other words, when one's own tradition has become problematic, the two traditions are perceived as conflicting and pluralism becomes a difficult or impossible arrangement. This is to say that the likelihood of conflict increases as the tradition weakens, provided it does not weaken to the point of being given up. If I were a deeply religious man, science would not threaten me, either because I honored its right, which I consider unquestionable, or, in a very different sense, because I completely disregarded or despised science; but if I came to have doubts about my religion, yet wanted to hold on to it, I might defend it violently against what I then perceived as the threatening claims of science—provided I did not abandon it and move, as it were, over into the scientific camp, looking back in glee at the superstitions I had left behind me. In this case conflict has disappeared with the disappearance of one of the parties to it.

Obviously, not all conflict is over traditions or intellectual matters. What is important here about this seemingly trivial reminder is that much anti-intellectualism, or hostility toward intellectuals, is not either, hence is called by the wrong name. A common phenomenon is the attack against intellectuals because, as Lewis Coser observes in *The Functions of Social Conflict*, they transform "conflicts of interests into conflicts of ideas." "It is precisely this function of the intellectuals," Coser continues, that, for instance,

> has earned them the enmity of those theoreticians of the American labor movement who are concerned with confining conflicts to immediate issues rather than extending them into political and ideological spheres.

The antagonism concerns the misplacement of ideas, their false insertion, not the ideas themselves. Anti-intellectualism here, as it often does, means hostility to misplacers, abusers, and squanderers of intellectual issues. It does so, for instance, in Julien Benda's "treason of the intellectuals"— their treason consists in their taking part in political and social affairs, which Benda thinks they should not—or in Bertrand Russell's warning to those who would call him an intellectual, for to him this is "a person who pretends to have more intellect than he has" [6], that is, a braggart or charlatan, who also is a misuser of things intellectual. So, indeed, it does in much of the talk about "eggheads," "double domes," "professors who have never met a pay roll," and the like, talk that betrays hostility and contempt for ideas that are irrelevant, ridiculous, phony, or highfalutin in relation to the *real* conflict, which is over political, social, or economic, not intellectual, matters.

Any example of our second form of anti-intellectualism, that directed against intellectuals, must be examined to determine whether it is genuinely that or rather the antagonism toward those who threaten certain nonintellectual interests or who symbolize the threat. If we remember what I suggest about the conflict between traditions, we will realize that genuine antagonism toward intellectuals is of two kinds: either toward those who stand for a threatening tradition, existing or emerging, or toward those who stand for the threat to tradition as such, either toward the enemy—such as the scientist perceived as the enemy by the person of weakened religious beliefs—or toward the stranger.

3

What, then, do we mean by intellectuals? Edward Shils suggests that they have their own traditions, of which that

> of awesome respect and of serious striving for contact with the sacred is perhaps the first, the most comprehensive and the most important of all [7].

If we recall the relation between ideas and the sacred, we find that Shils's definition may be understood as restating, in more comprehensive, history-conscious language, the popular definition of the intellectual as the man who is concerned with ideas. I would go a step further and submit a most *un*popular—and, inevitably, an ostensive—definition; that is a person who is devoted to the spirit.

It becomes immediately clear that such persons should not be expected to be identical to people in certain occupations, such as scholars, artists, philosophers, authors, some editors, and some journalists, who, in Seymour Martin Lipset's analysis of American intellectuals, are their hard core, because they create culture, although in his discussion Lipset also includes those who distribute culture, that is, performers in the various arts, most teachers, most reporters [8]. Only one of the five commentators on this analysis, Karl Deutsch, raises a question about this identification, commenting on

> the difficulty of defining intellectuals in terms of a social func-
> tion, rather than in terms of an inner attitude. One might
> consider an intellectual a person who takes a wide range of
> abstract symbols and ideas seriously, and who does so in
> relation to a wide range of topics outside his immediate field
> of professional specialization [9].

In comparison with Shils's definition and my own, Deutsch's strikes me as more modest and also as hardly distinguishable from that of an educated man. Of course—though Deutsch fails to mention this—if we did not identify intellectuals with social categories, we could not make the studies that Lipset made: we would have no available statistics. Yet we could make a study like Melvin Seeman's, previously referred to, for the number of intellectuals Seeman interviewed—the assistant professors in the humanities and social sciences in one university—was only forty. Seeman, too, preferred the use of categories to define and search for referents—which latter procedure might have had the advantage of yielding an even smaller, hence more manageable, number of interviewees. I suggest that at least one of the components in the attractiveness of such procedures is the predilection for making products that are considered scientific compared with the satisfaction of studying people or of finding out what is going on in our society—and that this component is another expression of what I consider the basis of our first form of anti-intellectualism, which is in all of us: the fear of persons, of "men of flesh and bone." The two studies mentioned are useful and interesting, but not in regard to the topic they claim to deal with—intellectuals—because they do not deal with that topic. They more nearly exhibit a conception of it.

Deutsch's proposed definition of the intellectual is more nearly, I ventured, that of an educated man. In the more recent period of our history Schopenhauer was probably one of the first writers to distinguish the two, and both from the specialist. The latter may

> be likened to a man who lives in his own house and never leaves it. There he is perfectly familiar with everything, . . . but outside it, all is strange and unknown.

By contrast, for the educated man

> it is absolutely necessary . . . [to] be many-sided and take large views; and . . . an extensive acquaintance with history is needful.

Finally, the intellectual, that is, the person devoted to the spirit, is Schopenhauer's philosopher, of whom he says:

> He, however, who wishes to be a philosopher, must gather into his head the remotest ends of human knowledge: for where else could they ever come together? [And he adds:] It is precisely minds of the first order that will never be specialists. For their very nature is to make the whole of existence their problem; and this is a subject upon which they will every one of them in some form provide mankind with a new revelation [10].

The specialist or expert, Ortega y Gasset's learned ignoramus [11], strictly speaking, is noncommittal in regard to tradition—he neither promotes nor fights it—and therefore there is no such thing as antiexpertism or hostility to specialists. When there *seems* to be a case of it, examination will show that the antagonism is directed toward the expert who is perceived as not remaining one, as illegitimately leaving his special field; for instance, toward Einstein, not the physicist but the social, moral, political commentator. It is directed, again, not toward a man's expertise but toward his activities, character, or personality, which, however, must be distinguished from it, as they often are—remember Robert Oppenheimer. Probably many if not most of these cases—and instances of red-baiting and egghead persecutions abound—are genuine anti-intellectualism—that is, expressions of hostility toward conflicting traditions, existing or arising.

4

Another form of anti-intellectualism will emerge from a brief consideration of two American comments on the Dreyfus affair.

> "Les intellectuels!" What prouder club-name could there be than this one, used ironically by the party of "red blood," the party of every stupid prejudice and passion, during the anti-Dreyfus craze, to satirize the men in France who still retained some critical sense and judgment!

William James, who said this, was proud to apply the designation to himself and the group he identified with, for he honored the critical sense and judgment to which the adversaries of those possessing them were blinded. Compare James's remark with Russell Kirk's:

> *Les intellectuels* was the term of contempt employed by the factions of the Right, during the Dreyfus controversy, to describe the café-revolutionaries, the men who had broken with tradition, the enemies of patriotism, order, and the wisdom of the ages. It implied an opposition between the life of the mind and the life of society—or, at least, an inimicality between "advanced social thinkers" and [the transition is breathtaking and disarming] the possessors of property and power.

Dreyfus was a military officer rather than an intellectual, but both James and Kirk, though almost fifty years apart and at opposite poles, are agitated by the anti-intellectual aspects of the affair. Both take it as an occasion to vindicate traditions—James that of men of critical sense and judgment, Kirk that of some variety of conservatism—and to fight other traditions: James the one of red blood and stupid prejudice and passion, Kirk that of rootlessness. Kirk's enmity is a mixture of the antagonism toward the person who threatens tradition as such, the stranger, a form of anti-intellectualism we anticipated, and another form, antagonism toward the bloodless or lifeless intellectual, which we indulge whenever we use "academic" or "academicism" in a pejorative sense. Nietzsche, of course, was full of this anti-academicism; much earlier the satirist and aphorist Georg Christoph Lichtenberg castigated the wordmongers, for which Kierkegaard thanked him:

> Thanks, Lichtenberg, thanks!, for having said that there is nothing so feeble as the conversation of learned literary men who have never thought for themselves but know a thousand historical-literary facts. Like Leporello [he adds] they keep a list, but the point is what they lack; while Don Juan seduces girls and enjoys himself—Leporello notes down the time, the place and a description of the girl.

This form of anti-intellectualism, antiacademicism, is also of two kinds. One is contempt for pretense, fuzzimindedness, or fakery; it plays a conspicuous role in Bertrand Russell's definition of the intellectual, quoted earlier, as the "person who pretends to have more intellect than he has," and finds expression in many derogatory terms, ranging from pompous ass, stuffed shirt, intellectual, thinker, and high-brow, in the derogatory sense of these words, to the professor who has never met a payroll, the egghead and double dome, the crackpot, charlatan, and the nut, with its numerous equivalents. However different from one another, none of the persons so designated is to be taken seriously inasmuch as he presents the less as the more, the obscure as clear, the spurious as genuine. Thus he strikes the person who calls him by these terms as disrespectful of what matters to that person and often as disrespectful of what he considers most important in the tradition of his group. The second form of antiacademicism, which is also reflected in the passage from Kierkegaard and in many other places, notably in "philosophies of life" and existentialist writing but also in the Nazi literature of "blood and soil," is hostility toward the man who presents ideas that he has not tested in experience, in his own life. Sometimes such a man is unfavorably compared with people who are thought to be closer to life—for instance, the peasants in many nineteenth-century Russian writers, most conspicuously Tolstoy. This form, too, as the examples suggest, has its range from the most admirable to the most obnoxious, depending on the admixture of nonintellectual elements —that is, the manifestations of political, demagogical, prejudicial, and destructive interests, which in the Nazi case all but overpower antiacademicism itself.

Antiacademicism is a strong ingredient of the culture of the United States. It is essential to the whole tradition of pragmatism, by which I mean far more than the philosophical school, namely, a basic characteristic of our outlook: the emphasis on practice and on improving practice, with an essentially practical if not utilitarian attitude toward tradition. Thus "almost all the great truths relating to society," writes Merle Curti in *American Paradox*, are (as Wendell Phillips said in his Phi Beta Kappa address at Harvard in 1881) ".... not the result of scholarly meditation, but have been first heard in the solemn protests of maryred patriots and the loud cries of crushed and starving labor." Much better known is Emerson, in *his* Phi Beta Kappa address, also at Harvard, more than forty years earlier (1837): "The so-called 'practical men,'" Emerson said,

> sneer at speculative men, as if, because they speculate or *see*, they could do nothing. . . . [Yet this is not so:] Action is with the scholar subordinate, but it is essential. Without it he is not yet man. Without it thought can never ripen into truth. . . . Inaction is cowardice, but there can be no scholar without the heroic mind. . . . Only so much do I know, as I have lived. Instantly we know whose words are loaded with life, and whose not.

Although Emerson called him the scholar, he is identical with the man devoted to the spirit. In a statement that is wholly compatible with Shils's view of the intellectual, Emerson calls the scholar

> the delegated intellect. In the right state he is *Man Thinking*. In the degenerate state, when the victim of society, he tends to become a mere thinker, or still worse, the parrot of other men's thinking.

His duties are

> such as become Man Thinking. They may all be comprised in self-trust. The office of the scholar is to cheer, to raise, and to guide men by showing them facts amidst appearances.

His everyday, minimal obligation is to search honestly and patiently for what is the case, since he knows that without honesty and patience his self-trust will not bless him with being "Man Thinking."

Neither Emerson's American scholar nor William James's college-bred (1908), who comes up to the best claim we can make for the higher education, namely, to enable us to know a good man when we see him, is an academician nor is he an expert or specialist. A century and a quarter ago, when Emerson delivered his address, and seventy years later, when James gave his on the college-bred, the American practice, with its pragmatism, optimism, and liberalism, had not yet been tested by world wars, the Great Depression, totalitarianism, Hiroshima, and Nagasaki, the rise of African and Asian nations, and automation, to mention only some of what has happened to this and other nations during the last few decades. It is so extraordinary an onslaught of novelties, one of them threatening the end of mankind, another the end of the West, a third the end of the white man's era, that it would be amazing if the meanings of intellectualism and anti-intellectualism had not changed as well. I have in fact remarked on one of the changes: the emergence of anti-intellectualism within ourselves, the first kind that I commented on. Why, indeed, should we not be afraid of individual human beings if recent years have produced such fearsome men as Stalin and Hitler and a harassing number of smaller destroyers? People often ask, most recently during the Eichmann trial, whether we would have been different if we had been where they were, and if we had been their victims would we have been nobler than many of their victims?

5

How did some students of man, professors of the social sciences, stand up to a minor monster, though the biggest in recent American history—the late Senator McCarthy? In *The Academic Mind*, Paul Lazarsfeld's and Wagner Thielens' study of more than 2000 such professors, the question is so operationalized into indices and subquestions and the professors' answers are therefore so submerged in their specificity to questionnaire items that instead of being answered we are bored and instead of bread we receive, not stones, but the cotton imitation we have long since become accustomed to accept as the real thing—another case of injury unsuffered [12], to borrow Harold Rosenberg's shattering description of the tone of some other recent sociological studies. This one is a fine example of academicism—quite a response to the McCarthys!—and its title, *The Academic Mind*, stares us in the face as a pun, referring not only to that mind investigated but also that mind laboring.

More than forty years ago, in his lecture on "Science as a Vocation," which he addressed to university students shortly after Germany's defeat, Max Weber sketched a picture of the college professor—distinct, noble, and moving. His mission, Weber urged, is to purvey knowledge and to teach students to think and not to indulge in value judgments, least of all by letting "facts speak for themselves." The many American adherents of this picture probably ignore the historical circumstances of its emergence. One of them was the chauvinism that had invaded many classrooms during the second *Reich*. Although it had just been overthrown, Weber's plea for objectivity on the lectern was still pointed at that misplaced patriotism. Another, more immediate circumstance was the reaction to the defeat in the form of a longing for leadership and personality. Against this longing Weber summoned all the passionate severity at his command to urge scholars and scientists, and the future scholars and scientists he was addressing, not to be tempted into playing the role of "prophet and leader." This plea could not turn German history, which had led to the enthronement of a prophet whose monstrosity Weber, with all his sense of the tragic, could not have foreseen.

A revision of Weber's picture of the professor might include his *right and duty* to transmit knowledge—that is, whatever to the best of his own knowledge and conviction is in fact the case—his *right and duty* to teach students to think—that is, to develop their knowledge and clarify their convictions so that they might learn even better the inexhaustible meaning of the phrase "to the best of their own knowledge and conviction." This meaning is always relative, but it can be clarified to the point at which, at a given time, it is relatively absolute. An example is the right and duty to tell the truth publicly as best we know it if we would be true to our profession as teachers, scientists, or scholars.

These rights and these duties entail sensitivity to threats and the announcement of such threats; cowardice, indifference, adjustment are acts of treason here. As far as *The Academic Mind* is concerned, the general impression I gained of American professors of the social sciences was more miserable and shameful than not. I have already quoted from Lionel Trilling's review of the book, with which I concurred and still do. Here, as in so many other places, academicism is the anti-intellectualism in ourselves that rises from our fear of human beings: we are back in the wild, enormous landscape in which we with our anti-intellectualism are located—in which, to quote Rosenberg again, "everyone has won a fairy tale luxury and lost himself."

To make this landscape commensurate with us, to make it fit human dimensions, instead of merely glancing at it and panicking, is the problem into which our ramble in that small part of it, anti-intellectualism, has led us. It gives us a task, both urgent and promising, in an unforeseeable future, and this in two very different, though intimately connected ways: sociological and human. Sociologically, the task is the clarification of what can from now on be accepted as public and what as technical issues. In public issues all citizens, and foremost men devoted to the spirit, must participate lest the expert not remain what he must, namely, an invaluable servant, and instead become his own demonic caricature, an impossible master [13]. The expert cannot be allowed, for instance, to decide whether nuclear tests should be resumed, and he should thank those individuals who have proclaimed it, keep on proclaiming it, and have acted on their proclamations, for no matter what the outcome they have infused some clarity into our landscape.

Humanly—and the example just recalled of the protests shows the connection with the sociological aspect—let us recall Emerson's definition of the scholar as "Man Thinking" who, when the victim of society, degenerates; or Poe's "The Man That Was Used Up"; or Melville's Confidence Man, whom he contrasted, not only with Ahab, but also, in the very "recesses of the office files," with Bartleby [14]. These are only a few among the writers who have warned us against the explosion of society, against the identification of person and social category. Surely, we are both persons and social beings, we make society as society makes us; but at a time when the social drowns out the human we must remember our faith in the human voice, no matter how pitiful, perhaps even unintelligible, its tune may be. Often it is not the courage to name that we lack, for the difficulty is far greater: we do not know what it is that we are expected to name or we do not know that we are expected to name anything at all. Courage takes only encouragement, but no matter how hard this may be to come by, to tear ourselves out of ignorance or pseudo-knowledge is much harder yet. In such a situation we have nothing to begin with but ourselves and therefore we must take ourselves seriously, trusting that the spirit to which we are devoted has not gone out of us. If it were not such a crisis, it would not be worthy of our unconditional effort and it would not be the extreme situation in which we are if it did not call on us whole.

IV

Thus in my second effort on intellectuals they emerged as men devoted to the spirit amid the horror, men in a maelstrom threatened by drowning but trying to preserve the light by forcing it up above the waters, voices whispering "Man," breathing this word in the roar of society. In the end there was a hint—now I see it—that I did not know, or knew only vaguely, what I was talking about: "we do not know what it is that we are expected to name or we do not know that we are expected to name anything at all." There followed a blanket entreaty, perhaps a desperate but perhaps a blank shot, to entrust ourselves to ourselves, a plea for the faith "that the spirit to which we are devoted has not gone out of us." Ambiguity: was the salvation I implored nothing perhaps but cathartic withdrawal?

The very possibility shows the flawed conception, the misplaced sentimentality, the writer's misunderstanding of his place in the world, his misinsertion in the world. It did not feel so then; it feels so now. Why?

Was it possible a few years ago to find hope in the appeal to the man devoted to the spirit, who was to be resuscitated out of the fallen intellectual—academician, professor, teacher? That the moral plea—which had also characterized my previous attempt, whose strongest component it had been—was still passionately or desperately clung to to get into the world, even though it had since become or shown itself as far more horrible, and to make it feel less horrible?

V

I must try to get over this ambiguity by consulting two searching and anguished descriptions of our world: Barrington Moore, Jr.'s "Revolution in America?" [15] and Herbert Marcuse's *An Essay on Liberation* [16].

Barrington Moore does not say whether he means that the question of the prospects for revolution in the United States must be asked in any diagnosis of this country today, but he would probably consider it inseparable from it—perhaps even more so than the diagnosis of the United States from that of mankind as a whole. At any rate, the result of his investigation is that although the prospects for revolution are dim "the prospects for any transformation of American society by purely peaceful and democratic means are dimmer still." Hence there is a very somber but not a passive and fatalistic sense of the world to come. Moore attributes, or recommends, it to the intellectual:

> One task of human thought is to try to perceive what the range of possibilities may be in a future that always carries on its back the burden of the present and the past. Though that is not the only task of the intellectual, it is a very important and very difficult one.

What possibilities emerge? Acting on his own injunction to intellectuals, Moore has reviewed those of revolution here. Is *this*—I find myself coming back to that hint in my earlier try—"what we are expected to name" if we would make our best diagnosis? What is the perception of possibilities based on? Optimally on a position in which the perceiver, the intellectual, takes as little for granted as he can manage. In the present instance he would *not*, for example, take for granted the limitation of possibilities to the alternative revolution or reform versus continuation of status quo or martial law or worse. He would not take for granted a traditional conception of revolution ("seizing and holding power") but would rather be guided by revolutionaries themselves who, Moore writes, to the extent that they "did succeed, . . . often did so in large measure by avoiding slavish adherence to past models and by displaying ingenuity in devising new policies for unprecedented situations." One reason for the thinker not to cling to the traditional definition of revolution might be the very "pathos of novelty," "the experience of man's faculty to begin something new" [17], that Hannah Arendt stresses as the essence of revolution.

I base this recommendation to take as little for granted as possible— or bearable—on at least three grounds. First is that we live in an unprecedented situation if only—to mention one of many reasons for saying this— because we can all be killed far more quickly and with greater probability than ever before in history. Second, the principles by which the student selects and orders his facts—as Barrington Moore himself writes elsewhere—"have political and moral consequences" [18]. The aspect of this proposition which justifies the advocacy of the maximum suspension of received notions is that the student's definition of his task, including the conceptualization of his subject matter, may also have consequences for the definitions, conceptualizations, and actions of his readers and for an unpredictable number of other persons: the kind of his understanding and the degree of his understanding make a difference; they are his awful responsibility. Third, the procedure argued makes the student who follows it perceive more than the more traditional student does. It is easy to understand, for instance, that in his frame of reference Moore has to say about "New Left semi-revolutionary movements" only that they cannot provide the "need for protection and continuing benefits" (furnished by "liberated areas" characteristic of peasant revolutions) "through such symbolic gestures as offering sanctuary to draft resisters or liberating a university through a student riot." Would a less traditional conception of revolution not predispose one to undertake a more expectant and dedicated exploration of possible influences on social change—let this term denote the broadest possible topic Moore is concerned with—which such phenomena as the "New Left semi-revolutionary movements," but many others as well, might have? Let their sphere be subjective or cultural, should it be a foregone conclusion that the subjective factor, the realm of culture, thought, the spirit, is irrelevant to social change, hence to its analysis—that there is no such thing as the cunning of reason?

VI

In contrast to Barrington Moore's diagnosis, Herbert Marcuse's *An Essay on Liberation* focuses precisely on the problem of the relation between the subjective and the objective factor, between culture and politics, between sensibility and social structure, organization, change. In this analysis, Marcuse writes, neither "critical theory" nor "political practice" can

> orient itself on a concept of revolution which belongs to the nineteenth and early twentieth century . . . [and] envisages the "seizure of power" in the course of a mass upheaval . . . (p. 79),

whereas now, if

> in the rebellion of the young intelligentsia, the right and the truth of the imagination become the demands of political action, . . . this apparently insignificant development may indicate a fundamental change in the situation (p. 30).

Obviously Marcuse's implied conception of revolution and of what is happening to consciousness and within consciousness—in the subjective conditions, in culture—differs from Barrington Moore's. Marcuse's chapter on "The New Sensibility," from which the last quotation was taken, analyzes movements or occurrences relevant to consciousness: art, language, drugs, and music. The attendant refusal of our society, Marcuse writes, "is affirmative in that it envisages a new culture which fulfills the humanistic promises betrayed by the old culture" (p. 10).

> This is the vicious circle: the rupture with the self-propelling conservative continuum of needs must *precede* the revolution which is to usher in a free socity, but such rupture itself can be envisaged only in a revolution . . . (p. 18).

There is "the striking contrast between the radical and total character of the rebellion on the one hand and the absence of a class basis for this radicalism on the other" (p. 79), so that "every step in the struggle for radical change isolates the opposition from the masses and provokes intensified responses" (p. 68). Therefore "the radical is guilty—either of surrendering to the power of the status quo or of violating the Law and Order of the status quo" (p. 70)—of the status quo whose "insane fea-

tures" are the "expression of the ever more blatant contradiction between the available resources for liberation and their use for the perpetu-
ation of servitude" (p. 83).

Guided by his "consciousness and conscience" (p. 71), Marcuse arrives
at a point in front of an impossible landscape (of the kind we encountered before: the world)—it arrests him, and thus us, who have accompanied him. What does he do? He remembers himself as an intellectual
who has memories of impossible situations and, speaking biographically,
as one who has been accused of claiming the right to draw the limits of
tolerance, of recommending a dictatorship by intellectuals [19]:

> But who has the right to set himself up as judge of an estab-
> lished society, who other than the legally constituted agencies
> or agents, and the majority of the people? Other than these,
> it could only be a self-appointed elite. . . . Indeed, if the alter-
> native were between democracy and dictatorship . . . , the
> answer would be noncontroversial: democracy is preferable.
> However, this democracy does not exist. . . . The representa-
> tion is representative of the will shaped by the ruling minori-
> ties. Consequently, if the alternative is rule by an elite, it
> would only mean replacement of the present ruling elite by
> another; and if this other should be the dreaded intellectual
> elite, it may not be less qualified than the prevailing one. To
> be sure, this has never been the course of a revolution, but it
> is equally true that never before has a revolution occurred
> which had at its disposal the present achievements of produc-
> tivity and technical progress. . . . Prior to its realization, it is
> indeed only the individual, the individuals, who can judge,
> with no other legitimation than their consciousness and con-
> science. . . . Their judgment transcends their subjectivity to
> the degree to which it is based on independent thought and
> information, on a rational analysis and evaluation of their
> society. The existence of a majority of individuals capable of
> such rationality has been the assumption on which democratic
> theory has been based (pp. 70–71).

A few years earlier he wrote:

> The question, who is qualified to make all these distinctions,
> definitions, identifications [among policies, opinions, move-
> ments] for the society as a whole, has now one logical answer,
> namely, everyone "in the maturity of his faculties" as a human
> being, everyone who has learned to think rationally and auton-
> omously. The answer to Plato's educational dictatorship is

the democratic dictatorship of free men. . . . In Plato, rationality is confined to the small number of philosopher-kings; in
Mill, every rational human being participates in the discussion
and decision—but only as a rational being. Where society has
entered the phase of total administration and indoctrination,
this would be a small number indeed, and not necessarily that
of the elected representatives of the people. The problem is
not that of an educational dictatorship, but that of breaking
the tyranny of· public opinion and its makers in the closed
society [20].

VII

Thus the point is not a Platonic academy, not a dictatorship by intellectuals but—to argue at least one legitimate and justifiable reading of these
passages—the elevation into consciousness of something spontaneous that
is going on and that we must develop into a principle of conduct and
policy; something that has long since been practiced but must be realized
as the revolutionary lever it can become. The clue to it is that "the existence of a majority of individuals capable of such rationality has been the
assumption on which democratic theory has been based." This, together
with the sentence preceding it and with other ideas contained in the
passages quoted, suggests that individuals, legitimated by their consciousness and conscsience and on the basis of independent thought and information, judge and assess their society, appealing to the reason in their
fellowmen. Let the former be called intellectuals (echo of Socrates, rather
than Plato); the latter are other people, unpredicated and unpredicable
beyond their endowment with reason.

Questions arising out of Barrington Moore's paper led to the recommendation that we, intellectuals and other people, take as little for
granted as possible—or bearable; thus that we not take a lowest common-
denominator conception of revolution as the basis for speculating on the
prospects for revolution now. Marcuse, we saw, does reject such a concept
of revolution for both critical theory and political practice. In thus suspending or bracketing a received notion he is intellectually more radical
than Moore, less deflected by tradition as he gropes for roots. Furthermore, his statement that *both* theory and practice must suspend received
notions hints at the close connection between intellectual and political
radicalness: they are two thrusts of one radicalism, for which practice, or
praxis, must be informed by theory, which is given life by praxis. In
Marcuse's words, both Moore and he engage, in the writings at issue and
in others, in "a rational analysis and evaluation of their [our] society."
For Marcuse, here and elsewhere [21], this is the analysis of "the problem

of the relation between the subjective and the objective factor, between culture and politics." The devotion to this analysis defines him as the intellectual: as the man devoted to the spirit, yes, but who thus devoted, thus legitimated, rationally analyzes and assesses his society, his shudder stayed by his faith that his followmen are, as he is, endowed with reason.

VIII

At this point we envisage the intellectual located between culture and politics—located in two senses: it is here that we must look for him in our search for a concept of the intellectual that we can answer for, and it is here that we would have him recall that he is active.

Medias in res: for me one of the most utterly unresolved questions—let everybody ask himself whether it is for him or her—is simply how to live with or without the daily news. I feel corrupt as I watch and hear continuous lying, killing, torturing, the evidence of insanity, obscenity, hypocrisy, crime, while doing no more than occasionally protesting in one form or another and sending money to fellow protesters or helpers, and I feel corrupt *not* watching and hearing, turning away from the horror. The only way I can imagine feeling less corrupt, just possibly even at peace, would be to devote all my waking hours and extending them as much as I could physically stand it to work on reducing at least one of the innumerable outrages that diminish the world. This is a piece of theoretical imagination; it does not change my practice, though surely my theory. That I am corrupt and not free is no more than a theoretical insight, for my arrogance—this *may* be a misnomer—lets me continue doing what I am doing instead of what that insight tells me would make me less corrupt: my arrogance, that is to say my conviction, that being as I am I must do what I do rather than what on *theoretic* grounds strikes me as morally superior. (There *is* comfort in knowing that others, too, do so.) Arrogance would be a misnomer if doing what one must because one is what one is were itself morally equal or superior to doing what one must on theoretic insight. To affirm doing because of one's being is morally the more bearable and justified, the more firmly it is based on the most thorough examination one can undertake of one's practice *and* theory as they impinge on one another—the more firmly it is based on the injunction, "know thyself" [22]—thyself as man, as "species being." To communicate this concept of theory and practice and this theory and practice is surely one meaning of the proposition that the "man devoted to the spirit rationally analyzes and assesses his society, his shudder stayed by his faith that his followmen are, as he is, endowed with reason." Communication with a partner or partners who suffer from similar unresolved questions as I do differs from communication with those who do not—in the first case it may and in the second it may not be indicated to discuss such questions. What in both cases is not only indicated but essential and what goes beyond communication in even the broadest accepted meaning is that we try with *all* partners to be at our best (which, of course, is not always the same) because we not only become better ourselves but make the world better, instead of diffusing our discontent that the world is not better than it is or that the better future has not yet arrived.

IX

To be at our best means to be not only kind, gentle, and considerate but also critical, and there is no end of occasions on which to be kind and critical. The fate of kindness in our society requires a large essay, which this one cannot be. I wish to make only one point, which I think important. The kindness I am referring to has not only an ethical but also an aesthetic aspect. Marcuse, and not only in the essay touched on, has much to say on aesthetics, though not in relation to kindness. What I mean is that to look at a painting, to walk, to listen to music, or to watch a play or movie can, whatever else it may be, also be a joy, and to give oneself or others joy is also to be kind. The question when to enjoy is again an unprescribable one of one's best "consciousness and conscience."

The kindness intrinsic to the intellectual's task is indicated by the fact (or definition) that his shudder is "stayed by his faith that his fellowmen are, as he is, endowed with reason." In accordance with what is most special to his task, however, we must now turn to him as critic. In moving between culture and politics, he may cry out, for instance, with Brecht: "Erst kommt das Fressen, dann kommt die Moral" ("First comes the grub, then comes morality"), a cry heard in the Weimar Republic in the late twenties, or with the French students in May 1968: "Soyons réalistes, demandons l'impossible!" ("Let's be realistic; ask for the impossible!")—or whatever his biographically or historically resounding cries may be: all he has to do is remember and a cry will rise in him that should be heard. These cries beat against aspects of society or result from somebody's, perhaps his own, assessment of society, which, of course, need not be his nation. The cries may reverberate only within the sphere of culture. Politicians, and not only tyrants and dictators, can by definition not hear them, in contrast to political men, including their professional variant, statesmen.

The excitement some intellectuals felt when they heard a devastating song from *The Threepenny Opera* sung or whistled in the streets of Berlin in the late twenties often was over an alleged or expected change in consciousness of ordinary people—the same excitement over consciousness now so often discussed with reference, for instance, to The Beatles [23] and comparable groups. Politically, it may be as irrelevant today as it was then, when a few years after Brecht-Weill came Hitler.

There are indications, however, that we have learned to understand this irrelevance; one example from the present exploration is the truth in Barrington Moore's cautionary comments on New Left semirevolutionary movements. The difficulty is that the sphere of culture, hence its relation to politics and its impingement on politics, changes historically—a circumstance, we noted, that is much more in Marcuse's thought than in Moore's. As we had occasion to say in different terms in connection with each of the essays of these two thinkers, the task of ascertaining, and *by ascertaining helping to constitute*, the boundary between culture and politics, hence of analyzing *and testing* the influence of culture on politics, is a task that can be attacked not only frontally but also in innumerable investigations and experiments which would be guided by the individuals' engaging in them. Therefore, whatever the tasks are, they are based on or contribute to a rational analysis and evaluation of the society they are done in or refer to. In many cases the exploration of the nature of this contribution is a part of the investigator's or experimenter's task of which he is quite aware [24].

X

Among the many areas of which we would do well to be critically conscious I mention only language—and no more than a single example: this morning—but any would do—I received an advertisement from the *Bulletin of the Atomic Scientists* which committed this offense against the merits of the journal and against language and people who speak and write:

> In the months ahead Bulletin readers will be enjoying such stimulating articles as
>
> RADIATION AND INCREASING INFANT MORTALITY [these words in red capital letters]—A horrifying (and probably controversial) assessment of a little-noticed phenomenon.

The entertainment value of the article on the consequences of radiation for the death of infants—the article is almost surely quite different—is heightened by the parenthetical wink at the potential reader's ambition to be an inside dopester. Such vicious babble, of course, also bombards us in almost every newscast, which in this country, furthermore, is interrupted, with inhuman timing, by the lies and idiocies of the commercials, the reaction to which seems not to be outrage—any more than it was the social-science professors' to Joseph McCarthy, as Lionel Trilling then observed—but indifference, apathy, cynicism, amusement, or the consumer's docile alertness: the news consumer *has* assimilated the message—never mind (*pace* McLuhan!) the medium. George Orwell is one of the few among the commentators on the decline of our language to relate it—a cultural phenomenon—to politics:

> one ought to recognize that the present [1946] political chaos
> is connected with the decay of language, and that one can
> probably bring about some improvement by starting at
> the verbal end. If you simplify your English, you are freed
> from the worst follies of orthodoxy. You cannot speak any
> of the necessary dialects, and when you make a stupid remark,
> its stupidity will be obvious, even to yourself [25].

Recognizing and rejecting cant and other sports of tradition, as well as traditions, as historically inadequate—sometimes because they feed on hypocrisy—a recognition and rejection that may be accompanied by the identification and acceptance of something else as real, seem to be at least an important part of the movement on the subjective, the cultural side of the change or revolution that industrialized and industrializing societies are variously undergoing. In the United States the two groups that exhibit these shifts in acceptance and rejection most obviously are students [26] (and an increasing number of teachers and other professionals [27]) and those who already as a result of these shifts call themselves blacks. In several places Marcuse has located our hope in these two groups [28]. Some of the rejection they share—of cant, hypocrisy, oppression, tutelage, exploitation, and mutilation—are even more manifest than are some of their common acceptances and affirmations, such as insistence on the search for new identities and the claim to them, shared and sometimes converging convictions and practices of liberation by music, dance, drugs, sex, love, free speech (and print), and attendant practices, new ways of living together ("pads," "communes," "communities"), membership in newly self-conscious groups [29], and stress on the importance of the body. Eldridge Cleaver so formulates part of this convergence: "Martin

Luther King, Jr., giving voice to the needs of the Body, and President
Kennedy, speaking out of the needs of the Mind, made contact on that day"
("when the Birmingham revolt erupted in the summer of 1963") [30]. The
importance of the body had, of course, been emphasized by philosophers
and psychologists —among the most recent Wilhelm Reich, in particular,
must not be forgotten—but it is only in the last few years that this attention has broken out of the sphere of culture into praxis and toward politics. That like other facets of student and black activities it also shows
irrelevant and self-defeating features, both of fashion and destructiveness,
is obvious, unfortunate, and understandable.

Even this insistence on the body is partly a reaction against the war in
Vietnam. Its fundamental importance for our social change—clearly not
only in the United States but all over the earth—has many more direct
manifestations. The most immediate is simply its rejection by draft resistance, desertion, sabotage, and the refusal of participation whatever, but
they range all the way to questioning our educational system at ever lower
levels and by ever younger students—this system supports the war or is at
least indifferent to it—and to analyses of our economy [31], including its
science [32].

XI

Here is a statement concerning the relation between culture and politics:

> Hitherto men have constantly made up for themselves false
> conceptions about themselves, about what they are and what
> they ought to be. . . . The phantoms of their brains have
> gained the mastery over them. . . . Let us teach men, says one,
> to exchange these imaginations for thoughts which correspond
> to the essence of man; says the second, to take up a critical
> attitude to them; says the third, to knock them out of their
> heads; and existing reality will collapse.
>
> . . . The first volume of this present publication has the aim of
> uncloaking these sheep, who take themselves and are taken
> for wolves; of showing . . . how the boasting of these philo-
> sophic commentators only mirrors the wretchedness of the
> real conditions . . . [33].

Compare this statement by Marx with one made 110 years later:

> As a type of social man, the intellectual does not have any one

political direction, but . . . his work . . . does have a distinct
kind of political relevance: his politics, in the first instance,
are the politics of truth, for his job is the maintenance of an
adequate definition of reality. . . . The intellectual ought to
be the moral conscience of his society, at least with reference
to the value of truth. . . . And he ought also to be a man
absorbed in the attempt to know what is real and what is
unreal. . . .

. . . If you ask to what the intellectual belongs, you must
answer that he belongs first of all to that minority which has
carried on the big discourse of the rational mind. . . . This
. . . is not a vague thing to which to belong—even if as lesser
participants—and it is the beginning of any sense of belonging
that free men in our time might have. And, just now, at this
point in human history, that is quite difficult [34].

Now compare this statement by C. Wright Mills with one made twelve
years later still, in 1967, by Noam Chomsky:

It is the responsibility of intellectuals to speak the truth and
expose lies. This, at least, may seem enough of a truism to pass
over without comment, Not so, however. For the modern intellectual, it is not at all obvious. Thus we have Martin Heidegger writing, in a pro-Hitler declaration of 1933, that "truth is
the revelation of that which makes a people certain, clear, and
strong in its action and knowledge"; it is only this kind of
"truth" that one has a responsibility to speak. Americans tend
to be more forthright. When Arthur Schlesinger was asked by
The New York Times in November 1965 to explain the contradiction between his published account of the Bay of Pigs
incident and the story he had given the press at the time of
the attack, he simply remarked that he had lied. . . . It is of
no particular interest that one man is quite happy to lie in
behalf of a cause which he knows to be unjust; but it is significant that such events provoke so little response in the intellectual community . . . [35].

Out of the many things that could be said about these three statements
on the intellectual between culture and politics I take only what strikes
me as most relevant to our concern—both in this essay and in our world
today.

1. Marx debunks the arrogance of culture (the philosophy of the Young
Hegelians) as a ludicrous mask of politics (the cause of the wretchedness
of the real conditions to which it is as indifferent as is that philosophy);
and he uncloaks its exhibitors, to recall the terms of one of the types of

anti-intellectualism (so misnamed) suggested before, as misplacers, abusers, and squanderers of ideas.

2. Like Mills and Chomsky (and many others), Marx wants intellectuals to tell the truth and, like them (and fewer others), above all the
truth about politics, society, economics, and—in a much longer range
than Mills and Chomsky—history.

3. It is easy to see that in addition to many other passages from Marx
this one shows him, or could show him, as one of the fathers of the sociology of knowledge,—which has been criticized most acrimoniously in its
development by Karl Mannheim [36], for (to use our own terms) not turning its attention to politics, society, and economics, for not breaking out
of the subjective or cultural sphere. Just as the philosophy of the Young
Hegelians was an object of Marx's critique, so the sociology of knowledge
itself would have been if Marx could have witnessed it.

4. The Marx quotation contains no explicit exemption of *some* thought
from its general debunking. If, however, there were nothing else in Marx's
writing—which on the contrary contains much—to convince us that he
was not a general debunker of thought, it is enough to recall his "Theses
on Feuerbach," written about the same time as the passage quoted, if not
shortly before, especially the famous eleventh, the last: "The philosophers
have only *interpreted* the world in various ways; but the point is to
change it." Far from advocating the abolition of philosophy, let alone of
philosophers, this on the contrary gives them—the intellectuals—a different and today more specific task than telling the truth. Both Mills and
Chomsky are moving in the direction of Marx's eleventh thesis. Mills, in
addition to pleading that intellectuals acknowledge and be loyal to their
tradition, "the big discourse of the rational mind," urges the political
relevance of truth, which is their politics. Chomsky does so more concretely by naming betrayers of this truth and this politics. The difference
between Mills and Chomsky, which may well reflect a difference between
the times in which they wrote, is that the later statement is more urgent
and specific than the earlier. The theoretical justification—in contrast to
the historical—of both Mills's and Chomsky's propositions can be found
in Marx's eleventh thesis on Feuerbach.

Part of how I read this thesis has also been expressed by Mills (in the
same essay), though without reference to Marx:

> In so far as he [the intellectual] is politically adroit, the main
> tenet of his politics is to find out as much of the truth as he
> can, and to tell it to the right people, at the right time, and
> in the right way. Or, stated negatively: to deny publicly what
> he knows to be false, whenever it appears in the assertions of

> no matter whom; and whether it be a direct lie or a lie by
> omission, whether it be by virtue of official secret or an honest
> error [37].

Marx's, Mills's, and Chomsky's message is this: get your culture into the
world and work in and at the world at whatever task your being, so
informed by the message, bids you do. Obviously, this need not be political in any technical sense; on the contrary, whatever you do as so defined
becomes political, at the very least, by contributing in this practice to a
new understanding of an old meaning of politics as activity for the common good.

In bringing my references even closer to today and to my home, the
university, I would argue that such an understanding informs a collection
of critical essays on the humanities and social sciences, *The Dissenting
Academy* [38]. It is at least as specific and concrete as Mills's critique of
sociology [39]; it contains incisive papers (some more than others) on
academic delinquency in general, on English, economics, history, international relations, anthropology, philosophy, the social consciousness of
the social sciences, political science, and the Catholic college, and a
reprint of Chomsky's "The Responsibility of Intellectuals." It illustrates
an expression of the desire—the historical necessity of this desire—to get
one's "culture into the world and work in and at the world."

One example must do. In her paper on anthropology, "World Revolution and the Science of Man," Kathleen Gough asks: "How can the
science of man help men to live more fully and creatively and to expand
their dignity, self-direction, and freedom?" and suggests

> that social science, like all science, becomes morally and so-
> cially either meaningless or harmful unless its skills and knowl-
> edge are periodically referred back to the question, "Science
> for what purpose and for whom?" If we cease to ask this
> question, we cease to seek wisdom and cease to be intellectuals
> in any meaningful sense of the word. With the loss of respon-
> sibility for our learning, we also cease to be fully social, and
> therefore human [40].

This is more consciously political than Robert S. Lynd's question almost
thirty years earlier, "knowledge for what?" [41]; several symposiasts, however, properly pay tribute to Lynd's book by that title.

XII

What have we found? That the intellectual is the man devoted to the
spirit,

who thus devoted, thus legitimated, rationally analyzes and
assesses his society, his shudder stayed by his faith that his
fellowmen are, as he is, endowed with reason.

That he is the man who does what he does on the basis of the most
thorough examination of his practice *and* theory as they impinge on one
another; that he is the man who ascertains, and by ascertaining helps to
constitute, the boundary between culture and politics, who analyzes and
thus tests the influence of culture on politics; that he is the man who
gets his culture into the world and works in and at the world, informed
by the historical necessity of his desire to do so.

These propositions contain definitional and historically diagnostic elements. The essential definition of the intellectual as the man devoted to
the spirit results from a taxonomic analysis undertaken to distinguish him
from other types of man with which clarity demands he not be confused.
The diagnostic elements concern our world: it is unprecedented in the
sense that we have to invent our beginning, since traditions are no longer
viable but must be suspended in the most thorough analysis of their status
relative to our own existence, our own theory and practice. It is the outcome of such an analysis that has resulted in the further findings just
passed in review: *here, now,* to be a man devoted to the spirit means to
be between culture and politics and thus to test the influence of the
former on the latter. I should add that failure to mention the reverse
influence,· of politics on culture, cannot mean denying its existence,
which would be absurd, but results from the diagnosis undertaken by an
intellectual and addressed to intellectuals and from the desire to alert
himself and them to an unrealistic assessment of the power or the
impotence of culture, to disregarding politics or cringing before it in
hopelessness. The idea of "doing one's being" is again the outcome of
the condition of doing anything at all in our unprecedented world.
It is to invent our beginning—we have nothing to begin with but ourselves, as I said before; and I add a new piece of diagnosis, that "doing
one's being" is informed by the historical necessity of the desire to get our
culture into the world. I mean this to be another way of referring to the
rational analysis and assessment of our society or the concern with the
boundary between culture and politics, thus suggesting unforeseeable ways
of implementing this activity, all of them to be invented.

This chapter is such a way. It is not political in any technical sense—
I said in general that it need not be—but in the sense that it might
contribute to activity for the common good. Now, then, let us talk with
others who would be intellectuals and with political men and other
people, unpredicated and unpredictable beyond their endowment with

reason, so that *all* of us can come closer to being each other's moral conscience and consciousness.

Acknowledgment. This chapter has greatly benefited from an unusually critical reading by Charles Nathanson to whom I am much indebted. It was prepared in 1969 for a symposium on intellectuals and power, edited by Godfried van Benthem van der Bergh and David Kettler, and published by van Gennep, Amsterdam, 1973.

NOTES

1. The Free Press of Glencoe, Ill., 1958. This review was printed in *The Ohio State Morning Lantern,* April 27, 1959.

2. See Wolfgang J. Mommsen, *Max Weber und die deutsche Politik, 1890–1920* (Tubingen: Mohr, 1959), especially Chapter IX.

3. In his essay on *The Academic Mind* in *The Griffin* (December 1958) p. 11.

4. *American Journal of Sociology* (July 1958).

5. "The Enemy Within: Anti-Intellectualism," *The Centennial Review,* 7 (Winter 1963), 46–63. An earlier version was presented at the annual faculty conference, Denison University, March 2, 1962. I acknowledge my indebtedness to George B. de Huszar, Ed., *The Intellectuals: A Controversial Portrait* (Glencoe, Ill.: Free Press, 1960), of which I made much use.

6. Bertrand Russell, quoted in Russell Kirk, "The American Intellectual: A Conservative View" (1965), in de Huszar, *ibid.,* p. 309.

7. Edward A. Shils, "The Tradition of Intellectuals" (1958), *ibid.,* p. 56.

8. Seymour Martin Lipset, "American Intellectuals: Their Politics and Status," *Daedalus* (Summer 1959), 460.

9. Karl W. Deutsch, "Comments on 'American Intellectuals: Their Politics and Status,' " *ibid.,* 489.

10. Arthur Schopenhauer, "The Art of Literature" (1851), in de Huszar, *op. cit.,* p. 116.

11. Jose Ortega y Gasset, *The Revolt of the Masses* (1930) (Mentor 1950), p. 82.

12. Harold Rosenberg, "The Orgamerican Phantasy," in *The Tradition of the New* (1959) (New York: Grove Press, 1961), p. 277.

13. Harold J. Laski, "The Limitations of the Expert," in de Huszar, *op. cit.,* p. 171.

14. Rosenberg, *op. cit.,* pp. 271, 282. (Rosenberg refers to Poe's story as "The Man Who Was Made Up.").

15. *The New York Review of Books,* January 30, 1969.

16. Beacon Press, Boston; 1969.

17. Hannah Arendt, *On Revolution* (New York: Viking, 1965), p. 27 and *passim*.

18. Barrington Moore, Jr., *Social Origins of Dictatorship and Democracy: Lord and Peasant in the Making of the Modern World* (Boston: Beacon, 1966), p. 521.

19. Particularly because of his essay, "Repressive Tolerance" (from which, however, note a quotation presently), in Robert Paul Wolff, Barrington Moore, Jr., and Herbert Marcuse, *A Critique of Pure Tolerance* (Boston: Beacon, 1965). See reviews by David Spitz (*Dissent*, September–October 1966), Nathan Glazer (*American Sociological Review*, June 1966), and Henry David Aiken (*The New York Review of Books*, June 9, 1966). For similar accusations see Herbert Marcuse et al., *Das Ende der Utopie* (Berlin: v. Maikowski, 1967), pp. 39 f.; "Democracy Has/Hasn't a Future . . . A Present" (a discussion by Nat Hentoff, Norman Mailer, Arthur Schlesinger, Jr., and Herbert Marcuse), *The New York Times Magazine*, May 26, 1968, especially pp. 31, 98; "Marcuse Defines His New Left Line" (an interview with Jean-Louis Ferrier, Jacques Boetsch, and Françoise Giroud of *L'Express*), *The New York Times Magazine*, October 27, 1968, especially p. 100; Sidney Hook, *The New York Times*, December 29, 1968, p. 36, and his review of *An Essay on Liberation*, *The New York Times Book Review*, April 20, 1969; and Irving Howe in *Harper's Magazine*, July 1969.

20. Marcuse, in Wolff et al., *op. cit.*, p. 106.

21. Above all in *One-Dimensional Man* and *Eros and Civilization*.

22. The alternative acting on theoretical insight and "doing because of one's being" is analogous to Stuart Hampshire's research "by rational calculation of directly useful and socially relevant results" and by "intellectual excitement," whereby the "law of displacement" may show retrospectively the relevance of the latter to the former. Hampshire's discussion, however, remains limited to cultural concerns without touching on politics. Stuart Hampshire, "Commitment and Imagination" in *The Morality of Scholarship*, by Northrop Frye, Stuart Hampshire, and Conor Cruise O'Brien, Max Black, Ed. (Ithaca: Cornell University Press, 1967), pp. 29–55.

23. See Richard Poirier, "Learning from the Beatles," *Partisan Review* (Fall 1967), reprinted in Jonathan Eisen, Ed., *The Age of Rock: Sounds of the American Cultural Revolution* (New York: Vintage, 1969).

24. This awareness appears to be more characteristic of Left radical than of liberal, conservative, or Right radical literature, for the first wishes to change the status quo, whereas the other three, despite obvious important differences, do not; cf. the importance given to the problem of the relation of the intellectual to the revolution by Marx, Kautsky, Lenin, Gramsci, and other Marxist theorists.

25. George Orwell, "Politics and the English Language" (1946) in *A Collection of Essays* (Doubleday, 1954), p. 177. Orwell has more specific advice in this article, although some of it borders on that given in style manuals. (In regard to German—Wilhelminian and Weimar-Republic—Karl Kraus is far more outraged and searching, but preoccupation with language was central to him and not to Orwell.)

26. An estimate of 12- to 25-year-olds on earth is 750 million now and a billion by 1980: Kathleen Teltsch, "Study Sees a Rise in Youth Protest," *The New York Times*, February 16, 1969, p. 10 (the reference is to a study by United Nations sociologists). The literature on the student movement is already large; cf. Alexander Cockburn and Robin Blackburn, Eds., *Student Power* (Penguin, 1969), with *Youth in Turmoil*, adapted from a special issue of *Fortune* (New York: Time-Life Books, 1969).

27. Cf. *Radicals in Professions* (Ann Arbor, Mich.: Radical Education Project, 1967), especially the contribution by Barbara Haber and Al Haber.

28. Cf. Chapter II of *An Essay on Liberation* and the end of *One-Dimensional Man*.

29. Most recent at the time of this writing (June 1969)—to my knowledge— and potentially important is women's liberation (cf. Peter Babcox, "Meet the Women of the Revolution, 1969," *The New York Times Magazine*, February 9, 1969); Beverly Jones and Judith Brown, *Toward A Female Liberation Movement* (Boston: New England Free Press, 1969).

30. Eldridge Cleaver, *Soul on Ice* (New York: McGraw-Hill, 1968), pp. 201, 200. Living through what has long preoccupied philosophers theoretically as the Mind-Body problem is related to the politicization of experience encountered by many young radicals, especially in the student movement, and above all convergence as well as contagion by Negroes who in the process and by virtue of it change into Blacks (or antecedent equivalents, particularly Black Muslims). See *The Autobiography of Malcolm X* (New York: Grove, 1964); Claude Brown, *Manchild in the Promised Land* (New York: Signet, 1965). A related experiential basis also underlies the therapeutic theory and practice of the British psychiatrist R. D. Laing; notice especially, including the title, *The Politics of Experience* (New York: Ballantine, 1967). Also related is the work of Norman O. Brown, from *Life Against Death* (Middletown, Conn.: Wesleyan University Press, 1959; Vintage) to *Love's Body* (New York: Random House, 1966); cf. Herbert Marcuse, "Love Mystified: A Critique of Norman O. Brown" (1967), and Brown's response (1967), both reprinted in Marcuse, *Negations*, with translations from the German by Jeremy J. Shapiro (Boston: Beacon, 1968), pp. 227–247.

31. Only two of many especially illuminating examples: David Horowitz and Reese Erlich, "Big Brother as a Holding Company" (on Litton Industries), *Ramparts* (November 30, 1968), and William D. Phelan, Jr., "The 'Complex' Society Marches On," *Ripon Forum* (January, March, April, May 1969, and continuing at the time of this writing).

32. Again only one of many examples: "What is it that these eminent dissenters [professors at M.I.T.] have in common with the student radicals at Berkeley, Columbia, and the Sorbonne or those quietly challenging the Soviet leadership in Moscow? It seems to be a conviction that the various societies of our planet are trapped in ruts of ideological dogma, nationalism, and power politics." Walter Sullivan, "Fighting the 'Misuse' of Knowledge," *The New York Times*, February 9, 1969, p. 7E. (The article deals with a day of research

stoppage, sponsored by a number of professors at M.I.T. and then planned to take place at various universities.)

33. Karl Marx, preface to Karl Marx and Friedrich Engels, *The German Ideology* (1845–1846), with an introduction by R. Pascal, Ed. (New York: International, 1939), pp. 1–2.

34. C. Wright Mills, "On Knowledge and Power" (1955), in *Power, Politics and People,* Irving Louis Horowitz, Ed. (New York: Oxford University Press, 1963), pp. 611, 612–613.

35. Noam Chomsky, "The Responsibility of Intellectuals," *The New York Review of Books,* February 23, 1967. (Regarding the last sentence of this quotation, cf. Lionel Trilling's similar observation.) See also Chomsky's incisive "The Menace of Liberal Scholarship," *ibid.,* January 2, 1969, responses, predominantly oppositional, by various writers, and Chomsky's rejoinder, "An Exchange on Liberal Scholarship," *ibid.,* February 13, 1969.

36. See many entries in the bibliography appended to Mannheim's *Ideology and Utopia,* translated by Louis Wirth and Edward Shils, preface by Louis Wirth (1936; Harvest, n.d.), IV. The Sociology of Knowledge, 2. Present Status. For a more recent example see Theodor W. Adorno, "The Sociology of Knowledge and Its Consciousness" (1935), in *Prisms,* translated by Samuel and Shierry Weber (London: Neville Spearman, 1967), pp. 35–49.

37. Mills, *op. cit.,* p. 611.

38. Theodore Roszak, Ed. (New York: Pantheon Books, 1967, 1968). By comparison, two thirds of *The Morality of Scholarship* (n. 22)—the articles by Frye and Hampshire—are written from a subjective or cultural point of view; only O'Brien's gets into politics: "The intellectual community to which we belong, and whose morality we are discussing, is that of the advanced, capitalist world" (p. 66). O'Brien's "Politics and the Morality of Scholarship" is a political analysis.

39. *The Sociological Imagination* (1959; Evergreen, Galaxy). (Its existence is used to justify the absence of a treatment of sociology in *The Dissenting Academy,* p. vii.)

40. Gough in Roszak, *op. cit.,* pp. 148–149. See also her (Kathleen Gough Aberle) *Anthropology and Imperialism: New Proposals for Anthropologists* (Ann Arbor, Mich.: Radical Educational Project, 1967).

41. Robert S. Lynd, *Knowledge for What? The Place of Social Science in American Culture* (1939; Evergreen Black Cat). (The less consciously political nature of this book is suggested by its subtitle.)

Reprinted from the *International Journal of Contemporary Sociology,* **8** (1971), 13–34, and *The Centennial Review,* **7** (1963), 46–53, by permission of the publisher. The essay has been edited and partially revised by the author.

2

SOCIOLOGY AND EVIL. 1969, 1967

Certainly in some, probably in most, very likely in all of
his activities *as a social scientist,* the social scientist by
what he does inevitably intervenes in, interferes with,
meddles in the social process.

If this "social science is social action theorem" (Seeley, 1963, p. 56) is
true, it follows also that social-science neglect makes itself felt in society.
Such neglect exists in regard to evil: to my knowledge no social scientist,
as a social scientist, has asked what evil is.

"What is evil?" is a question that has been raised (both in the East and
West) by philosophers and theologians as well as by uncounted, unclassi-
fied, unrecorded people since time immemorial. Here, however, most
social scientists, do not feel negligent but virtuous, and self-evidently so:
"Of course," they might put it, "the exploration of the nature or essence
or meaning of evil *obviously* is not our concern; it *is* the concern of the
philosopher and the theologian! All we do and legitimately *can* do is
ascertain (as well as possible) what men, what certain men *consider* evil.
We study beliefs about evil, conceptions of it, attitudes toward it, the
moral code of a given society or other group, and so on; in short, we
explore what is *called* evil, but as social scientists we do not and cannot
commit *ourselves* to a conception of evil, because if we did we would *by
definition* no longer be social scientists but precisely become philosophers
or theologians." As they might *not* put it, in their nominalism and the
practice attendant on it social scientists commit themselves to a science
that claims *not* to know what evil is, *not* to be responsible for knowing
or seeking to know it, and would, they are convinced, indeed lose its
scientific character if it founded its investigations of evil on its own
conception of it.

This social science is characterized not only by its neglect in raising the question at issue—as well as many others it considers equally non-scientific—but also by certain related, typically unacknowledged, theoretical consequences of conceptions of truth, particularly scientific truth, and of the relations between student and subject matter, Is and Ought, theory and practice, knowledge and its application, science and history, society, politics, and ethics.

Even more conspicuous are two other relations between social science, especially sociology, and the investigation of evil. On the one hand, there is the "classical tradition" which puts sociology at the service of improving the society studied, whether we think of Marx, Comte, Spencer, Durkheim, Max Weber, or others among its representatives. On the other, there is the plethora of research into social problems, that is, into evils, which are, however, conceived as such characteristically not by specified groups but by some sort of anonymous middle-of-the-road (American) society with which their student, probably in contradiction to the conception of sociology he would profess if he were pressed, might well agree. (For an attempt at specification, cf. Mills, 1963.)

The representatives of the classical tradition, no matter how different from one another, share an explicit conception of history. Both features, but particularly the latter, are not characteristic of the social pathologist. The one characteristic that the two groups have in common is a desire to ameliorate extant society—the classicists consciously and as an admitted task of their activity, the social pathologists blushingly, given their vaunted freedom from value judgments. The latter, and sociologists typically, in the United States probably more than elsewhere, do not judge what they study, or judge it unwittingly, but if they do at all it is more likely to be on the basis of their private views which, according to their conception of social science, ought not to contaminate it. They do not tell us, or do not tell us frankly, what they consider evil or, for that matter, evils: their conception of social science cannot tell *them*. Instead they take over the ideas of others and base their own studies on them, if not by contract or on order. Their position, role and professional type approach those of the "organization man."

I

These social scientists are unaware that whatever they may be studying, their nominalist position hides a twofold commitment. One of its aspects is evident: it is a commitment to a science that does not know what its subject matter is, does not hold itself responsible for such knowledge (to repeat), and fears to lose its character as a science if it bases its studies of evil (for instance) on its own conception of it. The second aspect may be less immediately obvious: it is that in his research, which he believes to be purely nominalistic, the sociologist (and, of course, not he alone) depends and cannot help depending on his own conceptions and convictions, not only concerning evil but quite generally whatever phenomena figure in the study he may be undertaking.

Suppose he is interested in the conceptions of evil existing in a given society. He tells himself that he does not know what they are, in any event that his own notion of evil, if he has one, neither matters nor enters his research. Because he is dealing with a society, he will have to use a sample. He finds, let us say, that he will have to choose between a random and a stratified sample. If he chooses a random sample, it means in his view that the distribution of concepts of evil is not tied, at least not significantly, to the social, economic, religious, or political characteristics that distinguish the groups or strata in his universe. That is, he bases the expected distribution on a notion of evil itself, namely, on one whose expressions vary more with individuals than with aggregates, which have other traits (age, sex, occupation, etc.) that might form the basis of a stratified sample. He expects these expressions to vary less between bankers and unemployed, between old and young, men and women, Catholics and Protestants, or painters and engineers than *among* bankers, unemployed, old, young, and so on, as *individuals*. Inversely, if he uses a stratified sample he is indicating his expectation of a stratified distribution of expressions or concepts. Moreover, regardless of his choice of sample, conceptions beyond those of distribution and evil itself necessarily play a role, particularly assumptions of the nature of the society he wishes to investigate and of the groups, strata, and individuals composing it. After all, it is on the basis of these assumptions that he justifies the kind of sample he has chosen. In short, even to begin nominalist research presupposes definitions, concepts, or convictions that are the researcher's own, even though he may fancy dealing only with other people's ideas for which he is not responsible.

The situation is the same if his universe is too small to require sampling, for here, also, figure notions of his own influence, the student's choice of technique (interview, questionnaire, scales, etc.), and so on.

The next question asks where these notions come from. Undoubtedly from socialization, including general and special education, and reflection. What distinguishes the social scientist is that in his professional education he has acquired the concept or concepts of social science that prevail in his society, among them, the one we have called nominalist.

Even in this approach, then, there is inevitably an element that might be called realist, a fact that may come to the student's attention if he finds that his concepts, which are based on his own socialization and education, are inadequate. Suppose he is troubled by the diversity of traditions that concern the very nature of the society he wants to study. He then has two options: either he chooses one of the traditions or reinterprets it in a way that is more acceptable to him or he feels that his trouble has less easily specifiable grounds—for instance, a diffuse distrust of tradition in general. Although the two cases differ, once the student comes up against the unavoidable presence of a realist element in his undertaking the basis of his concept can become a problem. If it does, once again he has two options: to affirm or to replace this basis. In the first case, if it is the plurality of traditions that bothers him, he may try to reaffirm a traditional basis. In the second, which is distrust of tradition in general, he may try to replace this basis altogether.

He proceeds by carefully examining the competing traditions in the hope of arriving at one of them, or at a synthesis of their elements, that strikes him as trustworthy. To reaffirm or affirm a basis means to take existing traditions for granted, not to call them into question, and to stay within their framework. What could it mean to leave their framework—what is there beyond tradition? How can the social scientist replace it instead of trying to affirm it as honestly as he can? It is possible to bracket the world (to use a phenomenological expression), that is, neither affirming nor denying but, precisely, calling it into question, suspending it. Such suspension of the world, which may be followed by its reaffirmation, redefinition, or reinvention, is an extraordinary experience, in which the whole being, not only the cognitive faculty, is at stake. The desire to have such an experience does not guarantee its occurrence because it is unforeseeable. The very consciousness that tradition no longer is viable may arouse the will to go beyond this consciousness to find in oneself the basis of his convictions. Because human beings are socialized, that is, because they would not be human beings without their traditions with which to orient themselves, it is clear that "oneself" cannot mean some kind of *tabula rasa*. Rather, it refers to that psychic state in which the question of tradition does not come up at all— that extraordinary state, that extreme situation, of which love, anxiety, solitude [cf. **Chapter 4**], **mediation**, **creation**, or **other unexpected** extraordinary experiences are examples—"extraordinary" meaning not ordinary, nonroutine, not everyday. If not simply enjoyed or suffered but undergone as cognitive experiences, they may be occasions of calling the world into question and reconstituting it; and this reconstituted, reinvented, new world gives the experiencer greater certainty about the world than he has had before. As far as he knows, what he has found is true, not in a nominalist sense of a truth for others that does not commit him, but true for himself. To distinguish this truth from scientific truth let us call it existential.

We saw that the researcher's own view also figures in the nominalist approach. He searches for scientific truth but cannot help availing himself of truths that, whatever their origin, are, for him, existential truths. Thus there is a relation between the two kinds of truth in the very act of research. This relation emerges as more systematic on the basis of the criteria for verifying the two kinds. The criterion for verifying existential truth is the outcome of the examination of received notions, which also include all the scientific truths at the examiner's command. They, too, consequently, are examined. It follows that existential truth, unverified by the examination of relevant scientific truth, is, properly speaking, merely idiosyncrasy. On the other hand, it also follows that scientific truth that disregards existential truth is empty. Let us come back to our example—research into the concepts of evil in a given society—in order to see concretely how these two kinds of truth, their relation and their interdependence, manifest themselves.

In this example scientific truth refers to concepts of evil found among certain people. We take it that the researcher has ignored what for him are existential truths, namely, a number of propositions he accepts as valid (propositions on the distribution of the concepts of evil in the society he wants to study, his own notions of evil, of that society, and of the groups, strata, and individuals making it up), for it is on the basis of these concepts that he has chosen his samples or adopted other techniques. He ignores them, however. It might be objected that the notions mentioned are not existential but scientific. If this is so, it is easy to understand that the researcher had to conceive them on the basis of decisions which, at some point, must be existential in nature, even though this point may not be the one envisaged here (the one at which the choice of sample or the interview, instead of the questionnaire, was made). Whatever the stage of the research, there is a moment, if only he is aware of it, when the student is bound to place his trust in existentially true propositions as the basis of his enterprise.

It is equally important to point out that existential truth that is indifferent to scientific truth is an idiosyncrasy. Suppose that in a study of concepts of evil a student bases the choice of his sample on the hypothesis (an existential truth for him) that his population must be classified by hair color, for he anticipates a significant correlation between the distributions of hair color and the concepts of evil. If such a hypothesis strikes us as idiosyncratic, if we do not believe it, it may be because we have the results of enough scientific studies to be convinced of its invalidity. If, instead of hair color we take ethnic or religious affiliation, we may in certain cases not know whether there is a correlation between ethnic and religious groups and evil. We may or may not be inclined to think so. In any event, we must examine our expectations, which can become existential truths provided they are controlled by the results of scientific investigation. Otherwise the growth of existential truth would be stunted.

Thus what is required is a conscious cooperative effort of the two kinds of truth, which figure in research anyway. We have seen that each suffers from the absence of the other and that each serves to correct the other. There cooperation thus resembles a virtuous circle, whereas if the student allows one of them to exploit the other, on the contrary, a vicious circle forms. It does if, instead of rigorously examining his existential truths, he chooses only those that he considers existentially valid. To give an absurd illustration: if he chooses among all his studies only that of a strange community in which redheads have an idea about evil that is different from that of all blonds and he generalizes on it in order to demonstrate his existential truth, the exploitation of scientific by existential truth, is nothing but the rationalization of a prejudice. There may, however, also be exploitation of existential by scientific truth. It occurs if the student assumes that scientific truth is all the truth there is: he may not distinguish between the two kinds or may believe that scientific truth can lead him to existential truth, or, far from not distinguishing them, he may maintain that existential truth cannot be analyzed rationally because it *is* idiosyncratic. The last is close to Max Weber's attitude, which, however, he prescribed more than he practiced. The first two of the three positions are varieties of scientism; the third is one of nihilism or absolute relativism. All three produce a vicious circle.

We must distinguish clearly between these types of misalliance of scientific and existential truth and cases in which the two are not even meant to meet. If we now say that there are studies in which not both of them figure, we speak from a psychological point of view, from that of the student and no longer from the systematic. So far we have made reference only to the most serious form of study, from the student's standpoint, in which he tries as best he can to honor the claims of both truths. His own aim, however, may be only one of them. If it is scientific truth, he will discover and collect facts that do not personally concern him and which he will relate to other facts in order to determine their structure for the purpose of comparison or generalization. If, on the contrary, he is seeking existential truth, he may proceed in an analogous manner but with reference to facts that do concern him: he will want to find out what he can truly hold to be good or bad, beautiful or ugly, right or wrong—what he must do. From a systematic point of view the difference between these two types of study is only in the distribution and emphasis of the two kinds of truth which are always present—a difference of degree. From a psychological point of view the first type is that of a pragmatic, hypothetical, stipulative, propositional, external, objective, theoretical study. From a social point of view, and only with respect to the relation between the study and the society in which it is done, this relation depends, in both cases, on the existential truth on which the study is based, because it alone can bring to light an attitude (positive, negative, or neutral) toward the society and, combined with scientific truth, can have a social effect, for scientific truth by itself is neutral, ineffectual, impotent, like Max Scheler's ideal factors, his "logos."

II

We began with the observation that the question "What is evil?" has been raised not in social science but in philosophy and theology. Why is this so? Perhaps we can try for an answer by glimpsing the history of the Western concept of evil and contemporary society.

This concept is marked, above all, by the Judaeo-Christian tradition, particularly its Christian component, whether original sin or glad tidings be considered the core of Christianity. The Western concept of evil would thus have dissipated with the dissolution of that tradition, especially of Christianity itself. Perhaps because of the personal and particular loyalties that characterize it—to Jesus, to saints and priests, to the Protestant's individual conscience—because of this "particularism," Christianity seems difficult to reconcile with the "universalism" (both terms in Talcott Parsons' sense) that characterizes industrial, technological, bureaucratic society, whether capitalist or socialist (despite the fact that a line connects certain features of universalism with certain features of Protestantism). This difficulty obviously accounts for much of the controversy and movement that has for some time agitated many churches—the Catholic Church notably since John XXIII. The heritage of the Christian concept of evil, at any rate, even though modified, diluted, and deformed, is rooted in us, and the combination of this heritage with the historical development that is hard to reconcile with it goes some way toward accounting for the incapacity of presumably a great many individuals today to form a viable concept of evil, one for which they—and we— could truly answer.

To put it differently, God has been replaced by other absolutes—state, race, the future of a given people, if not of mankind, to which the present generation must be sacrificed (cf. Camus, 1958, especially p. 282). Millions of men have been victimized by these absolutes and in their names have victimized others. The bad conscience or unease hovering about them remains to be ascertained. When infidels or witches were executed, bad conscience and unease were likely to have been covered up by the conviction that these acts were done in the name of God—although the persecuted died as irrevocably as if they had fallen prey to Hitler, Stalin, a traffic crash, or napalm. Recognition of mishandling the name of God, however, played its role in the Reformation, which, among other things, was a secularization of Catholicism in that it questioned previously unquestioned aspects of God and their abusive institutionalization on earth.

Yet the suffering inflicted in the name of more recent absolutes is much less limited than that perpetrated in the name of God: the numbers and categories of people that punishment, misery, and death can attain have grown enormously with democratization and technology, especially communications, transportation, and destruction. Modern social control thus is more nearly total and far more cruel, and efficient than ever before, when crimes against mankind had not yet been recognized as such. They were first named and punished at Nuremberg but have also been perpetuated for years in Vietnam by American "fire power," "especially air power (Harvey estimates . . . [its preponderance over the Vietnamese] at about 1000 to 1)." Crimes against mankind have not yet entered the consciousness and conscience of mankind, so that "American Huey troops at Vinh Long" (soldiers hovering in a Huey Hog, "a converted transport helicopter which has been remade into a floating firing platoon with the fire power of a World War II infantry battalion crammed aboard")

> didn't hurl impersonal thunderbolts from the heights in supersonic jets. They came muttering down to the paddies and hootch lines ["rows of houses along a road or canal"], fired at close range and saw their opponents disintegrate to bloody rags 40 feet away (Harvey, 1967, quoted by Crichton, 1968).

If ever these men conceive of their actions as evil, they fail to act in accord with their conception. Thus if "no poetry after Auschwitz," what social science in the face of such bestiality? Will there be a Nuremberg for the American military and their Washington directors or will it be impossible to distinguish the Eichmanns among all of us? Yet to

> be silent about what we cannot grasp is the only adequate mode of being; the only adequate mode of being before that which we cannot grasp is *not* to be silent about it. Between these two contradictory truths lies our dilemma, for we can neither be silent nor speak; we must speak but we cannot speak (Wolff, 1961, p. 14).

This dilemma has taken historical body in our paralyzing suspension between two impossible worlds: one in which we can no longer believe, a world ordered by religious directives and moderations, and one that we cannot bear, a world without these directives and moderations. We are alienated from both, yet there seem to be no others. This, perhaps, is the reason why we have not succeeded in articulating a concept of evil that would be adequate to the secularized world in which we live but which has left evil itself, in contrast to space, cancer, the Greenland Icecap, and innumerable other phenomena and problems, comparatively unexplored, ominously sacred and threatening. Evil is no longer committed in the name of God. It is less than ever legitimated by religious or even moral motives and is covered over for political, economic, and technological reasons on a larger scale than ever—but the cover can also be seen through, and is seen through, by more people than ever. There is evil, such as the suffering and death caused by famine and epidemics, that the technology and economy we have developed could eliminate if we applied them to this end instead of submitting to other orders we also have developed, notably the distribution of power and the distribution and, especially, the nondistribution of economic products.

The decisive difference between the two worlds is that the first is done with, whereas the second is there for us to work on to make it one we can affirm. Here Max Weber's work (Marcuse, 1968) can be helpful not only in its analytic power but also its symptomatic character. *The Protestant Ethic and the Spirit of Capitalism*, in particular, has a significance at once vaster and more specific than tends to be recognized, for it deals not only with the two phenomena indicated in its title but conjures up, for Weber as well as for us, a much larger complex, which profoundly troubled Weber himself, and which consists, in addition to the remnants of ascetic Protestantism and the spirit of capitalism, of the associated elements of bureaucracy, functional (technical, instrumental) rationality, secularization, impersonality, and control. In other words, it represents modern industrialized society, the second of the two worlds mentioned. It is this complex and those and related elements that make us feel frustrated, alienated, powerless, vicarious, or anonymous, as we so often say. Beyond analyses, discussions, and laments, however, are more active and practical responses, suffering, and political action. Max Weber's intent was to account for the rise of the spirit of capitalism, but what this account can mean for us was probably as unintended by him as was, from the point of view of Calvinism, capitalism itself [1].

Let us recall the features of the Protestant-capitalist complex: labor, work, making, producing, discipline, asceticism, control, specialization, bureaucracy, profit. Being parts of a whole, they are related, as are our responses to them. In terms of this list capitalism and the reaction to it, socialism, which has become the other variant of modern industrialized society, are much more alike than unlike.

This society goes back far beyond the present generation and so does its critique—it is enough to recall Marx, Kierkegaard, and Nietzsche, utopian communities, communist and socialist movements, and many other indications in the arts, philosophy, and theology. What is new is the extraordinarily accelerated development of this society during the last decades. Some of its results are Stalinism, nazism, and fascism, and, more generally, the A- and H-bombs, electronics, and the exploration of space. Perhaps the most common reaction to them is one of puzzlement, foreboding, and ignorance and, more recently, the protest against the proliferation of nuclear weapons and the war in Vietnam. There are many more indirect reactions that nevertheless are equally, if not more, instructive in regard to the society in which we live: the widespread feeling of alienation and concern with alienation; the resistance against control and manipulation on the part of younger people, particularly students; the distrust of their elders; the civil-rights struggle; the ecumenical movement; the formation of various groups who protest or withdraw, from Beats to Hippies and Diggers; developments in art—pop-art, happenings, and art in the service of politics; certain governmental programs, especially the antipoverty program; and developments in the social sciences—for instance, action anthropology [cf. Wolff, 1974, ch. 24]. A few words about some of them will show their relevance in our context.

Alienation places a distance not only between the individual and his society but also between himself and whatever he might believe reality to be (Keniston, 1967). Much of what the alienated encounters, including himself, is unreal, and he longs for the real. He may try to find it in psychic states induced by drugs; he may be tired of the centuries-old sermon on deferred, indefinitely deferred, gratification and seek it now; he may "turn on" (but notice the mechanical metaphor) by letting music, turned on full-blast, invade him. He may be less pervasively alienated and instead reject more definable and particular aspects of his society, notably people, especially his parents and his elders in general, who he believes suffer from this world as he does but whom he may also hold responsible for its horror. He may rebel against certain of the features he resents as particularly objectionable, such as control and manipulation— despite the official veneration of science, as if science were nothing but the highest expression of this control [2], or he may do more than rebel by joining others in trying to leave his society physically, socially, emotionally—perhaps founding a community. This may be no more than withdrawal or, as in the case of the Diggers, it may also entail action on concern and kindness.

Others react to this society by attempting to improve it, working, for instance, for civil rights or in the ecumenical movement. A few try to understand how certain children and adults risk their lives doing what strikes them as right—how *they* fight evil (Coles, 1967), or they attempt— as did the late C. Wright Mills, Herbert Marcuse, Barrington Moore, or Kenneth Keniston—to understand this society historically and critically, or they engage in political actions of many kinds.

Concerning our society, various forms of art, most obviously caricature and cartoon but also certain mime and pantomime plays, use irony and sarcasm; in other forms expectations are broken—from the *trompe-l'œuil* to the happening ("it isn't as you think it is"), which may, like the social "no," pass into a "yes," into the effort to feel real or to have an experience, if only to be shocked out of numbness. This consideration points to antecedent developments in art—surrealism, dadaism, and expressionism—and in literature, from the contemporary "new novel," in which the object replaces the subject, to Kafka, Joyce, Henry James, imagism, and stream-of-consciousness writing. Marshall McLuhan, too, finds his place here, with his insistence in favor of the appeal to all the senses, or, in Norman O. Brown's words, polymorphism.

The most obvious problem of modern industrial society lies in international relations, though less, despite its magnitude, in the precarious connection between the two variants of this society, capitalist and communist, than between both and those that are neither—the "developing nations," the "third world." The truth of Marx's adage that the root is not society but man shows itself when man comes to the fore and fights— most dramatically as a guerrilla—against the whole military-industrial complex. The political outcome surely is uncertain; thus in Vietnam an increasing number even of observers who are members of that complex admit that our machinery is not equal to guerrilla warfare; in Latin America the success of the guerrillas appears to have been set back by

Che Guevara's assassination; in the United States itself the future seems impenetrable but of more importance than almost anywhere else.

Max Weber's methodological tenets, notably his misleading and widely misread insistence on a value-free social science but also his dangerously elliptic formulation of the ethics of responsibility and of principle, suggest his position at the end of a period during which men took it for granted that the nation was the largest unit of social organization. Characteristic of Weber's position was that he felt urged to diagnose his society and his time but that he insisted on doing so outside sociology. "No one knows"—to recall a famous passage at the end of *The Protestant Ethic*— "who will live in this cage of the future" (the "iron cage" that the "light cloak" of the Puritans' "care for external goods" had become),

> or whether at the end of this tremendous development entirely new prophets will arise, or there will be a great rebirth of old ideas and ideals, or if neither, mechanized petrification, embellished with a sort of convulsive self-importance. For of the last stage of this cultural development, it might well be truly said: "Specialists without spirit, sensualists without heart; this nullity imagines that it has attained a level of civilization never before achieved." But with this [Weber checks himself], we get into the field of value judgments and judgments of faith, with which this purely historical presentation shall not be burdened (Weber, 1958, p. 182; my translation of the last sentence).

If we take Weber, the whole man, and not only that part of him that he himself admitted into his sociology, then by bringing his diagnosis to bear on ourselves we are acting on his intent. We placed Protestantism and capitalism into the complex of which they are a part and from which Weber had isolated them for scientific analysis, and we are trying to understand the whole of this complex today. The reactions to it we have sketched, to which many could be added, suggest that we are closer to the end of Weber's period than he was or are already into the beginning of a new one, of which we know as little as Marx could know about the reign of freedom that was to follow the reign of necessity.

On the basis of the diagnosis suggested, the task of the sociologist is to analyze and interpret the responses to our society that have been illustrated. To vary Marx's formula of the change from necessity to freedom we can adopt Marcuse's (in *Eros and Civilization*) of the change from life under the performance principle, which we all know, to life under the pleasure principle, of which we have only the most fleeting notions. Under the guidance and compulsion of the former we have produced so many things and so much knowledge that we can afford the most radical change in man's history: to a society that would be acceptable to an unprecedented majority of men because they would consider it good on mature reflection. Not only this change, but also its outcome is almost impossible to imagine. Still, it is quite possible, if not likely, that in the short run we shall be dead but that the prospects for those who come after us, if we ourselves attend to this change with everything at our command, are unimaginably better than is the world in which we live.

III

This suggests what one sociologist at least might argue as good: a necessary utopian society whose seed he recognizes in ours. *Evil*, therefore, would be the failure to recognize and fight all that would choke this seed: injustice, misery, and sham and the institutional arrangements that favor and facilitate them. A historically adequate concept of evil cannot locate it in the individual as evil deed, sin, or vice (which, of course, exist) nor in myth, religion, or philosophy (not that its mythical, religious, and philosophical dimensions are not relevant today) but must find it in society and in the individual's relations to society.

Hence the task of a *sociology of evil* is to study the various reactions to our society that have been mentioned, or others that are similar, in an effort to specify the corresponding characteristics of this society, thus the society itself, the changes it needs, and how they are to be made.

It may be stated that such an undertaking is possible without reference to evil, in another perspective or, indeed, without one that is explicitly formulated. It may also be stated that the undertaking, in whatever perspective, is superfluous because we know enough already and what is needed is not study but action. Both objections, if they are counter-suggestions, are to be welcomed. What recommends the proposal submitted here is this. It acknowledges and acts on sociology as morality and praxis, which has been neglected, thus helping to reconnect sociology with its historical task and thereby to re-establish, at least in one area of our intellectual concerns, a believable, affirmable continuity. It re-establishes a continuity also with the universal human preoccupation with good and evil. This continuity is expressed and denied—expressed, e.g., in nightmares, neuroses, psychoses, anxiety, aggression, violence; denied in the widely observable reluctance to use the word evil and to prefer, instead, less haunting words. The enterprise proposed thus has a therapeutic function for those who would act on it as well as for those who would in any way come in contact with it. The failure to study evil intervenes, and its study will intervene—if we recall Seeley's "social science is social action theorem"—in the social process. On the most modest scale those engaged in the study will find it meaningful, hence feel less alienated for it. This may also apply to some readers of their findings. Less modestly, the study may contribute to a change in the definition of the situation of contemporary society and thus perhaps to a change in the situation and the society.

I conclude with a few examples of study complexes that may serve to make the proposal more concrete by conveying its open and comprehensive character.

An example of one of the investigations envisaged by the general diagnosis suggested

In all countries perhaps, there are people who recognize certain aspects of our historical situation and act accordingly: resisting, protesting, rebelling, fighting, destroying, killing, building, planning, constructing, helping, writing, marching, analyzing, proclaiming, and preaching. It is always a "No" to aspects they have recognized and a "Yes" to others whose seeds they discover and want to cultivate, whether a peasant revolt or a civil-rights struggle, whether the actors are colonials, ex-colonials, or students. Is a new concept of evil—less Christian or religious in general, more secularized and more in line with our One World—in the process of developing? We could try to find out by studying the leaders of many of these types of activity and the participants at all levels; we would probably arrive at a number of concepts of evil. What are the social sources of these concepts and what are their social and political effects? Which are their common traits? Is it possible to ascertain a rather limited number of types, or even one, that would be diffused everywhere? What purposes would such studies serve, how could their utilization be justified, how could they be used and what could the consequences of their use be?

An example of research into sociology suggested by the sociology of evil proposed

The individual and sociologist who argues this sociology of evil is himself somebody who acts according to his recognition of certain aspects of the world in which he lives. His own concept of evil finds expression, for example, in his insistence that evil be recognized as a topic of social-scientific, especially sociological, research. What kind of sociologist is concerned with evil as a scientific topic; what kind is not? What has happened in the world that would account for the change from the second to the first? Is there, in addition to the precarious role of Christianity in a society partly described, partly predicted by George Orwell twenty years ago in *1984*, also the precarious situation of the white man and of Western domination predicted fifty years ago by Oswald Spengler in *The Decline of the West*? The social psychologist who studies socialization, aggression, resentment, and prejudice, the psychiatrist who studies neuroses and psychoses, the cultural anthropologist who studies the variety of cultures, including moral codes, and the sociologist who studies slums, crimes, and vice are probably more sensitive than others to the problematic and dangerous aspects of our world. Many of them separate their professions from their lives, hold on to a value-free social science, and try to practice it. What is the origin, beyond Max Weber, of this social science? (Recall the change from the Hegelian concept to positivism; Marcuse, 1960.) Its practitioners have spread not only their knowledge but also their personal sensitivity to social phenomena far beyond the social sciences themselves. Is this, however, comparable to knowledge diffused by the mass media in having contributed less to the enlightenment than to the disorientation of the general social consciousness and to its increased disturbance?

A few examples of sociological analyses of materials
not originally found in sociology but relevant to the inquiry

From sin to complex

Origin and development of the psychological interpretation of the infraction of moral norms, including changes in attitude toward such infractions, especially the shift from judgment and condemnation to understanding and explanation. Development of efforts to correct and improve the behavior of those who breach norms. Changes in the significance attributed to the thought of infraction as against the act of infraction. All these aspects are to be investigated in relation to social situations and structures and their changes. One of the lessons of the research could be the answer to the question that both the author and his readers might ask: what is a justifiable attitude toward his or their own behavior and that of others—critical or understanding, moral or psychological?

Mythology and practice of ordeals

What concepts of evil can be deduced from ordeals described in myths; what concept of evil, from ordeals that have in fact been practiced? What can we infer about the nature of ordeals and corresponding concepts of evil from an analysis of the mythical against the practical context (circumstances, explanations, frequency, and consequences) of ordeals? What does the study of ordeals suggest if we compare them with investigations that suspected persons undergo in our own society (examinations and cross-examinations, lie detection, brainwashing, punishment, and humiliation to discover the truth or obtain a statement)? To what extent can such studies change our own attitudes toward these measures?

Evil in dreams

Dreams about particular evils, their imagery of evil, inferences regarding the dreamer's concept of evil, and comparison of this concept with that of the awake person. Special attention should be paid to relations between evil and anxiety, fear, and the mechanisms by which what is feared becomes an evil or evil. What is the importance of these mechanisms to our understanding of the relations between anxiety, fear, mythical figures, and symbols of evil, of the phenomenon of the scapegoat and, more generally, of prejudice—including the importance to our understanding of these phenomena in ourselves?

When does who think about evil?

We could begin by studying socialization in which people acquire their ideas of evil. What are these ideas and what importance for the individual is given them? For which manifestations of evil, which the researcher knows from other sources, does socialization inadequately prepare the individual? A comparison of what the student knows about concepts of evil acquired in socialization and what he knows about evil or evils that exist in the world can furnish him with hypotheses concerning evil(s) for which socialization does not prepare, or insufficiently prepares, the individual. These hypotheses can then be examined by studies of cases in which the individual thinks about evil or otherwise encounters it. We could also begin with these cases, wherever they are found—in scientific literature, in novels, or short stories, or by direct investigation—in order to find an answer to this question.

What does the history of censorship teach us about the history of concepts of evil?

The inquiry that tries to answer this question should be accompanied, as far as available sources allow, by another into the diffusion of censored writings and their readers. Censorship, diffusion of censored books, and types of reader show perhaps marked changes according to the contents of the writings. Thus the history of pornographic books is possibly less variable, despite the variations in the criteria of pornography, than the history of books censored for theological or political reasons. In any case, what can we learn from such studies about the nature of evil that expresses itself in this fashion in its varied relations with social institutions and human traits—particularly in contemporary society?

Obviously, these examples could be vastly multiplied (for more, see Wolff, 1967, pp. 206–213). In addition to the concepts of evil and their differences and convergences, the examination of sociology and sociologists in regard to notions of evil and attitudes toward them, interpretations of the breaches of moral norms, ordeals, evil in dreams, occasions on which people think about evil, and censorship—what about comparative studies in the etymology and semantics of "evil" and cognate and contrasting words in one language, inquiries into the place of evil in the history of philosophy, into ideas of evil as counterconcepts to ideas of the good society in works of sociologists and other thinkers, into the antecedents, if they exist, of evil in prehuman animals, or into the vast relations between evil and technology or between evil and law—among many, many others? No matter how heterogeneous these areas of research may appear, drawing as they do on the literatures of sociology, social, child, and depth psychology and psychoanalysis, ethics and theology, cultural anthropology, law, linguistics, philosophy, history of ideas, social, economic, and intellectual history, animal sociology, ethology, and genetics, the histories of science and technology, literature and the other arts, and journalism—what makes them contributions to one central problem is the question that inspires them: the question concerning the seeds of a better society than ours. This, to put it mildly, is a *good* task for sociology.

Acknowledgment. Talks with Ruth Meyer, Juan E. Corradi, Roger Pritchard, Alice Stewart, and Barrie Thorne, friends and students, responses to the first version of this chapter in French (Wolff, 1967) by Carroll Bourg, S.J., Mihailo Marković, Barrington Moore, Jr., Paul Ricoeur, John R. Seeley, Hans Weil, and Walter A. Weisskopf, comments on an earlier draft in English by members of a seminar on the topic at Brandeis University, Fall 1967–1968, especially Stephen D. Berkowitz, Y. Michael Bodemann, Mario Montano, and Andrew Strickland, as well as by Milton Rokeach and Ralph K. White, and critical readings of this essay itself by Montano and Strickland have influenced and helped me. I wish to acknowledge my gratitude to all these persons.

BIBLIOGRAPHY

Camus, Albert, *The Rebel*, translated by Anthony Bower (New York: Vintage, 1958).
Coles, Robert, *Children of Crisis* (Boston: Little, Brown, 1967).
Crichton, Robert, "Review of Harvey," *New York Review of Books*, 9 (January 4, 1968), 4.
Harvey, Frank, *Air War: Vietnam* (New York: Bantam, 1967).
Hirsch, Walter, "The Image of the Scientist in Science Fiction," in Bernard

54

Beyond

Barber and Walter Hirsch, Eds., *The Sociology of Science* (New York: Free Press, 1962), pp. 259–268.

Keniston, Kenneth, *The Uncommitted* (New York: Delta, 1967).

Marcuse, Herbert, *Reason and Revolution* (1941), (Boston: Beacon, 1960).

Marcuse, Herbert, "Industrialization and Capitalism in the Work of Max Weber" (1964), translated by Kurt H. Wolff and Jeremy J. Shapiro, in Marcuse, *Negations*, translated by Shapiro (Boston: Beacon, 1968), pp. 201–226.

Mills, C. Wright, "The Professional Ideology of Social Pathologists" (1943), in Mills, *Power, Politics and People*, Irving Louis Horowitz, Ed. (New York: Oxford University Press, 1963), pp. 525–552.

Parsons, Talcott, *The Structure of Social Action,* (New York: McGraw-Hill, 1937).

Seeley, John R., "Social Science? Some Probative Problems," in Maurice Stein and Arthur Vidich, Eds., *Sociology on Trial* (Englewood Cliffs, N.J.: Prentice-Hall, 1963), pp. 53–65.

Weber, Max, *The Protestant Ethic and the Spirit of Capitalism* (1904–1905), translated by Talcott Parsons (1930) (New York: Scribner's, 1958).

Wolff, Kurt H., "Pour une sociologie du mal," *L'homme et la société*, **4** (April, May, June 1967), 197–213.

Wolff, Kurt H., " 'Exercise in Commemoration,' "*Jewish Quarterly*, **8** (1961), 14-17.

Wolff, Kurt H., *Trying Sociology* (New York: Wiley, 1974).

NOTES

1. Capitalism as what Robert K. Merton might call "an unintended consequence of purposeful social action" is suggested by Talcott Parsons: "one cannot say that the Calvinistic ethic or any of its legitimate derivatives ever approved money making for its own sake or as a means to self-indulgence, which was, indeed, one of the cardinal sins. What it did approve was rational, systematic labor in a useful calling which could be interpreted as acceptable to God. Money was, certainly in the beginning, regarded as a by-product and one by no means without its dangers. The attitude was, that is, an ascetic one. But even this served capitalistic interests since, on the one hand, work in economic callings would serve to increase earnings but, on the other, the fear of self-indulgence would prevent their full expenditure for consumption" (Parsons, 1937, pp. 526–527). Thus it looks like a double surprise: first, capitalism, then the meaning for us of Weber's analysis of it.

2. Despite this veneration, its more spontaneous distrust is shown, for example, in science fiction in the decreasing confidence in the scientist as the human type who solves "social problems" which are rather left to the natives of other planets, suggesting that faith in the magic of science had resurrected the older magic of the *deus ex machina* (Hirsch, 1962, p. 267).

Reprinted from *L'homme et la société*, No. **4** (1967), 197–213, and *Journal of Social Issues,* **25** (1969), 111–125, by permission of the publishers. The essays have been edited and partially revised by the author.

3

SOCIOLOGY
AND HISTORY;
Theory and Practice. 1959

In discussing the broad topics of sociology and history with sociologists it is hardly necessary, at least not at the start, to present an array of concepts of sociology. Instead, I shall begin with some observations on history.

I

The most obvious is the distinction, sometimes overlooked, between history—in W. H. Walsh's formulation—as "the totality of past human actions," or history proper, and history as "the narrative or account we construct of them now" [1], or historiography. In this distinction the last word, "now," has an importance that Walsh seems not to have accorded it, for if it were left out of the second definition the distinction between it and the first would disappear, inasmuch as narratives or accounts surely belong among human actions. Thus historiography accomplished is part of history proper, or only historiography-in-the-making is historiography, for once made, it is history.

Now, in the first place the present moves ineluctably, not, as it is so often put, into the future, but into the past [2]. As you read this sentence, now—the "now," once spoken, no longer is—is becoming past. As I write the history of yesterday, even of today, my historiography is becoming part of the time in which it was written, part of history. Yet not all of me, not all of man and mankind, is historical; not all of us is composed of an ever receding present and an ever growing past; not all of us is intrinsically temporal. There are situations, for instance, in which we forget time, in which, were we reminded of it, we should be struck as if by an incongruous and irrelevant noise; for example, the situation in which we think. When we think, we make connections that are not temporal. They are logical. Their judge is not time but logic or reason, which apply atemporal standards of judgment. Thoughts, ideas, their connections, their judgment, and its standards are atemporal. This does not mean that they are timeless, for, obviously, they change in time. Ineluctably, they are located in time. Causal sequences are temporal; sequences of ideas are not [3].

In the second place we have just seen that ideas are parts not only of atemporal, acausal sequences but also of temporal, causal sequences, being causes and thus having effects, being effects and thus having causes. As I am thinking, my idea, willy-nilly, becomes part of the past and only thus takes on the character of a candidate in a causal sequence. While I am thinking it it is wholly atemporal, wholly caught in the realm of ideas, wholly outside the realm of time, but once thought it can be inspected—I or somebody else can inspect it and can ask not only logical but also causal, temporal questions about it. One can ask atemporal questions such as these: What are its premises? Is it consistent with them? What are its implications? Now that it is before us, no longer in the making but made past, we also can ask temporal questions: How did I get this idea? What effect may its communication have? In the present's moving into the past, ideas take on the dimensions of causality and temporality. If this were not so, historiography of whatever subject matter, including intellectual historiography or, as it is usually called, intellectual history, would not be possible. Historiography, as we have already seen, has this characteristic of all ideas, that in the making it is *only* an atemporal, acausal process of ideas but that once made it is also a temporal event which has its cause and effect.

A third observation which has to do with the movement of the present into the past concerns a distinction between theory and practice. Theory is looking, contemplating; practice is doing, acting, making. As attitudes, the two—theory and practice—are not differentiated in the present. They become differentiated only by the present's moving into the past. Whether I am thinking a thought or making a tool, my attitude is inextricably both watchful, inspecting, reflecting, and fashioning, changing, combining, recombining. Although my purpose may be predominantly theoretical or predominantly practical, in the present, even if I am conscious of it, purpose is an atemporal element in an atemporal complex. Once I have thought the idea or done or made the thing, the thought—as we have already seen—and the deed or product become links in a causal chain and may be inspected in reference to their effects in the realms of both ideas and actions. What is more, they may be inspected in reference to other men's ideas or actions or to my own. If I look at them wholly in reference to other men's, I am, whatever else I may be, not practical, for I exclude from my reference the core of the present, which is myself. Full practice is acting on theory, on my theory, my looking, my contemplating. This is expressed, even if elliptically or inaccurately, in the saying that the theorist is the most practical of men.

The past, then, with which historiography deals, may be approached as a reservoir of atemporal ideas or of causal sequences, and it may be approached theoretically or practically. If we take atemporal ideas out of the past in which we find them (rather than think them ourselves), we may deal with them either atemporally, in logical analysis, or in their temporal dimension, either in explicit causal analysis, that is, explanation, or implicit causal analysis, or, as we might call it, probability analysis. So for our dealings with causal sequences, for we may take them, too, as atemporal ideas or in their temporality. All are theoretical, for in all of them I look to see and understand relations and phenomena. They are practical if I undertake them in order to learn about myself as a person who must act. In this case I deal with ideas atemporally, yet not in logical analysis but in ontological, moral, or aesthetic analysis, and I deal with causal sequences, in explanations or probability analyses or other interpretations, in order to understand myself better as a person who must act and the time in which I live and must act. Intellectual disciplines, such as the various branches of philosophy, historiography, and social science, have, of course, not developed according to this scheme of distinctions and relations, for their development has surely not resulted, as this scheme has, from an observation of the relations between present and past and attendant observations of ideas and causal sequences and of theory and practice.

John C. McKinney writes:

> It is obvious that the research tasks of sociology and history are different as *disciplines,* for their procedures answer to their respective research purposes. Nevertheless, since all data are historical in one sense, the data of history and sociology are the same. The logical difference lies in what they do with the data. The research task of the sociologist is to generalize; that of the historian, to individualize. . . . The historian is concerned with processes and structures that are singular in their space-time occurrence; hence he does not conceive of

them as being repeatable, whereas the sociologist adopts the opposite view. The sociologist is concerned with the repetitive and constant factors, or tendencies to regularity, of human society [4].

II

Many other writers who have discussed the relations between sociology and historiography likewise follow, more or less closely, the distinctions made by Windelband, Rickert, Dilthey, Troeltsch, and others between sociology as generalizing (nomothetic, a *Naturwissenschaft*) and history as particularizing or individualizing (idiographic, a *Geisteswissenschaft*) [5].

Still others are not so much concerned with analyzing the nature of the two disciplines as with pointing out or advocating the advantages of their cooperation. Thus Arnold M. Rose reminds sociologists that in some branches of their science (e.g., the study of social change, social movements, social trends, and migration), historical data alone provide content; that the investigation of national characteristics is impossible without recourse to history; that "a knowledge of history is essential . . . in providing . . . a cultural premise for any hypothesis" [6]; that is, in making us realize that our findings, based as they are on culture- and time-bound data, have no transcultural and transtemporal validity and that we can learn methods from historians, the use of documents, for example, and the synthesis of wide varieties of facts. On the other hand, historians may learn from sociologists the usefulness of such techniques as descriptive statistics and content analysis, some concepts and findings, and the relevance of grasping contemporary phenomena for studying past periods. Similarly, though in more general terms, Maurice Mandelbaum says:

> History . . . depends for the furtherance of its analysis upon principles which only sociology and the other theoretical social sciences can disclose; sociology depends upon historical investigation for the material upon which it works, examining and comparing historical instances in order to discover the laws which may be implicit within them [7].

What is common to all these disquisitions is their positing historiography and sociology as having coordinate status, neither occupying a position that is in any sense preferred. Not so, however, for Franz Oppenheimer. For him the two are not equally legitimate scientific enterprises, one seeking the particular or unique and past, the other, the regular or general and atemporal, for, in contrast to sociology, historiography is not a science at all, nor, for that matter, is it an art. Instead, it is a "descriptive doctrine of the ideal." This concept, Oppenheimer believes, "fits in beautifully with the very common idea that history should and can be the schoolmaster of mankind . . . [and] even better, with the utterances of important historians and philosophers of history" [8].

The distinction between Oppenheimer's concepts of history and historiography and those mentioned above is that Oppenheimer's is practical, whereas the others are theoretical. Oppenheimer's is the conception of a man who is "doing," "making," and "acting," who must act, whereas the concepts referred to previously are those of men who "look" and "contemplate." As Oppenheimer says, there are many historians and philosophers of history who hold a practical view of their subject. Thus for Arthur Child, a more recent writer, practical history is "an imitation of the processes of decision . . . a choosing once more among alternative lines of conduct which themselves, in deliberation, are evaluated," and the historian's assessments form a part "of that massive disputation, of that vaster dialectic, within which society as a whole discusses the problem of its practice" [9].

Of particular relevance for our purposes is R. G. Collingwood, who asks, "What is history for?" and answers:

> "for" human self-knowledge. . . . [And knowing] yourself
> means knowing, first, what it is to be a man; secondly, know-
> ing what it is to be the kind of man you are; and thirdly,
> knowing what it is to be the man *you* are and nobody else
> is. Knowing yourself means knowing what you can do; and
> since nobody knows what he can do until he tries, the only
> clue to what man can do is what man has done. The value
> of history, then, is that it teaches us what man has done and
> thus what man is [10].

This statement assigns to the study of history the task of throwing light on man's house with its three mansions (mankind, group, and individual) and, by implication, of applying the changes that such illumination may entail. This is the same house that appears in another contemporary but ahistorical theory of personality in which we find the proposition that "every man is in certain respects a. like all other men, b. like some other men, c. like no other man" [11].

III

To sharpen and enrich the distinction between practice and theory as it bears on the relations between history and sociology two other contrasts, in addition to that between a practical view of man and a theoretical view of personality, may be mentioned. The first is between a practical and a theoretical use of pluralism. In the context of Frederick Woodbridge's *The Purpose of History*, the pluralism of history means that a single purpose is not discoverable in history but that there are many purposes; that, for man, "the study of his own history is his congenial task to which all his knowledge of other histories is contributory; and for him the conscious, reflective, and intelligent living of his own history is his congenial purpose" [12]. Compare this with Mandelbaum's "historical pluralism" [13], which "consists in the view that . . . we shall always find that in themselves all of . . . [the] components [of the historical process] are not related to each other in any save a temporal manner." Clearly, Woodbridge's interest in the purpose of history, as serving a practical end, contrasts with the interest of Mandelbaum and others in the methodology of history as serving theoretical ends.

The second contrast is that between the typical contemporary social-scientific studies of national character on behalf of theoretical interests and Américo Castro's study of a given people's "dwelling-place of life" and "living structure" on behalf of practical interests. By "dwelling-place of life," Castro means "*the fact of living* within certain vital possibilities (preferences) and impossibilities (reluctances)"; by "living structure," "*the mode according to which* men live within this dwelling-place." It is his conception of history that imposes the investigation of these two aspects of a people, for, in history, in Castro's view, "are realized . . . man's possibilities for achieving great deeds and works that endure and radiate their values afield . . . that can affect the mind, the imagination, or the soul" [14]. Thus Castro is arguing that we study history in order to learn who we are by realizing what various kinds of men, of our own and other kinds, have been. This is what Collingwood and Woodbridge say, the former focusing on universal and particular man, the latter, on universal and particular history. The practical sides of these three contrasts show kinship—as do, from the standpoint of practice, their theoretical sides.

IV

All this is not to suggest, not even indirectly, the abandoning of sociology conceived as a theoretical discipline or a plea for historical sociology. The first may be eliminated by saying that I advocate not the abandoning of theoretical concerns but their formulation on the basis of a historical diagnosis of our time [15], that is, on the basis of a practical concern. Such a program, far from contaminating or weakening the two components of sociology, purifies and strengthens each, and, although neither can be eliminated, either can be and has been played down, exaggerated, and otherwise sinned against. In the most recent past the sinning has been done more against the practical than the theoretical component, yet surely a practical concern gave rise to sociology in the first place, whether our disciplinie is said to have begun with Hobbes, Montesquieu, or Comte, with the eighteenth-century philosophers of history, with the economists [16], or whenever else. Always there were concrete phenomena of Western society that called for illumination and action, and this has been true for the further development of sociology until the last two or three decades [17]. (As to this view, one of the most outstanding American sociologists in this classical tradition is C. Wright Mills [18], and some writers who are not professional sociologists, such as David Riesman and William H. Whyte, Jr., share it more than many, if not the majority of, sociologists. The widespread interest in the work of these men is to the sociologist interested in a diagnosis of our time an obvious problem for sociological investigation, but I am not aware of its having been explored [19].)

The aims of historical sociology are not relevant here, except for the one that, in Raymond Aron's interpretation, characterizes some of its German representatives (Oppenheimer, Alfred Weber, Mannheim, and Scheler), who consider sociology as "akin to a theory of universal history and as undertaking the tasks of the philosophy of history; namely, the provision of the answer to present anxieties out of the experience of the past" [20]. In this country, to judge by the work of its foremost advocates, Howard Becker and Harry Elmer Barnes [21], historical sociology consists in the attempt to discover regularities in the past and to derive generalizations from them. Although in neither German nor American usage can one easily distinguish historical sociology from historiography or from philosophy of history [22], the Americans evidently see it as predominantly theoretical, whereas the Germans admit a practical component of much greater significance.

Oppenheimer—one of the German historical sociologists treated by Aron—concludes his analysis of the relations between history and sociology by saying that "the writing of history ceases to be the *opponent* of sociology and becomes its *subject of study*" [23]. Such a conception parallels Howard Jensen's concept of the sociology of knowledge, which must provide a sociological analysis of the history and present status of general epistemology. Jensen sees far more clearly than Oppenheimer (perhaps in part because of the intervening work of Karl Mannheim and the considerable critical discussion of it) that this concept presupposes the acceptance of "the autonomy of logical principles and the possibility that conceptual systems can transcend cultural relativity," for otherwise the sociology of knowledge (and, we may add, sociology in general) "undermines the basis of its own validity" [24]. Despite this acknowledgment, however, Jensen's argument is theoretical, as it intends to be. What would a practical argument look like here?

V

I propose that the practical argument is a plea for raising questions in the face of recognition of the overwhelmingly and inescapably practical character of history. For we are historical in the most practical sense—not exhaustively so but much more profoundly and pervasively so than our historical moment will allow us to see. Even so, we may realize that one of its most practical manifestations is history as terror [25]. The terror of history follows from our failure to master our arsenal of machines. We have built it, but we understand it so little that it may terrorize us. This terror has not yet shown enough signs of passing for us to replace this concept of history with another toward which we are drawn with equal force. We are, as Hannah Arendt has put it, "where man, wherever he goes, encounters only himself," where

> the Kantian and Hegelian way of becoming reconciled to reality through understanding the innermost meaning of the entire historical process seems to be quite as much refuted by our experience as the simultaneous attempt of pragmatism and utilitarianism to "make history" and impose upon reality the preconceived meaning and law of man [26].

In grasping history, sociology appears both impotent and arrogant, in need, therefore, of both strength and humility. Not that there are no strong and humble sociologists—Max Weber, surely, is one of them. He could, wrote the historian Friedrich Meinecke, "motivate his unrealistic project of value-neutral historical research with the most value-laden goals: 'I wish to see how much I can endure.'" As a whole man even Weber was stronger and humbler than the prescriptions laid down in his methodological pronouncements [27].

In respect to the sociology of knowledge, a transformatino from theory into practice is suggested by Mircea Eliade:

> It is certain that none of the historicistic philosophies is able to defend . . . [man] from the terror of history. We could even

imagine a final attempt: [in order] to save history and establish an ontology of history, events would be regarded as a
series of "situations" by virtue of which the human spirit
should attain knowledge of levels of reality otherwise inac-
cessible to it . . . such a position affords a shelter from the
terror of history only insofar as it postulates the existence at
least of the Universal Spirit. . . . It is only through some such
reasoning that it would be possible to found a sociology of
knowledge that should not lead to relativism and skepticism.
The "influences"—economic, social, national, cultural—that
affect "ideologies" . . . would not annul their objective value
any more than the fever or the intoxication that reveals to a
poet a new poetic creation impairs the value of the latter.
[They] . . . would, on the contrary, be occasions for envisaging
a spiritual universe from new angles. But it goes without saying that a sociology of knowledge, that is, the study of the
social conditioning of ideologies, could avoid relativism only
by affirming the autonomy of the spirit—which, if we understand him aright, Karl Mannheim did not dare to affirm [28].

The theoretical autonomy of logical principles of Jensen and others
among Mannheim's critics is being transformed here into the practical
autonomy of the spirit, the attribute of a man who acts in a world that is
common to men—past, present, and future. The former is what a man
sees who looks and contemplates; the latter, what a man acts on who must
act. How, as sociologists, must we learn to see? As practical men; but this
means as reasonable men.

Acknowledgment. This chapter is a revision and expansion of a paper prepared
for the meeting of the American Sociological Society, Seattle, Washington,
August 1958.

NOTES

1. W. H. Walsh, *An Introduction to Philosophy of History* (1951) (London:
Hutchinson's University Library, n.d., 1956), p. 14. See also Michael Oakeshott,
Experience and Its Modes (Cambridge: The University Press, 1933), p. 93, dis-
cussed by R. G. Collingwood in *The Idea of History* (1946) (New York: Oxford
University Press, 1957), p. 153.
2. Cf. Frederick J. E. Woodbridge, *The Purpose of History* (New York:
Columbia University Press, 1916), pp. 36–40.

3. Cf. Robert M. MacIver, *Social Causation* (Boston: Ginn, 1942), pp. 21–22.

4. John C. McKinney, "Methodology, Procedures, and Techniques in Sociology," in Howard Becker and Alvin Boskoff, Eds., *Modern Sociological Theory in Continuity and Change* (New York: Dryden Press, 1957), pp. 228–229.

5. See, for example, Nicholas S. Timasheff, *Sociological Theory: Its Nature and Growth* (Garden City, N.Y.: Doubleday, 1955), pp. 5–7; Karl R. Popper, *The Poverty of Historicism* (London: Routledge & Kegan Paul, 1957), especially pp. 143–147; Morris Ginsberg, "History and Sociology" (1932), in *On the Diversity of Morals* (New York: Macmillan, 1957), especially p. 179. See also S. F. Nadel, *The Foundations of Social Anthropology* (Glencoe, Ill.: Free Press, 1951), pp. 8–17 ("Anthropology, Sociology, and History"); Talcott Parsons, *The Structure of Social Action* (New York: McGraw-Hill, 1937), p. 771.

6. Arnold M. Rose, "The Relationship between History and Sociology," *Alpha Kappa Deltan*, **26** (Spring 1956), p. 33. See also Kenneth E. Bock's analysis of the pervasive and unexamined acceptance by social scientists of evolutionism in *The Acceptance of Histories: Toward a Perspective for Social Science* (Berkeley: University of California Press, 1956), especially Chapter VII, p. 116.

7. Maurice Mandelbaum, *The Problem of Historical Knowledge: An Answer to Relativism* (New York: Liveright, 1938), p. 265; see also Richard Hofstadter, "History and the Social Sciences," in Fritz Stern, Ed., *The Varieties of History: From Voltaire to the Present* (New 'York: Meridian, 1956), pp. 359-370.

8. Franz Oppenheimer, "History and Sociology," in William Fielding Ogburn and Alexander Goldenweise, Eds., *The Social Sciences and Their Interrelations* (Boston: Houghton Mifflin, 1927), pp. 227–228.

9. Arthur Child, "History as Practical," *Philosophical Quarterly*, **4** (July 1954), 209, 215. Important but little noted among similarly oriented writers is Georg Simmel, who is not treated in this respect by Mandelbaum (*op. cit.*, pp. 101–119). Among Simmel's writings on history see particularly "Vom Wesen des historischen Vertehens" (1918), reprinted in *Brücke und Tür*, Michael Landmann, Ed., in collaboration with Margarete Susman (Stuttgart: Koehler, 1957), specifically pp. 59–82. See also Child, "Five Conceptions of History," *Ethics*, **68** (October 1957), 28–38, and for "history as imitation" *ibid.*, 28–30; "History as Imitation," *Philosophical Quarterly*, **2** (July 1952), 193–208; Mircea Eliade, *The Myth of the Eternal Return* (1949), translated by Willard R. Trask (New York: Pantheon, 1954), especially pp. 34–35.

10. Collingwood, *op. cit.*, p. 10. See Karl Marx, *Selected Writings in Sociology and Social Philosophy*, with an introduction and notes by T. B. Bottomore and Maximilien Rubel, Eds., translated by T. B. Bottomore (London: Watts, 1956), p. 72; and Friedrich Nietzsche, "The Use and Abuse of History" (1874), in *Thoughts out of Season*, translated by Adrian Collins (Edinburgh: T. N. Foulis, 1910), p. 16.

11. Clyde Kluckhohn and Henry A. Murray, "Personality Formation: The Determinants," in Kluckhohn and Murray, Eds., *Personality in Nature, Society, and Culture* (New York: Knopf, 1948), p. 35.

12. Woodbridge, *op. cit.*, pp. 49, 57.

13. Mandelbaum, *op. cit.*, p. 274. Similarly, David Bidney, "On the So-called Anti-Evolutionary Fallacy: A Reply to Leslie White," *American Anthropologist,* **48** (April–June 1946), 293, quoted in Bock, *op. cit.*, p. 119.

14. Américo Castro, *The Structure of Spanish History*, translated by Edmund L. King (Princeton, N.J.: Princeton University Press, 1954), pp. 33, 31.

15. Cf. Kurt H. Wolff, "Before and after Sociology," *Transactions of the Third World Congress of Sociology* (1956), **7** , 157.

16. Cf. Karl Polanyi, *The Great Transformation* (1944) (Boston: Beacon, 1957), pp. 111–129.

17. Cf. John W. Bennett and Kurt H. Wolff, "Toward Communication between Sociology and Anthropology," in William L. Thomas, Jr., *Yearbook of Anthropology—1955* (New York: Wenner-Gren Foundation for Anthropological Research, 1955), p. 330; reprinted in Thomas, Ed., *Current Anthropology* (Chicago: University of Chicago Press, 1956), p. 330; and Wolff, *op. cit.*, p. 155.

18. For his own assessment of the matter see his "IBM plus Reality plus Humanism Equals Sociology,"*Saturady Review of Literature* (May 1, 1954), 22 ff., and *The Sociological Imagination* (New York: Oxford University Press, 1959).

19. Cf. Michael S. Olmsted's remarks at the end of his review of John Kenneth Galbraith's *The Affluent Society, American Sociological Review,* **23** (December 1958), 753.

20. Raymond Aron, *German Sociology* (1936), translated by Mary and Thomas Bottomore (London: Heinemann, 1957), p. 37.

21. Howard Becker, "Historical Sociology," in Harry Elmer Barnes, Howard Becker, and Frances Bennett Becker, Eds., *Contemporary Social Theory* (New York: Appleton-Century, 1940), pp. 491–542; Howard Becker, *Through Values to Social Interpretation* (Durham, N.C.: Duke University Press, 1950), pp. 128–188; and Harry Elmer Barnes, *Historical Sociology: Its Origins and Developments* (New York: Philosophical Library, 1948). Similarly, Howard E. Jensen, "Developments in Analysis of Social Thought," in Becker and Boskoff, *op. cit.*, p. 53. Also W. J. H. Sprott, *Science and Social Action* (Glencoe, Ill.: Free Press, 1954), pp. 123–140.

22. This, in several places in this brief essay, is perhaps the most plausible in which a more thoroughgoing discussion would require the analysis of some of Hans Freyer's writings, especially *Soziologie als Wirklichkeitswissenshaft* (1930). Cf. Ernest Manheim, "The Sociological Theories of Hans Freyer: Sociology as a Nationalistic Program of Social Action," in Harry Elmer Barnes, Ed., *An Introduction to the History of Sociology* (Chicago: University of Chicago Press, 1948), Chapter XVIII, pp. 362–373; also W. E. Mühlmann, "Sociology in Germany: Shift in Alignment," in Becker and Boskoff, *op. cit.*, Chapter XXIII, pp. 664–665; René König, "Germany," in Joseph S. Roucek, Ed., *Contemporary Sociology* (New York: Philosophical Library, 1958), pp. 788–789.

23. Oppenheimer, *op. cit.*, p. 230.

24.   Jensen, *op. cit.*, p. 58. See also his lucid critique of Mannheim's perspectivism, pp. 55–56.

25.   Cf. Eliade, "The Terror of History," *op. cit.*, Chapter IV, pp. 139–162.

26.   Hannah Arendt, "History and Immortality," *Partisan Review*, **24** (Winter 1957), 31 and 34.

27.   Friedrich Meinecke, "Values and Causalities in History" (1928), translated by Julian H. Franklin, in Stern, *op. cit.*, p. 284. The prescriptions may have had more influence on contemporary sociology than has that part of the man Max Weber which he himself did not admit into them; that part of Weber is alluded to by Meinecke when he contrasts Weber's neutral project with his passionate goal. Cf. Leo Strauss, *Natural Right and History* (Chicago: University of Chicago Press, 1953), pp. 35–80.

28.   Eliade, *op. cit.*, p. 159 and n. 15. This position is closer to Scheler's than to Mannheim's. See also Kurt H. Wolff, "A Preliminary Inquiry into the Sociology of Knowledge from the Standpoint of the Study of Man," in *Scritti di sociologia e politica in onore di Luigi Sturzo* (Bologna: Nicola Zanichelli, 1953), Chapter III, especially pp. 612-618 [Chapter 7].

Reprinted from *The American Journal of Sociology*, **65** (1959), 32–38, published by the University of Chicago, by permission of the publisher. The essay has been edited and partially revised by the author.

4

MAN'S HISTORICITY
AND DUALISM:
The Significance
of Hannah Arendt's
The Human Condition
for Sociology. 1961

EXPOSITORY

The title of Hannah Arendt's book, *The Human Condition* [1], was to have been *Vita Activa* [2]. It is an analysis of the *vita activa*, of its vicissitudes in Western history, and therewith of much of the story of Western man.

I

Arendt begins, however, with a systematic rather than historical description of the *vita activa*. This is the term she chooses to refer to the three human activities of labor, work, and action, each of which "corresponds to one of the basic conditions" (p. 7) of human existence.

Labor corresponds to life itself. It is the activity man must engage in if he would live on this earth, where he is neither immortal nor self-sufficient. In laboring, the human body "concentrates upon nothing but its own being alive, and remains imprisoned in its metabolism with nature" (p. 115; cf. 209) or "matter" (p. 183, n. 8).

Work, on the other hand—a term that Arendt uses synonymously with making and fabricating—corresponds to man's worldliness. It is the activity of producing the human artifice, that is, all the things that are used, enjoyed, revered, or contemplated. They are not consumed, however, for to be consumed is precisely the fate of the products of labor, not of work. Within the "artificial world of things" provided by work, "each individual life is housed, while this world itself is meant to outlast and transcend" (p. 7) the life of the individual.

The third human condition, plurality (simply the fact that man is not one but many), is the condition of action—"the only activity that goes on directly between men without the intermediary of things or matter" (p. 7)—hence of all political life. Plurality must not be confused with society, which is not a human condition but only one of the historical forms of plurality.

II

To understand the distinction between plurality and society and to understand the rise of society itself we must explore the distinction Arendt makes between the public and private realms. It is the distinction between the *polis* and the family household, made in "all ancient political thought" (p. 28), in which the *polis* was the (public) realm of freedom, to which the mastery of the necessities of life in the household entitled one, and the household was the (private) realm of necessity, in which the man labored for individual maintenance and woman for the maintenance of the species.

The rise of society signifies the rise of economic activities—of private activities characteristic of the household—"to the public realm" (p. 33). Society is essentially a phenomenon of the modern age, which began "in the seventeenth century [and] came to an end at the beginning of the twentieth century" [in contrast to "the modern world, in which we live today" and which was born "with the first atomic explosion" (p. 6)].

Society replaces action with behavior and it equates the individual with his social status (which determines his behavior)—rank in the eighteenth-century half-feudal society, title in the nineteenth-century class society, "or mere function in the mass society of today" (p. 41). In the earlier stages of society its science was economics, which introduced and developed statistics to describe behavior—but only parts of the behavior of the population. This germinal, though modest, beginning was to develop

> into the all-comprehensive pretension of the social sciences which, as "behavioral sciences," aim to reduce man as a whole, in all his activities, to the level of a conditioned and behaving animal (p. 45).

Members of modern societies are indeed laborers or jobholders, people who "consider whatever they do primarily as a way to sustain their own lives and those of their families" (p. 46). The society of jobholders, "the last stage of the laboring society" (p. 322), no longer belongs in the modern (p. 319), but in a later age (cf. p. 6).

As behavior and labor go with society, so does the division of labor, the organization of laboring, which presupposes (as image perhaps even more than as the individual's activity) a gigantic household wherein all members are harnessed to one or another of myriad mechanized labor processes. This mechanization of labor has gone so far that it allows us to forget "the verbal significance of the word [labor], which always had been connected with hardly bearable 'toil and trouble' " (p. 48) [3].

Public refers, first (as an adjective), to what "can be seen and heard by everybody" (p. 50), second (as a noun), to the man-made world common to men, including the affairs that go on among them; and this world contrasts with "our privately owned place in it" (p. 52). By virtue of this common man-made world men are related and separated; by virtue of it they *can* relate to one another and distinguish themselves from one another. Such a public, as against private, space "cannot be erected for one generation and planned for the living only; it must transcend the life-span of mortal man" (p. 55).

Historically, Arendt claims, the most conspicuous proof and exemplification of the private realm has been property, which had the same obscurity—as contrasted with publicity—as the other essential features of the household (the laboring of the man and woman). We are likely to forget this because of the modern identification of property with wealth. Wealth, however, is the individual's "share in the annual income of the society as a whole," whereas property, originally, meant "to have one's location in a particular part of the world and therefore to belong to the body politic" (p. 61). The interior of the household, as well as birth and death, remains hidden from the public, but its exterior appears as the boundary that separates one household from the next; and the original meaning of the law of the *polis* was the boundary line between the private and the public (pp. 63–64 and notes 63, 65).

Thus, in addition to labor (and the division of labor) and behavior, a third characteristic of modern society is wealth and propertylessness. Their simultaneous rise has meant the extinction of the difference between the public and private realms, hence their simultaneous disappearance in the social realm and their replacement by it. The modern age has emancipated both women and laborers, the two types of man who had not been part of public life but had been private, laborers in the two senses of the term; and "the few remnants of strict privacy even in our own civilization relate to 'necessities' in the original sense of being necessitated by having a body" (p. 73).

III

The products of labor are destined to be consumed; they are consumer goods. Hence to speak of our society as one of consumers or one of laborers is merely to single out one or the other phase of the same process. The "thing character" of our world is guaranteed by the work of our hands, the main products of which are use objects; and without use objects we might not even know what a thing is (cf. p. 94). Labor produces no things. It is a process, repetitive, self-perpetuating, and fertile, which has emerged for conceptualization ever since the seventeenth century. That was the time when political theorists were first "confronted with a hitherto unheard-of process of growing wealth, growing property, growing acquisition" and thus turned "to the phenomenon of a progressing process itself, so that . . . the concept of process became the very key term of the new age as well as the sciences, historical and natural, developed by it" (p. 105).

Labor is the only activity into which we can translate, and which corresponds to, the life process in our bodies that we know by introspection. The discovery of introspection in philosophy coincided with that of process in the natural sciences. Modern philosophies of labor, followed by philosophies of life, have equated productivity with fertility, but the philosophies of life have lost sight of labor, which is the activity needed to sustain the life process, and labor, having become more effortless than ever before, has indeed become "more similar to the automatically functioning life process" (p. 117).

To labor and to consume are so overwhelmingly the activities in whose terms we conceive of our lives that every other activity, all that is not making a living, is a hobby. This dichotomy is anticipated in the several types of modern labor theory, all of which contrast labor with play.

Leisure, which has increased and spread by the mechanization and division of labor, has engendered the crucial problem "how to provide enough opportunity for daily exhaustion to keep the capacity for consumption intact" (p. 131). Still, no matter what forms labor takes, it remains in the realm of necessity. Its elevation to unprecedented status is the elevation of necessity to such status.

IV

Homo faber, the maker of things and objects—in contrast to the man of action—"is master of himself and his doings" (p. 144). Labor, as compared with making, has no beginning or end, and action inevitably involves others. *Homo faber* is different from both laborer and man of action also in distinguishing between means and ends in respect to his activity, making or fabricating. Both he and the laborer may use tools or machines. The *problem* of the machine, however, has developed with the function of the machine in the service of labor rather than in the service of fabrication. Because everything, natural or man-made, enters the conditions of man's existence, the problem of the machine is not one of adjustment: man adjusted himself to the machine the moment he designed it (cf. p. 147). Rather the problem of the machine is that "as long as the work at the machines lasts, the mechanical process has replaced the rhythm of the human body" (p. 147). If the present stage of machine technology channels "natural forces into the world of the human artifice, future technology may yet consist of channeling the universal forces of the cosmos around us into the nature of the earth" (p. 150). The tools and implements of *homo faber* primarily serve to erect a world of things. The question of machines today is not so much whether we are their masters or their slaves as whether they still serve such a world or whether, "on the contrary, they and the automatic motion of their processes have begun to rule and even destroy" it (p. 151).

   It could be that the dialectic that governed the replacement of *homo faber*, man the maker, with *animal laborans*, man the laborer, was released by the failure of Western man to realize that, "while only fabrication with its instrumentality is capable of building a world, this same world becomes as worthless as the employed material . . . if the standards which governed its coming into being are permitted to rule it after its establishment" (p. 156); that is, the means-end scheme, which controls the making of the world of things, does not control it once it is made. Instead it controls the public realm of *homo faber*, namely, the exchange market (cf.

p. 160), which is the arena of values in the authentic historical, hence the only legitimate sense of this term:

> The much deplored devaluation of all things . . . begins with their transformation into values or commodities, for from this moment they exist only in relation to some other thing which can be acquired in their stead. Universal relativity, that a thing exists only in relation to other things, and loss of intrinsic worth, that nothing any longer possesses an "objective" value independent of the ever-changing estimations of supply and demand, are inherent in the very concept of value itself (pp. 165–166; cf. p. 235, n. 74).

The reason that every man-made thing once made (as contrasted with the thing-in-the-making) transcends the means-end scheme is that it "must appear, and nothing can appear without a shape of its own." Consequently everything in some way transcends "its functional use, and its transcendence, its beauty or ugliness, is identical with appearing publicly and being seen" (p. 173).

V

Man may be human without laboring (but allowing others to labor) or working (but enjoying the things made by others); but a "life without speech and without action . . . is literally dead to the world; it has ceased to be a human life because it is no longer lived among men" (p. 176). To speak and act is to insert ourselves into the world, not by necessity, as when we labor, nor by utility, as when we work, but by virtue of that beginning which was our birth; it therefore is like a second birth (cf. p. 177 and n. 3).

Speech plays a much greater role in action than in any other human activity in which it has the function of communication. Indeed it must not be confused with communication, although in modern society, including much of modern social science and philosophy, the two are often, if not characteristically, no longer distinguished—just as labor and work and behavior and action have lost all clear differentiations. Unlike communication, which, along with making, is governed by the means-end scheme, speech and action are not. They disclose the person who engages in them and is willing to risk being disclosed. This can, however, be done only in the public realm: neither the doer of good works nor the criminal can, since their deeds and words must remain hidden. Neither is such revelation possible when people are for or against one another rather than simply together, for then speech and action become means to an end as, for example, in war.

Only a man's biography—the story in which he is the hero—tells us *who* he was or is; hence "we know much better and more intimately who" Socrates was "because we know his story than we know who Aristotle was, about whose opinions we are so much better informed" (p. 186).

We cannot know human nature or who man is because *his* story is history, or the storybook of mankind, and mankind is an unidentifiable agent (cf. p. 194). Even the individual agent cannot know the meaning of his action: it can be revealed only by the storyteller, who has the advantage of hindsight. The reason is that action is boundless and unpredictable: "it acts into a medium where every reaction becomes a chain reaction and where every process is the cause of new processes" (p. 190). The resulting frailty of human affairs was transcended by the Greek *polis*, which assured "the mortal actor that his passing existence and fleeting greatness . . . [would] never lack the reality that comes from being seen, being heard, and, generally, appearing before an audience of fellow men" (p. 198).

That which keeps the public realm, that is, the space in which acting and speaking men appear, in existence, is *power*. Power passes away when it is not actualized, and it

> is actualized only where word and deed have not parted company, . . . where words are not used to veil intentions but to disclose realities, and deeds are not used to violate and destroy but to establish relations and create new realities" (p. 200).

Power, inseparable from action and politics, is unknown to *homo faber*, who is convinced that man's products may be more than himself, and to the *animal laborans*, who believes that life is the highest of all goods. Power, instead, accrues to the man of action, for whom "the greatest that man can achieve is his own appearance and actualization" (p. 208).

Because action is unpredictable in its outcome, irreversible (products can be destroyed), and anonymous in its authorship, the attempt to substitute making for action is as old as recorded history. Fundamentally, it is the attempt to have one man, modeled after *homo faber, make* political life. This attempt is at the bottom of all arguments against democracy—the political form that most fully recognizes the human condition of plurality—and thus is "an argument against the essentials of politics" (p. 220) itself.

We have seen that in the modern age the seeming elimination of labor has resulted in work being performed in the mode of labor, and the products of work, that is, objects, being consumed like consumer goods. Similarly, the attempt at eliminating action and replacing it by producing has resulted "in channeling the human capacity for action . . . into . . . a [new] attitude toward nature" (p. 231)—the nature into which we have begun to act.

Still, the fact that man is both free and not sovereign, that is, he can act, start something new, and yet cannot control its consequences, does not justify the existentialist conclusion that human existence is absurd, for action is not only irreversible it is also forgivable, and the remedy for its unpredictability is "the faculty to make and keep promises" (p. 237). Forgiveness terminates a chain of action and reaction, when vengeance promotes such a chain, and forgiveness is as revelatory as action itself. The force of mutual promise, or contract, is the power that keeps the public space in which people can act together in existence. What is mastership in the realm of making and the world of things is sovereignty in the realm of action and human affairs, but although the former is conceivable only in isolation, the latter can only be achieved by the many bound together (p. 245).

VI

Throughout most of the parts of her book on which I have expounded so far Arendt has written in a historical vein more implicitly than explicitly. She has told us, for instance, of the (historical) rise of society and of the (historical) confusion between private and public, property and wealth, behavior and action, labor and work, consumption and use, values and a great many things, communication and speech, power and strength, force, or violence, action and work (and, as we shall see, truth and truthfulness). In the last part of her book "The *Vita Activa* and the Modern Age" she faces, equipped with the frame of reference with which we have acquainted ourselves, more explicitly the nature of the modern age and its history.

The modern age is characterized by world alienation, or the loss of a common human world. In social life the first phase of this age was marked by the cruelty toward ever-increasing numbers of laborers deprived of family and property, of a place in the world; its second stage, by the rise of society that replaced the family as the subject of the new life process.

In physics and philosophy the center of the universe, at one time the earth, later the sun, has disappeared in the Einsteinian "centerless world view" (p. 263). We have transcended the age of natural science, which looks on nature from a universal standpoint and thus acquires complete mastery over her, and have entered that of a universal science, "which imports cosmic processes into nature even at the obvious risk of destroying her and, with her, man's mastership over her" (p. 268). Our thought is still dominated by the Cartesian doubt and its two nightmares: that reality may be a dream and that an evil spirit, rather than God, rules the world—a devil who has created a creature which harbors a notion of truth but which "will never be able to reach any truth, never be able to be certain of anything" (p. 277). Thus, in religion, Protestantism has resulted in the loss of the *certitudo salutis*, and, in regard to cognition, modern man has lost the certitude of truth (and has substituted for it the ideal of truthfulness). Introspection, or "the sheer cognitive concern of consciousness with its own content" (p. 280), has dissolved objective reality into subjective mental processes and has transformed common sense into "an inner faculty without any world relationship" (p. 283). Modern science deals exclusively "with a hypothetical nature" (p. 287); scientific and philosophical truth have parted company; and "the philosopher no longer turns from the world of deceptive perishability to another world of eternal truth, but turns away from both and withdraws into himself" (p. 293).

The loss of a common human world was first indicated by the elevation to predominance of making and fabricating. Man who made instruments and experiments no longer asked what or who but only how. The objects of his knowledge no longer were things or eternal motions, but processes; no longer nature or the universe, but their history. Ever since Vico the despair of human reason made itself felt in the conviction that only man-made things were understandable to man.

Yet there was a second shift or reversal: *homo faber* was replaced by *animal laborans*; making by laboring; means-end-product by process; the principle of utility by that of the "greatest happiness of the greatest number," that is, by the principle of life itself. The reason for this second reversal, a reversal in the *vita activa*, is the very medium within which it took place. This medium was the Christian society with its traditional immortality of the individual life, as against the pre-Christian immortality of the body politic. This medium, however, had been secularized, and secularization had deprived man of faith in individual immortality, which was still believed in during the Middle Ages. Now, the one thing of potential immortality "was life itself, that is, the possibly everlasting life process of the species mankind" (p. 321). The concept of life unifies all processes, from subatomic through human to terrestrial and galactic. The reason

> why the behavior of the infinitely small particle is not only similar in pattern to the planetary system as it appears to us but resembles the life and behavior patterns in human society is, of course, that we look and live in this society as though we were as far removed from our own human existence as we are from the infinitely small and the immensely large which, even if they could be perceived by the finest instruments, are too far away from us to be experienced (p. 323).

Nevertheless men keep on making things and have not even lost the capacity to act, although this capacity is largely limited to the scientists. The scientists, however, act into nature by releasing processes. Their action therefore lacks, "the revelatory character of action as well as the ability to produce stories and become historical" (p. 324).

In line with both the premodern and modern tradition Arendt has omitted thought from her reconsideration of the *vita activa*, but she concludes her book with a few remarks on it. "As a living experience," she writes,

> thought has always been assumed, perhaps wrongly, to be known only to the few. It may not be presumptious to believe that these few have not become fewer in our time. This may be irrelevant, or of restricted relevance, for the future of the world; it is not irrelevant for the future of man. For if no other test but the experience of being active, no other measure but the extent of sheer activity were to be applied to the various activities within the *vita activa*, it might well be that thinking as such would surpass them all. Whoever has any experience in this matter will know how right Cato was when he said: . . . "Never is he more active than when he does nothing, never is he less alone than when he is by himself" (p. 325).

In her end she thus comes back to her beginning: "What I propose," she then wrote,

> is a reconsideration of the human condition from the vantage point of our newest experiences and our most recent fears. This, obviously, is a matter of thought, and thoughtlessness— the needless recklessness or hopeless confusion or complacent

repetition of "truths" which have become trivial and empty—
seems to me among the outstanding characteristics of our time.
What I propose, therefore, is very simple: it is nothing more
than to think what we are doing (p. 5).

INTERPRETIVE

We should miss the nature of Hannah Arendt's book were we not to
analyze it as communication *and* thinking. In respect to the former we
examine two facets: factual statements and theoretical claims [4]. For
purposes of this chapter I disregard Arendt's factual statements, although
many of them, especially those contained in her extensive comments on
Plato, Aristotle, Marx, and other thinkers, warrant sharp scrutiny. Nevertheless, they are of secondary importance in light of my purpose, which
is to bring home the significance of Arendt's book for contemporary
sociology. As I see it, this significance lies above all in the exemplification
of an attitude toward history and our time. The power of this attitude is
related to the viability of the theoretical claims that Arendt advances in
its behalf and, to be sure, but more indirectly, to the correctness of the
factual statements that she makes in support of her theoretical claims.
My interpretation, which omits the factual statements, thus is incomplete,
but incomplete, I think, in regard to the less important, the relatively
least important part of Arendt's work.

By interpreting this work I mean commenting on its theoretical claims,
which, along with its factual statements, here disregarded, make it up as
a piece of communication, and on its attitude, which, I hold and shall try
to show, far exceeds the author's factual and theoretical concerns and
reveals her to us as the thinker she is. To appreciate this second task of
interpretation we should recall, to paraphrase Arendt (pp. 170–172), that
thinking is autonomous, self-contained, without end (both without purpose and without terminal point), whereas communication, like cognition,
is patterned after the means-end scheme. Thinking, we go on, tries to
accept no distinctions man has ever made (including the many Arendt
makes); it is a maelstrom that engulfs whatever ordering the world may
exhibit; it shows man at his most unconditioned, and this means at his
most practical—as open and exposed to the world as he can be, with no
holds barred, no outcome certain, even the fact of any outcome at all
uncertain. Thus to think is the extreme meaning of the practical reaction,
including that of the sociologist, to Arendt's book.

As she says with Cato, however, to think is to be by oneself, and to
speak, and certainly to write, is to add an element of making to thinking—

an element that increases from speaking to writing. When in the following I enumerate some of the propositions I wish to submit for inspection, perhaps even thinking, by others, it is a sure sign that I am submitting cognitions and tentative outcomes, that is, interruptions of thinking yielded to under its onslaught, and made, but only somehow, into entertainable propositions—I cannot do the impossible, submit thinking itself.

The first part of these halts in thinking—all of which I consider relevant to the social scientist—concerns (we recall) theoretical questions, including the definitional and methodological, some of which require answers in order to decide the items in the second section, which are practical.

Theoretical

THE RELATIONS AMONG THE CONDITIONS OF THE THREE ACTIVITIES OF THE VITA ACTIVA. To say that the human condition of *labor* is life itself means that man (though not necessarily every man) must labor if he wants to live. To say that the human condition of *work* is worldliness means that man (with the same qualification) must work if he wants a world beyond nature. Yet, of course, he must live in order to be able to work and must labor in order to live. It thus appears that the two human conditions, life and worldliness, are not coordinate and mutually irreducible but rather hierarchical: labor makes life possible, which in turn makes work possible; but although life is possible without work (though not without labor), work is possible only if there are labor *and* life. Furthermore, labor is biologically necessary, work is not.

As to plurality, the predicate "condition" does not mean what it does in life and worldliness. Man can choose not to live and not to be worldly, but he cannot choose not to be plural: plurality, as the word says, is not an individual trait, and its abolition is the abolition of mankind, which, on the contrary, is left intact by both the individual's death (including suicide and murder) and other-worldliness (in whatever sense of this term). Plurality, in fact, is the condition of the denial of life by man-made death, whether suicide or murder, and of other-worldliness. Durkheim has shown this in suicide. It is obvious in murder. Other-worldliness, even in the form of withdrawal from mankind, is a withdrawal, an activity "that goes on directly between men" and was preceded by similar activities [5]. Plurality, in fact, is the condition without which man cannot survive long enough to reach the maturity needed for choosing death or other-worldliness. Even if there were authenticated cases of feral children (I am not aware of any), they would not be of human children, who, like many other animals, need adults of their species to bring them up.

It turns out that all three of the human conditions—life, worldliness, and plurality—corresponding to the three human activities of labor, work, and action, are not coordinate and mutually irreducible for neither life nor labor is possible without the other. Both life and labor are necessary prerequisites of work, but not vice versa, and neither life nor worldliness is possible without plurality, which therefore is necessary not only for action but for labor and work as well.

LABOR AND WORK.   Labor is private, necessary, repetitive, and for consumption, whereas work is public, spontaneous, with a beginning and an end, and destined to last. Yet we have seen that work can be performed in the manner of labor and the products of work can be consumed like consumer goods, which suggests that the above predicates of labor (private or necessary) and work (public or spontaneous) are not intrinsic to these activities but dependent on man's attitudes; that a man is not laboring or working by virtue of what he does but by virtue of what he thinks he is doing. Thus an assembly-line laborer in an automobile factory is laboring if he expects that the car on the production of which his effort is expended will be consumed, but he is working if he thinks that he is contributing to making a use-object. Whether an item is a consumer good or a use-object likewise appears to depend on the attitude one has toward it. Thus, if I use my car as a vehicle in the service of my everyday life, including my occupation, it is a use-object, but what can it mean to say that I consume it, that it is a consumer good, other than that I feed it, as it were—not into my stomach but into my system of thrills or prestige? Something like voraciousness, whether literal or figurative, thus appears to be the attitude that determines an item's status as a consumer good. The only other entertainable criterion for distinguishing between use-object and consumer good is even more inarticulate. This is the matter of the time that an item is to last: if brief, it would be a consumer good; if longer, a use-object. This time element does enter into Arendt's distinction—things, for instance, have durability, but by this criterion how long must a car last to transcend its status as a consumer good and become a use-object?

The result of our questions seems to be that labor and work are ideal-typical extremes of a continuum which, as we move, in this order, from one to the other, descreases in privacy, necessity, repetitiveness, consumptive character, perishability, as well as in the intent for the product *not* to have these characteristics, or, to put it positively, which increases in public nature, spontaneity, beginning-and-end character, durability, as well as in the intent for the product to have *these* characteristics. In other words, labor and work are, in this view, not different in kind but different in the degree to which they possess not one but a number of characteristics [6].

Surely this is not what Arendt means. A reversal such as that from *homo faber* to *animal laborans* is not a quantitative affair. At least what Arendt wants to convey is the change in *kind* from one to the other, never mind the difficulties of formulation and demonstration that a more careful conceptual analysis might uncover. Hers is a practical, a rhetorical concern, and indeed, kind or quality is, above all, an inevitable category of practice. At this point (and we shall see others) Arendt's theory appears in the service of practice but much in need of clarification; she wants "to think what we are doing": the thinking and cognizing are for the sake of the doing.

ACTION. Like work, action is public and spontaneous; like work, it has a beginning, but it has an end in a sense other than in which work has an end. Again, like work, it produces lasting things, its "stories," that correspond to work's use-objects. Although work is ended when its purpose is achieved, Arendt would probably admit that an action also has a terminal point, which is a feature of the empirical (though not the analytical) referent of Parsons' unit act [7]. This is quite irrelevant compared with the fact that action is boundless and unpredictable. It is difficult to understand the difference between these two attributes unless the first means infinitely interpretable. This reading is suggested as the result of juxtaposing the boundlessness of action with the idea that action, by virtue of being free and in this sense an absolute beginning (cf. p. 177 and n. 3), is part of a unique person who, being unique, cannot be exhaustively or definitively interpreted—cannot even tentatively be interpreted before his death, that is, before he ceases to act, before we have all his actions from which to make our stories. This reading, however, would make the story, or historiography, of any people not yet extinct impossible—not only that of mankind, as Arendt says. The death of a people, say, the Roman people, would, in turn, be a matter of interpretation: we might have no historiographies at all.

The meaning of boundlessness as infinite interpretability must not rest on the impossibility of historiography—after all, there *is* historiography—but on the initiatory character of action. I suggest that this character refers to the uniqueness of action, its sheer "thereness," to the total absence of the element of fabricating, making, working, purposing. To put it differently, action, like thinking, is the purest state of human elementarity we know of and for this reason we can "make" anything out of it, not just one thing—exactly as in thinking. The only difference between action and thought is what might be called externalization or objectification: action is externalized thought.

Arendt also calls action unpredictable, that is, it is unpredictable in both its occurrence and consequences. Let us take these two subjects of unpredictability in this order. Does the first mean that when a person does something that I predict he is not acting but, say, behaving? Does it mean that if he does something other than I predict he is acting? I predict that my friend will show up at noon. He does; hence, he does not act. He does not show up; hence he acts. This, of course, cannot be Arendt's meaning. Might it be that we have action when rather than any of the predictions we can entertain on the basis of our best knowledge something else happens? I can predict a number of things my friend might do other than show up; but he will have acted only if, instead of keeping his appointment with me, he does something I could not have predicted. This is tautologous; it merely says that the unpredictability of action means the unpredictability of action. Again this cannot be what Arendt means. Perhaps unpredictable does not mean not predictable at all but rather *that* in respect to which the question of predictability or unpredictability is irrelevant; that is, in action the dimension of predictability-unpredictability is overshadowed by another dimension: once more, by its uniqueness, "thereness," novelty, its initiatory character. The nature and location of the criterion of this characteristic remain to be worked out, but we shall see, on the basis of the fact that action presupposes plurality in a way that labor and work do not, that this criterion is located neither in the agent nor in the witness alone.

What about the unpredictability of the consequences of action? Because we do not know all causal laws, we cannot predict these consequences. For the same reason, however, we cannot predict the consequences of anything, including labor and work. Does Arendt mean that the regularity of labor and work eases their predictability and that the irregularity (if this term be permitted) of action makes its predictability more difficult? Probably not, for this again would be a quantitative matter to be discarded for the same reasons that we thought we had to discard it in distinguishing between labor and work. Here, too, we may surmise, the unpredictability of the consequences of action derives from its novelty: action brings something new into the world, something intrinsically unpredictable, not only difficult to predict. If predictable and unpredictable were understood as causal concepts, Arendt would probably mean not that action has no part in any causal matrix but that because of its novelty we can anticipate neither the emergence of its cause nor its effect. In this sense it is a miracle, as man as man of action himself is [8].

The counteragent of the boundlessness of action is that it can be forgiven; of its unpredictability that it can be hedged in by promise. The forgivableness of action raises problems in our interpretation of its boundlessness and unpredictability, for if these conditions are interpreted as infinity of interpretability and novelty, respectively, what then is to be forgiven about action? The unprecedented, unique, unforeseeable lies outside the realm of forgiving or not forgiving, which is the realm of ethics. It is at this point that we must remember plurality as the condition of action, and we realize that there *are* limits—precisely those set by plurality—to the uniqueness, the sheer "thereness" of action. Only when action exceeds these limits (recall that plurality is not society) does forgivability become a criterion applicable to it. Action then emerges, as it were, as an experiment in the ethical character of plurality such that, for instance, the prophet's action needs no forgiveness, although he transcends the ethics of plurality as grasped before his emergence, whereas a Raskolnikov does. It is clear that Arendt's conceptions of ethics, plurality, and action and their interrelations call for much more explicit treatment than she has given them.

In regard to the faculty to make and keep promises as the remedy for the unpredictability of action there is a related difficulty if we would preserve action's uniqueness, for contract, or the force of mutual promise, surely follows the means-end scheme and thus is more a case of making than of acting. Here, again, the way out of the apparent contradiction must lie in the fact that only *that* promised doing and not-doing is action which is limited, not by a purpose, by something to be achieved or avoided, but exclusively by the ethics of plurality as such.

Although this, too, obviously needs explication, it will be clear that the criterion of the uniqueness or novelty of action, that is, the question when a given activity is or is not action, lies *both* in the agent and his witness: this criterion itself is developed and applied by the plurality such as it exists at the moment when it confronts the activity. Thus it is a practical, and both a collective and a historical, criterion.

PUBLIC AND PRIVATE.   Action, we have heard, is public, whereas labor is private. Here, too, we must argue that both may appear to be matters of degree and of attitude. First, how public is "public," and how private is "private?" We do know from experience and observation of others in our own society and in other societies that here again there is a continuum that ranges between the poles of a completely public and a completely private character. This is true in either of the two senses of "public" that Arendt distinguishes—the adjective ("public" is what "can be seen and heard by everybody ... by others as well as by ourselves," where the quan-

titative element is implied in the question *which* others and *which* ourselves) and the noun (the man-made world common to men, in which the
quantitative element is implied in the question of *which* men, which how-
brought-up men). The answer to the quantitative question is the attitude
or intent of the doer, who wants his activity to be public or private within
the limits that he intends to draw.

We can only repeat what we said after we brought out the quantitative
and attitudinal character of work and labor. We did not think then that
Arendt was engaged in an ideal-typical construction of a continuum but
in persuading us of the reversal from work to labor, from *homo faber* to
animal laborans. Similarly, now we think that she is concerned with driv-
ing home the emergence of the household as the organizing principle of
society, the rise of the private to public recognition. Again the theory in
the service of her practical concern needs clarification.

What about the identification of privacy with the household and with
necessity? This may be an apt description of the *polis* but surely does not
cover all meanings of privacy, notably the privacy of feeling [rather than
only of feelings that issue into bodily activities, to which Arendt alludes
(p. 73)], and of thinking [which she also mentions (p. 325)]. The necessity
for labor as a condition of life (and vice versa) is one thing; the necessity
of feeling by which one is overcome is quite another; the necessity of the
thinking that is begun in freedom is different yet. Nevertheless, all three
are private: my having to make a living is private, my love and hatred are
private, my thinking is private. What makes us call these three things,
all of which are necessary in three very different senses of the term, by one
name, "private?" Surely only the first has anything to do with the household, and necessity has such different meanings for each of them that to
take it as their common characteristic strikes me as playing with words.
Private itself means something different in each of the three. In the first,
it means, precisely, of no public concern, of no relevance to action or to
history—a technical condition without which man can neither work nor
act. In the second, it does not mean that man cannot work or act unless
his bodily needs are met but that he cannot work or act unless he feels,
that his feelings become of public concern only insofar as they become
transformed into publicly inspectable works or deeds. Private in the first
case refers to a necessary condition of work or deed but in the second only
to a possible source. In the third, finally, private refers to that solitude in
which man is least alone, for then he is most human, he is as close to being
a representative of mankind as he can be. That we do apply the term
private to all three—making a living, feeling, and thinking—suggests that
we see man at once as an organism, as a potential maker, and as a member of mankind.

POLITICS AND POWER.   To be able to act demonstrates man's freedom. In our discussion of action we found it necessary to limit this freedom by the ethics of plurality. A further limitation is imposed by Arendt's locating the realm of freedom in politics, that is, by her tendency to equate action with political action (e.g., p. 220) [9]. Freedom in the sense of starting something new by virtue of one's birth (p. 177) and in the political sense of starting something new (by virtue of one's birth) in behalf of society surely is not the same thing; nor is it clear why man can act (the pre-requisite for disclosing himself) only if he is with, rather than for or against, other men (p. 180). An unanalyzed infatuation with the *polis* or with an image of the *polis* may be at work here, but perhaps there is something of more than biographical interest, namely, the fact that, *polis* or no, man's freedom can be realized only in common with other men. This means that what has vaguely been called the ethics of plurality becomes explicated to some extent: it comes to mean that to act truly in freedom is to act for mankind's good. This, however, is difficult to recon-cile with the discussion of the irreversibility of action (p. 220), its inevi-table incurrence of guilt (pp. 223–235), and the attendant distinction between man's freedom and his nonsovereignty (pp. 234–235). In Arendt's conception of political action we have the desire for the demonstration of the continuity of mankind rather than the demonstration itself as we have it in the remembering of etymology [10], that is, in our speech and its history.

What is to be understood as political itself is not clear either. "The Latin usage of the word *societas*," Arendt writes (p. 23), "also originally had a clear though limited political meaning; it indicated an alliance between people for a specific purpose." She gives examples—*societas regni, societas sceleris.* Is it the character of what in contemporary sociology is often called an interest group that makes a group political or is it this character that makes it political in a limited sense? Surely, an interest group has a purpose and to achieve it uses certain means—all of which have the ear-marks of making not of action. Perhaps the solution to the puzzle is that to the extent that the effect of the group's activities—to rule, to commit a crime, to do business—enters the surrounding plurality the group is political, even if its procedure is work rather than action. If so, it would have clarified matters if Arendt had made this argument explicit, although explication might not have validated it. At any rate, it would parallel our understanding of promise as action, despite its contractual, that is, means-end, character.

What keeps the public realm in existence, we are told, is power, the attribute of the man of action, but not of the maker, for whom his prod-ucts, nor of the laborer, for whom life, is the highest good. Power, apparently, is engendered only by public action, by action publicly perceived, taken up, carried on, and transformed. Power is the power of freedom, of beginning, it would appear, and it is, as we saw, to an astonishing degree independent of material factors, either of numbers or means; it is a potentiality that can be actualized but not fully materialized (p. 200), and unlike force, Arendt says elsewhere [11], it grows rather than decreases if divided. Power, apparently, is the contagious humanness disclosed by action. There is nothing that man cannot do if the spirit moves him. Unfortunately, here again, the practical-rhetorical nature of Arendt's enterprise is indicated, among other things, by the imprecision of the concept. Applying it, as she does elsewhere, to the power of the federal government of the United States, which, she claims, is increased rather than diminished by the power of the states, she finds herself recommending that the matter of school segregation or desegregation be left in the private sphere, which, apparently, is meant to be championed by the states rather than nationally [12]. Such practice suffering from unclarified theory complements the withdrawal from practice that appears characteristic of much contemporary social science. If the latter shows what Arendt calls world alienation, perhaps the former betrays the desire for a world *à tout prix*—in her terms, it displays not so much power as violence.

SOCIETY AND BEHAVIOR.　What are the social scientists' "societies" that existed before the rise of society and when was society formed? The two questions are interrelated; that is, the fact that Arendt does not propose a term to designate presociety "societies" is connected with her failure of clarity on the time period in which society itself emerged. We have heard that this happened in the modern age, with "the rise of the 'household' . . . or of economic activities to the public realm" (p. 33), when society replaced the family as the subject of the new life process (p. 256). Although society is a modern phenomenon, and the modern age began in the seventeenth century (p. 6), still Arendt speaks of the medieval "society of the faithful" (p. 31). Perhaps this is no contradiction but an easily corrected failure to explicate the beginnings and the history of society. If so, this failure, in turn, may have something to do with the importance Arendt gives to etymology. Is the historical and sociological significance of Livy's *societas regni*, of Cornelius Nepos' *societas sceleris*, of Aquinas' *societas* of risk-sharing investors, of the medieval society of the faithful, of Locke's society of property owners, of Hobbes' acquisitive society, of Marx's society of producers, of our society of jobholders, and of the totalitarian laboring society (p. 23, n. 3; p. 31) even comparable except in a distorted and misleading sense? Theoretically it is clear that a much more careful tracing of continuity and change is needed in which a terminology would accurately designate the results of the analysis. Perhaps even before that one would have to decide on what to call groupings (by one name, by many names?) that do *not* figure in this enterprise. Hence the interrelation between the vagueness concerning the rise of society and the failure to give presociety "societies" a name or names. It would also appear that Arendt has here succumbed to one of the dangers of etymology, namely, the tendency to assume that the same word means, if not the same thing, at least something related. The question of a defensible attitude toward etymology comes up in our consideration of what she has to say about values.

Similar observations must be made in respect to behavior, which, in society, as we have seen, replaces action. What other than laboring, working, acting, thinking, and contemplating does or can man do and what are the relations between his activities in the *vita activa* to whatever these other things may be? What were people engaged in (besides laboring, working, acting, thinking, and contemplating) before, with the rise of society, they started to behave? Both questions parallel one of those we raised about society itself, namely, that concerning the lack of nomenclature for presociety "societies," which corresponds to the lack of terms for both prebehavior "behavior" and human conduct other than that discussed. It is tedious to call attention once more to the practical nature of Arendt's undertaking—here to her desire to carry home the nature of our society, the nature of our behavior—and to her theoretical inadequacies.

Intrinsic to Arendt's observations on society, of course, are her observations on labor. Labor, we are told, is the only activity into which we can translate, and which corresponds to, the life process in our bodies that we know through introspection—hence (logically or psychologically and historically) the modern labor philosophies and their succession by the various philosophies of life (p. 117). Neither her argument nor experience shows that labor rather than thought (p. 325) is the only activity that corresponds to the introspectively perceived life process and the only activity into which we can translate this process. Is she not missing something to clinch her argument—a sociological rather than a psychological point? Might this point not be the distrust of thinking rather than the objective impossibility of discovering it through introspection (recall Descartes, otherwise so importantly drawn on by Arendt), which is relevant if we would account for the availability of life, and the fascination by it, in the various philosophies of life? In respect to labor philosophy might a quite different feature not be less intellectual than social and political, lying in the area, to use a Marxian term, of class struggle, of shifts in the relative claims and powers of labor and capital?

NATURE.   Arendt distinguishes between nature and the cosmos or universe (pp. 150, 268). Nature is not only that which is not man-made, for this also applies to the universe, but it is, most explicitly suggested by the equation of "terrestrial and 'natural' laws" (p. 268), the earth. Hence Arendt's distinction between natural and universal science, the former looking at nature—the earth or man's traditional habitat—from a universal standpoint, the latter importing cosmic processes into nature itself (*ibid.*). We have seen the considerations into which this distinction enters (VI, above) and thought it appropriate to record it explicitly rather than having to glean it from widely scattered passages in Arendt's book.

Practical

The matters discussed in the section just concluded were theoretical, that is, largely questions of conceptual and, by implication, factual clarification. In our efforts to answer these questions we found ourselves led back, again and again, to Hannah Arendt's attitude and concern, which we have called predominantly practical and rhetorical. We have now come to a point in our preoccupation with her book at which we ourselves take a practical attitude, which focuses on what we must do—what we, as social scientists, must do.

Our focal points are behavior and action, value, the means-end scheme, and man's historicity and dualism.

BEHAVIOR AND ACTION. We have commented on some of the difficulties inherent in Arendt's use of these terms. Now we disregard these theoretical matters and instead consider the meanings of behavior and action as used by contemporary social scientists, on the one hand, and by Arendt, on the other. We have seen that Arendt holds behavior to be a historically specific term, which it is not in contemporary, nor for that matter in past, social science. There are other differences, however, between the two uses of these terms. A number of adjectives may serve to suggest them.

1. Noncommittal-committal. Social scientists do not commit themselves to pass judgment on the merits or demerits of man's activities which they call behavior and action, whereas Arendt does.

2. Operational-substantive. For them the terms are what their operational definitions stipulate; Arendt means to get at their nature.

3. Observational-participatory. The social scientists set up their definitions and observe the empirical referents of these definitions; Arendt's relation is more to behaving and active individuals with whom she is participating than with the behavior and action abstracted from them.

4. Theoretical-practical. For social science the terms are concepts in theory; for Arendt they refer to human fates.

5. Nonhuman-human. For social science behavior and action can be predicated of any item in the universe, even of concepts (not only of animals but of prices, rates, or telephones); the terms do not refer to exclusively human activities; hence the question concerning their place within a concept of man does not come up, whereas for Arendt it is central, no matter how implicit.

6. "Out-group—in-group." Social scientists are not members of a group of people or things that behave or act; Arendt is.

7. Extrasystemic-intrasystemic. Social scientists do not intend to conceptualize themselves and have the concepts thus obtained enter the system in which behavior and action are located; Arendt does.

8. External-existential. The terms refer to matters external to the social scientists; for Arendt, to characteristics of human existence, including her own.

9. Neutral-affective. These terms are affectively neutral, both intrinsically and regarding the social scientists' relation to them; the opposite is true in both respects of Arendt's use.

10. Scientific-humanistic. For social scientists behavior and action are abstracted from their apperception mass; for Arendt they are real and of real concern.

11. Non-normative—normative. In social science the referents of the terms lack any character of requirement or obligation; for Arendt they have such a character.

12. Systematic-historical. In social science the terms function not only in theories but in systematic theories (of man's social and psychological life); in Arendt the terms function in a concept, philosophy, or theory of history. They may also be called nomothetic and idiographic.

There is also, however, a difference between the distinctions that social science and Arendt make *between* behavior and action. If social scientists make one at all, it is in the form Max Weber gave it, for whom action was

> human behavior (no matter whether external or internal
> doing, failing to do, or suffering) if and insofar as the acting
> person or persons connect a subjective meaning with it [13].

which includes all but reflexive and other unconscious behavior under the category of action and within this category makes no contentual distinctions. What the two terms mean for Arendt, and consequently how she distinguishes between them, we saw in the preceding part of this section and in the last paragraph.

It is clear that as sociologists we have to make a decision about two competing concepts—we must reject or accept them both or accept the current or Arendt's use. I have gone to great lengths in assembling adjectives intended to show the differences between the two (many of these adjectives are synonyms or severally imply each other logically) in order to make the need for the decision more plausible. It is clear that most of the adjectives used to characterize the first of the two concepts of behavior and action mark it as scientific. To recognize this allows us to formulate the decision we have to make as that between being scientific-theoretical and not scientific but, say, practical, although the four options (accepting both, rejecting both, accepting the first, accepting the second) remain open. If we view social science, as I do [14], as both theoretical and practical, we must make our decision accordingly: we must choose the first option, that is, accept both conceptions.

This decision itself, however, changes their status, namely, from competitive to cooperative. The question now before us is, for what purpose, in what situation, must we use one or the other? The most immediate answer is that we use the theoretical concept for theoretical, the practical for practical, purposes. This answer needs a qualification that is entailed by our analysis of Arendt, who we found in her more practical orientation fell short on theoretical clarity, hence on scientific soundness. To reformulate our criticisms, even if in oversimplified fashion, Arendt's practical results would perhaps not have changed but would have been more persuasive or powerful if she had asked how far and in what ways theoretical weakness has influenced them. This observation illustrates the cooperative status of the components. As to the difference between behavior and action, which in social-scientific usage is, with some exceptions, comparatively unattended, we have been struck by the power of Arendt's propositions, despite their theoretical inadequacies. We must try to make up for them, although here, of course, we can only attempt to suggest the direction that improvement might take.

I propose to preserve the customary social-scientific use of behavior which answers a number of questions we asked about Arendt's application of the term. What Arendt calls behavior, then, might be qualified by an appropriate adjective, for example, administered, but before we can find one more accurate an inspection of the relevant literature on the difference between the behavior in "presociety societies" and contemporary society, and, depending on the outcome of such inspection, perhaps actual research, would seem indicated. To read the literature intelligently and engage in research, however, we must also be clear on Arendt's use of "society," which is the locus of her "behavior." Here I suggest something similar to the proposal concerning behavior itself: to preserve society in its social-scientific usage as the most general term to designate global human wholes and to refer to Arendt's society, once more, by a restrictive adjective, possibly the same as the one suggested for behavior, namely administered. As in that earlier case, however, corresponding preparatory inquiries are called for.

Action, because it has, on the whole, a hardly specific definitional status in social science (despite, of course, the antibehaviorist action theorists, notably Parsons), needs more conceptual work to become theoretically tenable. First, it must be distinguished precisely from behavior; then, when properly defined, Arendt's action must be further distinguished from it—whereas in the cases of behavior (as well as society) the first of these two steps had already been taken in social science itself.

Here it helps to recall Weber's typology of action (traditional, affective, purpose-rational, and value-rational). If we allow subjective meaning to be one of the requirements with which to distinguish action from behavior, then, strictly speaking, both traditional and affective action are not action but precisely behavior, as Weber himself admitted without, however, eliminating them from his typology [15]. We propose to speak, instead (conceptually or ideal-typically) of traditional and affective *behavior*. What is left of Weber's offerings are purpose-rational and value-rational actions. Let us ask ourselves—let everyone ask himself—when it is that we think we have acted. We shall probably find that we think we had either when we did something which at the time or in recall had more than customary meaning or when we did something that had what we considered, or have come to consider, important consequences—however we may define either meaning or consequences.

If this is correct, we have two quite different criteria of action: heightened meaning and important consequences. On the first criterion, for instance, I act when I think (in Arendt's sense of thinking), when I write a poem or perform a piece of music. We immediately have several, easily augmented kinds of action: thinking, artistic action, performing action, always provided, of course, that the first criterion is met. The feeling of particular meaningfulness may often be accompanied by a state of heightened consciousness or self-consciousness or the assignment of meaning may be accompanied by the recall of such consciousness. By the first criterion decisions that the agent considers especially meaningful are actions. On the second criterion, we have, perhaps more often than not, actions only in retrospective definition, and probably more often than not, we have chains of action or processes rather than single actions. Suppose a sociologist asks himself how he came to be one rather than something else he once planned to be: chances are that he will recall a number of things he did rather than any one, that one thing led to another, and that in his mind all together make up a sequence whose elements he may call actions, although none may have been particularly meaningful or a particularly meaningful decision (if he recalls any decisions at all).

Let the most generic term for behavior that is action by the first criterion (meaningfulness) be significant action. We have, almost at random, already listed several types (thinking, artistic action, and performing action). Let the most generic term for behavior that is action by the second criterion (important consequences) be consequential action.

Meaningfulness, clearly, is a subjective criterion. Again we can follow Weber's procedure [16] by introducing the distinction between analyzing *particular* cases that, if distinguished by heightened meaning felt or recalled about them, are actions and cases *typically* not so distinguished, which we therefore list under behavior. Thus the fact that yesterday Smith's piano practice was especially meaningful to him does not make American piano practicing an action, for, in reference to the United States (during a certain period), to practice the piano is for certain people (types of people) traditional, hence falls under the category of behavior. Similarly for consequential action. Aside from the fact that Harry's getting married was particularly meaningful for him, it is likely to have had considerable consequences for him, his bride, and perhaps others. Again this does not make marrying in the United States an action; in reference to the United States it is, once more, behavior.

We should note that, unlike meaningfulness, for whose presence or absence we have only the agent's word (although we can, within limits, check on his statement), important consequences is a criterion that can also be applied by the observer—most rigorously if it is understood in the causal sense of the term.

In short, whether certain behavior is an action depends on its intrinsic criteria, meaningfulness and consequences, as perceived by the agent, and on the social unit or period in reference to which the analyst considers it [17].

What about Arendt's action in the light of these suggestions? The element of special meaningfulness is contained in her associating action with freedom and disclosure. If we reconsider the unpredictability of her action, we discover still another dimension of this term (which caused us so much difficulty)—namely, that action is unpredictable in the sense that it may have important consequences. In our terms Arendt's action would appear to be such by virtue of its intrinsic properties—uniqueness, "thereness," initiatory character, novelty—just as our significant action is such by virtue of the intrinsic property of particular meaningfulness (rightly or wrongly located, as we said, by the agent himself).

When it comes to predicating this intrinsic property, there is an important difference between Arendt's action and our significant action. Our procedure is scientific or theoretical (in the sense of finding out what is the case), whereas for Arendt it is practical (in the sense of wanting to know what we must do in consequence of what we have found out). We must add that she has not told us the full story that made her try to persuade us that it is the intrinsic properties she discusses that transform behavior into action. Here we are led back to her theoretical insufficiency.

Within our framework we have to drop Arendt's properties of action and instead define, as the theoretical parallel to her action, the type that is characterized either by a maximum degree of meaningfulness, by maximum consequences, or both. The colloquial term "historical act" connotes both characteristics [18].

It is up to the interpreter to argue the term maximum. Theoretically the scientist reports what others have considered to be maximally meaningful and maximally consequential actions; practically, he arrives at his own commitment concerning them. In most instances most people, including scientists, cannot collect the scientific knowledge that would enable them to use it as a basis for commitment (they lack time, interest, energy, and competence); instead they use secondhand knowledge (obtained, for instance, from parents, teachers, or books).

VALUES.   The history of the term value and its occurrence in various contexts remains to be written. As far as I know the term originally meant exchange value, which is redundant for value, short and simple. The referents of the word have multiplied far beyond this clearly demarcated usage—conviction, norm, principle, standard, criterion, preference, rationalization, goal, aim, end, purpose, taste, things important, not indifferent, desired, desirable are surely not all of them. Such expressions as use values, intrinsic values, and ultimate values are self-contradictory. If my relation to an item is that of use, it is not that of exchange. Something intrinsically valuable is not valuable in relation to something else, and if something ultimate can be bartered for another ultimate neither of them is. To designate the many different things, not all of which have been mentioned, by the one term, value, suggests that they have something in common, precisely the element of exchangeability. Unawareness of this may account for the difficulty encountered by those more self-conscious users of the term who try to define it [19]. Such broad, relievingly broad, as it were, definitions as "any object of any interest" [20] or "a conception ... of the desirable" [21] homogenize not only all matters toward which one is not indifferent or which are desirable to one but also all ways in which something may be of interest or desirable. Finally, there is the ubiquitous use of the term and the difficulty, especially, it seems, for academic people, of getting along without it. All of this—the multiplicity and heterogeneity of referents, the vacuousness of definitions, and the compulsive character of the use—betrays the exchangeability element, the means element, in all things to which the term refers, whether we are aware of it or not. Values are difficult to distinguish from valuables.

This means-character accounts for what ever since Weber social scientists have called the irrationality of values, particularly when understood as ends. In this view a value or end has no intrinsic worth that can in any sense be rationally assessed, and all science can do, as Weber insisted, is to make clear that

> *If* you take such and such a stand, then, according to scientific experience, you have to use such and such a *means* in order to carry out your conviction practically [22].

In short, if you want X, you must pay Y for it, but X is only one of the many values available in the market, and I can tell you the price of each of them, but not which of them you ought to buy or sell. That is altogether your private business. The stand the person questioning the scientist takes is private; only the area of means, the commodities or exchange market, is public. It is a conversation between two brokers (a species of *homo faber*), the less experienced one asking, the more experienced one answering.

Max Weber was so experienced that he was tempted to consider a variety of progress, namely, technical progress, altogether outside the market, that is, to deny technical progress status as a value and to elevate it to that of fact [23]. Thus he held that if the historian of art means by progress in art the technical improvement of the materials the painter uses—canvas, pigments, and brushes—he does not cease to be a scientist; neither does he when he designates as progress the advent of perspectival drawing. The reason is that improved canvas, pigments, and brushes make painting more efficient; they are better means to an end. In perspectival composition the end in reference to which it constitutes progress is complexity of vision: to see perspectively adds depth to the previously available two-dimensional way.

Here, again, Weber is talking as *homo faber*, for whom the end of technology, that is, efficiency, is beyond analysis. Weber admittedly could not argue with another type of man for whom efficiency is not the end—say, a contemplative man, a man of action, or a poet. Weber did recommend that the term progress, even if it means technical progress, be dropped from the vocabulary of the scientist. He also recommended it for the wrong reason: in view of the great difficulty of being quite unambiguous about its purely technical meaning. The legitimate reason is that even this meaning does not transcend *homo faber*; hence the irrationality of his ends, including that of technical progress.

Our analysis of the term value suggests that what Weber in effect did was to warn social scientists not to be duped by the market. He allowed them to speculate there, of course, but only after hours, privately. In his own terms they must guard against values that parade as facts such as progress (other than technical), trends, and adaptation [24]. They were not to use these terms at all, but if there were any excuse for the use of progress it would be in its technical sense because there is universal agreement on *its* aim—efficiency. Thus Weber verged on getting into the market after all, both by applying an irrelevant criterion—universal agreement—to establish factual status and by declaring efficiency intrinsic to things [25].

The fact that social scientists should in recent years have gone all out for the study of values is quite in line with our analysis: they study what people in the market, as it were, what different kinds of people in different situations, are willing to pay for and how much they are willing to pay to get something else; value systems or value patterns are fashioned after economic or financial inventories and marketing habits [26]. The sociologist, like the market analyst, keeps himself entirely out of his own investigations; he studies other people's values, not his own. The reason is that the student's own values are scientifically irrelevant because they *are* private and irrational. Still, although the scientist does not intend to be part of the system he is studying but to remain external to it, purely theoretical and scientific, we have tried to show that he, along with the subjects he studies, is involved practically in a much larger system than he imagines, namely, the time in history in which he and they are located— the time that has given his activities meanings that he is not aware of and does not control.

What must we do? The first thing, I should think, would be to eliminate the term value from our vocabulary, except for its original meaning of exchange value. Second, whenever we are tempted to use the term we must ask ourselves what we mean, which might be one or more of the things already mentioned—convictions, norms, principles, and so on. Third, and in comparison the two preceding steps amount to no more than an imposed diet, we must change our concept of the world in which we live and practice our profession and recognize it as a common way of life of which we are part; that is, we must recognize, acknowledge, and act on our nature, hence our scientific enterprise, which is ineluctably both theoretical *and* practical.

We now raise the question about a "defensible attitude toward etymology that we anticipated. For in respect to the preceding discussion the objection may be lodged that it is beside the point, that in its contemporary usage value does not, of course, mean exchange value, and that everybody knows and understands it. The situation is the reverse of an aspect of that in which we analyzed behavior and action. There, among other things, we found that in one sense of their meaning both terms referred to the same phenomenon—what in Arendt's view is simply behavior. To call attention to it makes a plausible case for terminological revision—here, simplification. On the contrary, we now find that one term, value, stands for many different things and the need for advocating terminological revision, here, differentiation, would appear to be equally plausible. The objection anticipated is not based so much on theoretical as on practical argument. It urges—to continue its argument—that value is a term that has come to stay in our vocabulary and that no *theoretical* argument will ever be able to dislodge it, that our concern is unwarranted anyway because we have many other words that have changed their meanings, occasionally even into their opposites.

The question of a tenable attitude toward etymology raised by this argument is which one we should take toward linguistic change. The answer would seem to be that when we know of change and have an arguable interpretation of it we should act on this knowledge and interpretation. First, we should call attention to the change and its nature, as we see it; second, if, as in the case of values, the change reflects a trend we wish to control and alter, we should do so, rather than allowing it to victimize us. The minimum step in this procedure is to put our own terminology in order, hence to say more nearly what we mean, instead of what we don't know who means.

THE MEANS-END SCHEME.   It is fair, if somewhat oversimplified, to say that the users of the means-end scheme in recent sociology—chiefly Max Weber and, developing him, Talcott Parsons [27]—do not focus on the question of its area of proper application and, particularly, nonapplication and nonapplicability. Rather it is a model to which to relate whatever action may be examined. Ends (other than as means to further ends) cannot be analyzed with its help; they fall outside its range of competence and in this sense are not subject to rational analysis. It should be noted that whatever modification of the scheme has been introduced by structural-functional analysis, notably in Parsons' own later writings, is no more than that, for the structural-functional analysis of ends changes them into means—means of maintaining, disturbing, and integrating the system in which they are located. In regard to the end of the system itself—typically it is its survival—it is an end cognate to the laborer-consumer's view of the world (or nonworld).

What those fascinated by the means-end scheme tend to forget is that, to repeat a quotation from Arendt,

> while only fabrication with its instrumentality is capable of building a world, this same world becomes as worthless as the employed material, a mere means for further ends, *if the standards which governed its coming into being are permitted to rule it after its establishment* (p. 156, italics added).

As she also puts it, utility is identified with meaningfulness; that is, meaningfulness is lost (cf. p. 158). *Homo faber*

> will judge every thing as though it belonged to the class . . . of use objects, so that, to follow Plato's own example, the wind will no longer be understood in its own right as a natural force but will be considered exclusively in accordance with human needs for warmth or refreshment—which, of course, means that the wind as something objectively given has been eliminated from human experience (p. 158).

It is clear that in the means-end scheme the wind figures only instrumentally or functionally. To this extent the scheme is authored by *homo faber*.

What happens as we move historically from *homo faber* to *animal laborans* is that to the former's lost understanding of meaning is added the latter's lost understanding even of instrumentality. Further,

> just as the implements and tools *homo faber* uses to erect the world become for the *animal laborans* the world itself, thus the meaningfulness of this world, which actually is beyond the reach of *homo faber*, becomes for him the paradoxical "end in itself" (p. 155).

The end in itself is the survival of the structural-functional system. In the society of *animal laborans* man labors in order to consume—regardless of how little and ever less he may have to labor. For him there is, strictly speaking, no longer any world, whether of durable things or of speech and stories; both work and action have disappeared, and necessity, the earmark of both labor and its counterpart, consumption, reigns more absolutely than it has ever before in history (cf. pp. 126–135, especially pp. 133–135).

Let us continue from here. We spoke of necessity once before, of its different referents when the term is used in connection with labor, with feelings, and with thinking. The meaning of instrumentality, of the means-end scheme, may receive new light once we realize that in relation to it necessity is located in the connection between means and end, this connection being causal and a causal connection being a necessary connection. As the man of action is free to act, so *homo faber* is free to make what he wants to; necessity enters once he has started fabrication. The *animal laborans*, on the other hand, is never free but always under the necessity to labor. Yet for man, the burden of necessity is relieved only by the freedom to choose necessity—in the activity of thinking and in creative action, the two are inseparably mixed. Hence the reports that thinking, or writing a poem, is at once the most glorious and the most gruelling experience.

It may be that the ascription of irrationality to value in contemporary social science, combined with the insistence on the means-end scheme, whether in the analysis of action or modified in structural-functional theory, wishes to preserve both freedom (in the irrationality of ends) and necessity (in the espousal of the means-end scheme). If so, however, the relation to both freedom and necessity is essentially a relation of consumption—to have one's cake and eat it, too. Once the means-end scheme is embraced as the most conspicuous avenue for exploring the world the sociological *homo faber*, forced as he is to espouse the idiosyncratic character of ends, transcends himself in the direction of *animal laborans*, and both meaningfulness and the instrumentality he celebrates are in danger of being lost to the necessity of labor.

MAN'S HISTORICITY AND DUALISM.   In *The Human Condition* Arendt shows in many instances how men have not so much penetrated, as having been penetrated by, their time and place. The question of man's historicity— the possibility of his transcending it and the nature and extent of this possibility—has, of course, been a major preoccupation of historicism, the sociology of knowledge, and, in a certain sense, cultural relativism. The new complexion this question takes on in Arendt's view gives it a new cogency. This view appears to be that we do not know the meaning of a story, of part or all of man's history, until it is over—but we must add that when it is over the question is not exclusively a matter of causal analysis but also one of interpretation, through which the end of the story reveals itself to us along with its meaning, as integral to this meaning. We must add this in view of Arendt's concept of action and our analysis of it as well as her discussion of the two major historical reversals she describes—the replacement of the *vita contemplativa* by fabrication, that is, one of the activities (that of *homo faber*) of the *vita activa* [28] and the replacement of *homo faber* by *animal laborans*. In fact, many of our preceding questions concerned the tenability of parts of her interpretation of Western man's history. Aside from these criticisms, however, to generalize from the two historical reversals as we did is another way of formulating her proposition that man is both free and nonsovereign, that is, not master of the meaning of what he is free to do.

Man is free within the world of necessity, but nonsovereign within the world of freedom. To realize this brings us closer to an answer to our question about the limits of man's historicity. Man is free to deal with the world to the extent that this world is characterized by necessity and he knows this. I am free to fell a tree, provided I have all that is necessary to do so (e.g., a keen axe and a strong body) and provided the infinite number of causal nexuses that result in the tree and its characteristics (e.g., its species, height, quality of timber) necessitate its falling under my axe. Furthermore, I am free to cut the tree down to the extent that the contract I made to do so is binding and thus enters the world of necessity (e.g., buying the land on which the tree stands, the purchasing contract containing no clause against tree feeling, or contracting with another person to cut the tree as a paid service or as a favor). On the other hand, I am not free to cut it down if I do so as a poacher because then I deny the world of social necessity, whether I try to escape or to change it (though not of natural necessity, as long as my body is strong and the axe keen). To generalize, I am free to act within that part of the world of necessity in which I find myself; let us call it the "relevant world of necessity." No matter how variable this world is—my private room in which I compose while having or not having a headache; the prison from which I try to escape; the mathematical problem that I am trying to work out; the necessary premises of my thought which set limits to it—it is always characterized by necessity.

I am neither sovereign within the world of freedom nor master of the meaning of what I am free to do. The important point here is not to confuse meaning with causal consequence [29], because causal consequence belongs in the world of necessity, and if I am not master of the consequences of my doing it is only because of insufficient knowledge of this world or insufficient interest in it. Meaning, on the other hand, belongs in the world of freedom and is uncontrollable, precisely, because not only I am free but all men are free, that is, free, within the limits of the world of necessity, to interpret and act on my actions in at least more than one way, for as soon as there is more than one way necessity no longer rules alone. How many ways there are is indeed codetermined by necessity, by all the causal nexuses, as in the case of the tree, that result in the particular persons that all the interpreter-actors are; but unlike trees, persons are also characterized by freedom, the freedom to raise questions, to imagine, to explore and try.

The historical moment is the conjuncture of the worlds of necessity and freedom at a given time. Our question concerning the limits of man's historicity, can now be formulated as the question of the changing, as against permanent, nature of his freedom and his nonsovereignty. Both being characteristics of man, they are, in this sense, permanent. The question, therefore, is whether the *relevant* world of necessity within which he is free and the *relevant* world of freedom within which he is nonsovereign are, in turn, permanent or whether they change. Once we have formulated the question we see immediately that the relevant world of freedom is the world of freedom itself. Not being a world of necessity but of meaning, it is not located in space and time, as the world of necessity is; the world of freedom which enters the conjuncture of the historical moment as one of its two components does not change. Man is not only permanently nonsovereign, the very meaning of this nonsovereignty is permanent.

In other words, man's nonsovereignty is not subject to history; only his freedom is historical. The question regarding his historicity, therefore, is limited to that concerning the historicity of his freedom. It is subject to limitations from two sources, the relevant world of necessity and the world of freedom itself.

The relevant world of necessity is a source, in turn, of two kinds of limitation: those imposed by its own nature and those imposed by our ignorance of this nature. On the one hand, coal is such that we cannot eat it; on the other, we may not know its combustibility. In general, whenever we speak of beating our heads against a wall or use a similar expression, the chances are that we refer to the limitations imposed by the nature of things; when we speak of unexpected results, side effects, unanticipated consequences, and the like, chances are that we refer to the limitations imposed by our ignorance. Our freedom changes (i.e., increases) with our knowledge of the world of necessity which, insofar as it restricts us by virtue of our ignorance, decreases in relevance with our increasing knowledge. The nature of the world of necessity remains an ultimate source of limitations on our freedom, but its relevance depends on our knowledge. *Savoir est pouvoir* is qualified by the fact that both knowledge and strength are lodged in the world of necessity; it means "to know the necessary is to be able to find our bearings."

The world of freedom, of meaning, action, will, thought, and imagination, clearly is another source of limitations on our freedom. Examples are commands, intentions, decisions, and arrangements, made by other

persons or by ourselves, which bind or hinder us, or our own beliefs,
desires, ideologies, and prejudices; in short, large sections of our culture.
The difference between our freedom *vis-à-vis* the world of necessity and
our freedom *vis-à-vis* the world of freedom itself is the difference that
results from the fact that the world of necessity is, precisely because it is
not the world of freedom, nonhuman, whereas the world of freedom is
human. Gravity we share with nature, and the necessities of our bodies
with all organisms, but will, intent, and meaning are shared only with
other men. *Vis-à-vis* necessity we can only accept (whether the necessary
be a part of nature, like sunshine, or a man-made object, like a house),
reject (escape a thunderstorm or fight a political régime), or know (sunshine and thunderstorm, house and political régime). *Vis-à-vis* freedom
or, better, within the world of freedom, we can talk, think, act, persuade
and be persuaded. Action and speech are closely akin and both are
located in freedom, as we have already been told by Arendt.

Necessity and freedom, however, are mixed because man lives in the
world of both, although, to repeat, only the latter is exclusively human.
Determinisms of all kinds stress necessity or even deny freedom outright;
some philosophies of life emphasize freedom. Although it seems incon-
trovertibly true that man is both free and limited by necessity—no matter
how his situation has been formulated—the actual mixture of the two
elements is subject to investigation in respect to individuals, groups,
societies, and times. We have many proclamations on the subject but
neither a scientific discipline nor even a program that is devoted to it.
Yet myriad investigations exist in all disciplines, in the natural and social
sciences and in the humanities which the enterprise could draw on;
particularly important among them are efforts made in the sociology of
knowledge [30].

To conclude, man's historicity is the changeability inherent in his
freedom, which, with his unchangeable nonsovereignty, makes up his
dual nature. Changeability inheres in his freedom because he lives in
two worlds, those of necessity and freedom, and he is free to reduce the
limitations from them with knowledge, acceptance, or rejection and
thought, speech, or action. How he has done so in the past and may
perhaps in the future, hence what is the nature of the relations between
the two components of man and their relative weight, is the subject
matter of a not yet existing science.

Our analysis of Arendt's *The Human Condition* has urged revisions
that we must make as social scientists if we would clarify our practice, our
place in the world, our attitude toward it, the nature of our chances to
act in it—just as the failure to make such revisions would muddle our
practice, giving theoretical sanction to our world alienation, to our point

in history, exhibiting our time that we may have thought we were analyzing, and evincing, unbeknown to us, our loss of a common human world. These revisions would increase our freedom by shrinking the world of necessity relevant to us.

In line with our distinction of theory and practice which we stated at the beginning of this chapter and have maintained since (and which is related to that of freedom and nonsovereignty), we arranged our dealing with Arendt's book in theoretical and practical parts. In the part on theory we tried to signal some things, at least, that need determination. Many were matters of conceptual clarification, but some, as well as what we said at the very end of the part on practice just concluded, need little developing to appear in the form of areas (vast areas, to be sure) of research. I shall merely list them, in recapitulation, as the terminal point of our inquiry occasioned by Arendt's book.

1. Behavior in past societies and in contemporary society.

2. Past and contemporary societies analyzed in terms other than behavior.

3. History of the term value and its colloquial and academic uses.

4. Analysis of cybernetics, game theory, information and communication theory, operations research, and similar developments in contemporary social science in respect to elements of *homo faber* and *animal laborans* operative in them.

5. The nature and historically changing relative weights of freedom and necessity in man (this suggests the beginnings of a new science).

NOTES

1. Hannah Arendt, *The Human Condition* (Chicago: University of Chicago Press), 1958. Figures in parentheses refer to pages of this book. An earlier version of this paper was developed in connection with a seminar on "The Means-End Scheme in Contemporary Sociology and Its Relation to an Analysis of Nonviolence," conducted at the Institute for Social Research, Oslo, August 1959; for helpful suggestions I am indebted to members of this seminar, particularly to Gene Sharp. An earlier version of the first part was presented at the annual meeting of the American Catholic Sociological Society, Notre Dame University, December 1958.

2. Personal communication from Hannah Arendt. *Vita Activa* is the title of the German edition of the book (Stuttgart: Kohlhammer, 1960).

3. In support of this point Arendt discusses the Latin, English, Greek, French, and German words for labor (pp. 48, n. 39; cf. 80, 81, n. 5; 101).

4. The beginning of such an examination has been made by Ralph Ross and

John W. Bennett in their respective reviews of the book in *The New Leader*, September 29, 1958, and *American Anthropologist*, August 1959.

5. Arendt herself illustrates this with the case of the hermit (p. 22).

6. The difficulties inherent in the logic of ideal-types have been well known, at least since Max Weber. See a recent essay, with bibliography, by Don Martindale: "Sociological Theory and the Ideal Type," in Llewellyn Gross, ed., *Symposium on Sociological Theory* (Evanston, Ill.: Row, Peterson, 1959), pp. 57–91.

7. Talcott Parsons, *The Structure of Social Action* (New York; McGraw-Hill, 1937), pp. 733, 740 (henceforth *Structure*).

8. On Arendt's conception of "miracle" (*Wunder*), see her "Freiheit und Politik," *Die neue Rundschau,* **69**, 4 (1958), 1–25, especially 20–22.

9. More centrally and in more detailed and explicit argument in her article on freedom and politics, *ibid.*

10. As in the remarks on the etymologies of *zöon politikon* versus *animal socialis* (p. 23), society (p. 23, n. 3), labor (referred to before), *polis*-"law"-city (pp. 63–64 and n. 65), *homo faber* (p. 136 and n. 1), object (p. 137, n. 2), nature (p. 150), action-beginning (referred to before), and power (p. 200).

11. Hannah Arendt, "Reflections on Little Rock" *Dissent,* **6** (Winter 1959), 54.

12. *Ibid*, 54–56.

13. Max Weber, *Wirtschaft und Gesellschaft* [Tübingen: J. C. B. Mohr (Paul Siebeck), 1925], p. 1 (henceforth *WuG*); cf. *The Theory of Social and Economic Organization*, translated by A. M. Henderson and Talcott Parsons, Ed., with an introduction by Talcott Parsons (New York: Oxford University Press, 1947), p. 88 (henceforth *Theory*).

14. Space limitations prevent me from doing more in support of this view than to refer to a paper in which I attempt to argue it: "The Sociology of Knowledge and Sociological Theory," in Llewellyn Gross, Ed., *op. cit.*, pp. 567-602 [Chapter 9].

15. Cf. *WuG*, pp. 12–13; *Theory*, pp. 116–118.

16. Developed in his comments on understanding; cf. *WuG*, p. 4, *Theory*, p. 96.

17. The second point similarly applies to the question whether an event constitutes change. The birth of a child is almost certain to be so considered by the members of the child's immediate family, but it is not if, instead of the family, their country is the social unit in reference to which the event is assessed [cf Kurt H. Wolff, *Trying Sociology, op. cit.*, ch. 5].

18. It should also be noted that *"Wertbeziehung"* and causal efficacy, the two predicates either of which determines a historical unit for Max Weber, are intimately related, respectively, to our meaningfulness and consequences; cf. Weber, "Critical Studies in the Logic of the Cultural Sciences" (1905), in *On the Methodology of the Social Sciences,* translated and edited by Edward A. Shils and Henry A. Finch (Glencoe, Ill.: Free Press, 1949), especially p. 59 (henceforth *Methodology*).

19. See, for example, Ray Lepley, Ed., *Values: A Cooperative Inquiry* (New York: Columbia University Press, 1949), which contains the essays of 13 philosophers. A reading of this volume pointedly shows the divergence of opinion even among scholars of somewhat the same school of thought. The editor remarks, with a note of defeat, in his preface: "At one stage of the inquiry it was hoped that agreement might be reached upon a common glossary of fundamental value terms . . ." (Louis A. Ryan, O. P., *Value Judgments in Selected American Introductory Sociology Textbooks, 1947–1950*, Ph.D. dissertation, Ohio State University, 1957, p. 11, n. 5).

20. Abraham Edel, "The Concept of Levels in Social Theory," in Llewellyn Gross, *op. cit.*, p. 189 (paraphrasing R. B. Perry).

21. Clyde Kluckhohn and others, "Values and Value-Orientations in the Theory of Action," in Talcott Parsons and Edward A. Shils, Eds., *Toward a General Theory of Action* (Cambridge: Harvard University Press, 1951), p. 395.

22. Max Weber, "Science as a Vocation" (1918), in *From Max Weber: Essays in Sociology*, translated and edited and with an introduction by H. H. Gerth and C. Wright Mills (London: Kegan Paul, Trench, Trubner, 1947), p. 151.

23. Max Weber, "The Meaning of 'Ethical Neutrality' in Sociology and Economics" (1913–1917), *Methodology*, p. 38.

24. *Ibid.*, pp. 22–27.

25. See also "The Means-End Scheme" below.

26. More recent developments in social science, especially cybernetics, game theory, information and communication theory, and operations research, need study in this connection. Note such pivotal terms as input-output, feedback, and strategies, all of which are taken from economics and engineering, the realms of various types of *homo faber*.

27. For minimal references cf. *WuG*, pp. 12–13 *(Theory*, pp. 116–118); *Structure*, pp. 648, 733. For a less technical textbook presentation see Kingsley Davis, *Human Society* (New York: Macmillan, 1949), pp. 120–146.

28. We have not discussed this first reversal in this paper; on the history of contemplation consult *The Human Condition*, index under "Contemplation," and especially pp. 14–17, 20–21, 291, 301–302.

29. This is a distinction Weber took great pains to clarify; cf. *Methodology*, especially p. 158.

30. Cf. Kurt H. Wolff, "A Preliminary Inquiry into the Sociology of Knowledge from the Standpoint of the Study of Man," *Scritti di Sociologia e politica in onore di Luigi Sturzo* (Bologna: Nicola Zanichelli, 1953), Vol. III, pp. 585–618 [Chapter 7]; "The Sociology of Knowledge and Sociological Theory," *loc. cit.*

Reprinted from *Inquiry*, **4** (1961), 67–106, published by Universitets-forlaget, Oslo, by permission of the publisher. The essay has been edited and partially revised by the author.

II
THE SOCIOLOGY OF KNOWLEDGE

5

THE SOCIOLOGY
OF KNOWLEDGE:
Emphasis on an Empirical Attitude. 1943

INTRODUCTION

Two distinct attitudes have been adopted by investigators in the field of the sociology of knowledge [1]. One may be called speculative, the other, empirical. The central interest of an investigator having the speculative attitude lies in developing a theory of the sociology of knowledge [2]. The central interest of an investigator having the empirical attitude lies in finding out or explaining concrete phenomena; the theory is employed, implicitly or explicitly, for this purpose [3]. The existence of the two attitudes may be explained in part, as far as the German sociology of knowledge is concerned, by reference to the history of this school, which has grown out of and been determined by a Marxist and materialistic philosophy and especially by the use of this philosophy as a political instrument in the struggle of the emerging proletariat against the bourgeoisie [4]. This statement, however, must be supplemented by a short location of the four most important contributors to the theory of the German sociology of knowledge. Max Scheler approaches the problem phenomenologically; he was the first and only one to ask the fundamental question, "What is knowledge?" [5]. Karl Mannheim, though markedly influenced by the Marxist viewpoint, particularly by Lukács, seems to me more adequately characterized by stressing his development from a more exclusively speculative to a more decidedly empirical attitude, which latter is especially evident in his most recent book, *Man and Society in an Age of Reconstruction* (1940). Alexander von Schelting's main contribution is his thorough logical analysis of Mannheim's theory in the light of Max Weber's methodology. Ernst Grünwald has given the most complete survey of the forerunners, the history, and the various contributions of the sociology of knowledge [6]. These four thinkers are indirectly dependent on the historically determined emphasis of the movement on ideology in that they remain on the level of a theoretical discussion without arriving at factual research [7].

The historical setting sketched above accounts for the fact that the sociology of knowledge has continued (rather anachronistically) to limit its subject matter to ideologies, theories, and, at most, ideas [8]. Even after the public at large had accepted the fact of the existence of a limited and characteristic bourgeois ideology, the sociology of knowledge has not undertaken a general examination of the nature of knowledge and of the social element as it possibly determines this nature [9]. Such historically intelligible one-sidedness, which results in a lessening of its chances of perception (Mannheim's *"Sichtchancen"*), does not mean, of course, that this discipline has not discovered and formulated important problems; without it, we should not have had the basis for the particular form of the empirical attitude, an outline of which I am trying to give in this chapter.

The empirical sociologist of knowledge believes that the subject matter of his discipline will become ever clearer and more differentiated with a great number of empirical investigations. He is conscious that the basic concepts occurring in his field must be treated as hypotheses which have to be verified by research. He therefore includes a large number of projects that might be claimed as belonging to other disciplines, but he meets the objection of imperialism by pointing out that only the completion of his projects will determine whether they belong to his field or should be ascribed to other fields. He thus proceeds according to the principle of inclusion and exclusion. This must be kept in mind when the subject matter and the method of the sociology of knowledge, as typical of the empirical attitude, are dealt with later in this paper.

This brief introductory statement may have sufficiently indicated the character of the empirical attitude, which seems to me at once more general and more concrete than the speculative. Unless, however, I am to seem just as naively determined by history as the observers whose historical conditions I have described (assuming my particular use of the word empirical to be universal), I must qualify the adjective empirical. I do not deny my own inability to escape historical determination, but I do believe that my proposal belongs to the "relatively natural *Weltan-schauung*" [10] of the (American) social scientist today, that is, to what we accept as an unquestionable basis for discussion, namely, that the task of science is to find out things of defined interest [11].

In further discussion of this empirical attitude in the sociology of knowledge I develop an outline of the system of this discipline. This outline is divided into four parts: Range of the Subject Matter, Interest and Method, Suggestions of Concepts to Be Tested in Research, and Conclusion.

RANGE OF THE SUBJECT MATTER

"Range of the subject matter," as I use the term here, describes the totality of the phenomena in which the sociology of knowledge may do research, that is, concerning which a sociologist of knowledge may want to find an explanation with respect to a particular problem in question and thus to make a contribution toward the solution of the fundamental problem of the sociology of knowledge, which may be characterized as the relation between knowledge and social setting [12].

Within the subject matter we have to distinguish between facts (understood as phenomena capable of sense perception, "literal facts") [13] and relations. For the sociology of knowledge the facts are communicated mental events; the relations [14] are those existing between communicated mental events and social units [15].

Mental event is a term that serves as a general denominator for all emotional-intellectual processes, productive or not, ranging from a flash-like feeling, association, or intuition to the creation of a philosophical system or a painting. "Communicated" is a term that serves as a general denominator for all ways of conveying a mental event, ranging from an observer's inference of an observee's flashlike feeling (on the basis of the observee's behavior) to the reading of a book in which a philosophical system is printed or to the contemplation of a painting. The term mental event, which covers, roughly speaking, all acts of knowing, thinking, and feeling, does not imply, by any means, the proposition of its identity with knowledge. If, however, the sociology of knowledge limits its investigations to manifestations of knowledge—as the mental presence of contents of the consciousness or as contents of the consciousness to which the qualification of "I know" can be attached—it excludes thinking and feeling from the beginning. This is unfortunate because in its attempt to contribute, through investigation of concrete phenomena, to the solution of the problem of the relation between knowledge and social setting it pretends, by means of an anticipating hypothesis, to be able to solve this problem on the basis of the limited research material offered by manifestations of knowledge alone. Any research in the sociology of knowledge also involves manifestations of thinking and feeling. This fact may indeed explain why no sociologist of knowledge has yet attempted to define knowledge from a sociological standpoint, and it may also explain, in particular, why thinking and knowing have not been distinguished in the existing contributions to this discipline. We may even say that, although the workers in this field pretended to be founding a sociology of *knowledge*, actually they were developing a sociology of *thinking* or rather of certain types of thinking [16].

The expression of a mental event, when communicated, may become susceptible of sense perception, and, if so, becomes factual. A list of types of factual communicated mental events includes written communications (books, magazines, newspapers, leaflets, posters, manuscripts of all kinds, including diaries and notes, inscriptions, statistical and other tables, maps, charts, and diagrams); oral communications (conversations, interviews, speeches, addresses, lectures, and sermons); works of the fine arts and of music (paintings, drawings, prints, etchings, illustrations, ornaments, architecture, sculpture, and of instrumental, vocal, and mixed music, photographs, and moving pictures); and, if these are looked on as communicated mental events, also implements made by craft or industry (tools, instruments, and other objects) [17].

A social unit is an individual, a group (i.e., a numerical aggregate as well as a social group, from family to nation and culture), or an institution [18].

The subject matter of the sociology of knowledge is the material with which it has to deal according to its interest and method. Interest and method determine the selection of this material in a double sense: they guide the choice of the facts on which to operate in a specific research task as well as the aspects of each fact, that is, the conceptual scheme on the basis of which the sociologist of knowledge sees the facts and with which he operates on them. The two types of selection are interdependent.

INTEREST AND METHOD

The method of the sociology of knowledge is that of understanding as realized by its interest in the huge and vague complex of knowledge and social setting. It may be explained as (1) the appropriation of the subjectively intended (immanent [19]) meaning of a given communicated mental event for the universe of discourse [20] of the investigator and of his public, and (2) the sociological interpretation of the results of (1), that is, their direct or indirect reference to social units as selected on the basis of the particular problem under examination—again within the universe of discourse of the investigator and of his public [21].

The typical chronological course of this process of understanding is as follows.

1. The sociologist of knowledge finds himself in a situation in which he discovers a certain object [22].

EXAMPLES. (a) He is listening to a statement by an acquaintance which tempts him to examine it with respect to other topics treated by the same person in order to obtain a fuller picture of his attitudes or of the status of his rational knowledge in a certain field. (b) The sociologist is reading a newspaper and is struck by the similarity between an article and a statement made sometime before by one of his friends.

2. He formulates the facts, those elements in his still vague enterprise that he takes for granted as a basis from which to start his research. Facts in this sense are psychological facts, as distinguished from the literal facts mentioned above; that is, they are items of the content of consciousness which are accepted as such in a specific situation or which are taken for granted after they have been examined as thoroughly as possible [23]. Thus a relation can be, and frequently is, a psychological fact.

EXAMPLES. (a) the sociologist of knowledge takes it for granted that he has discovered a certain attitude toward a value in his acquaintance's remarks and examines other comments made by this person with respect to this attitude, trying to establish a relation between them and the nature of this relation. (b) The sociologist has found out that there is no personal relation between anybody connected with the newspaper in which the article appeared and his friend; he is trying to collect similar statements and to determine how he can characterize the individuals who have made them and how he can classify the relations, personal and other, that obtain among them. (This will not be possible without clarifying a number of concepts that will thus indirectly contribute to the establishment of a scheme of the sociology of knowledge in that their applicability can be tested in further research.) Many similar steps follow, but their common property, readily seen, is the passing from facts and relations to new facts and relations within the limits of the situation as it determines and is determined by the developing problem and the simultaneously developing solution, including specific methodological questions. It may be stated that the solution is not always a definitive answer to the eventually clear-cut formulation of the problem but may also consist in the satisfaction of the investigator's desire for penetration so that he finds himself in a new problemless situation. Throughout this process the investigator uses concepts he assumes are understood unambiguously by his public in close connection with the contexts in which they appear and which he otherwise endeavors to define. (In these illustrations, for instance, the concept of attitude may need elucidation.)

The objection may be made that the process of understanding as indicated here is not exclusive to the sociology of knowledge, just as the range of the subject matter was shown to be shared by other sciences (cf. n. 17). All I can answer to this objection is that I think that the method— that is, *the logical and psychological operations evolved in carrying out research*—is indeed the same in the sociology of knowledge as in other social sciences. It is the synthesis of method, interest, and conceptual apparatus that is distinctive and will eventually produce a distinctive method—that is, *mental operations plus conceptual tools*—and a distinctive subject matter of the sociology of knowledge. I cannot see how, from the empirical, that is, scientific, viewpoint both can ever be more than temporarily definite (though ever more thoroughly analyzed), for there will always remain some new concept to be tested and some new type of material to be examined [24].

SUGGESTIONS OF CONCEPTS TO BE TESTED IN RESEARCH

The concepts that can be found in the literature of the sociology of knowledge (and elsewhere), especially in Max Weber, Scheler, and Mannheim, as well as those mentioned in various passages of this chapter, must, in my opinion, be tested in research before they can be considered part of the conceptual apparatus of the sociology of knowledge and thus of its method in the empirical sense. The same certainly holds true for the concepts I propose in the following paragraphs.

Concepts Pertaining to the Methodology of Understanding. The concept of central attitude may best be introduced by an extract:

> The first pages of philosophical books are held by the reader in special respect. . . . He thinks they [philosophical books] ought to be "especially logical," and by this he means that each sentence depends on the one that precedes it, so that if the famous one stone is pulled, "the whole tumbles." Actually this is nowhere less the case than in philosophical books. Here a sentence does not follow from its predecessor, but much more probably from its successor. If one has not understood a

sentence or a paragraph, he is helped but little by reading it
again and again, or even by starting all over, in the conscien-
tious belief that he is not allowed to leave anything behind
that he has not understood. Philosophical books refuse such
methodical ancien-régime strategy; they must be conquered
à la Napoleon, in a bold thrust against the main body of the
enemy; and after the victory at this point, the small frontier
fortresses will fall of themselves. Therefore, if one does not
understand a certain point, he may most securely expect an
elucidation if he courageously goes on reading . . . [It is] as
Schopenhauer said: his whole book contained only a single
thought, but he could not convey it in any shorter way than
in the whole book [25].

This extract may be freed from its restriction to philosophical writings
and applied to mental events in general. It implies the distinction between
the literal understanding of a specific element in a communicated mental
event (a word, sentence, gesture, or any other single part of a whole) and
an understanding of the entire context in which that element occurs that
will, in the same act of understanding, make understandable the function
of that element in the whole (communicated mental event). I propose
attitude as a term in the frame of reference for the understanding of an
element.

If by attitude we mean a prefixed selective scheme of action and reaction (including mental actions and reactions), each time we study a single
element we touch an attitude that we consider more comprehensive than
this single element, for we conceive of the latter as a function of the
former. The central attitude, then, is one that through our continuous
efforts in the process of understanding a given communicated mental
event reveals itself as that which renders understandable all single attitudes (each of which, in its turn, renders understandable single elements).
Concrete acts of understanding deviate from this scheme of gradual
understanding in that the central attitude is determined also by our individual approach, including the intensity of our interest, our logical capacity, and our own attitudes engaged, and by the general, though individually varying, capacity for intuition by means of which we jump from
elements to whole complexes of attitudes or even, in rare cases (of poetic
inspiration and, possibly, of "love at first sight"), directly into the grasping of the entire central attitude, or as much as we could probably ever
grasp in a patient step-by-step process.

The extremes of this process of understanding, irrespective of its actual
course, are the feeling of complete strangeness in front of the communicated mental event in question and that of identification with it (which

implies the capacity of re-creating it). In most concrete acts of understanding neither extreme is attained; usually there is some element that we understand from the beginning and some elements that we cannot understand even after the most careful study. (If we think we understand all, we usually have not examined some elements carefully or have overlooked some.) Often, we implicitly or explicitly carry out our study of a phenomenon from a standpoint that is less comprehensive than we are capable of adopting, the comprehensiveness of our standpoint being determined by the particular character of the study in which we are involved. Frequently, too, we are interested in studying only certain properties or aspects of a phenomenon. If, however, as sociologists of knowledge we wish to study something for which the highest degree of understanding is desirable, this aim may be more clearly envisaged if the central attitude is kept in mind as a frame of reference for our efforts. If, for example, we want to understand why a thinker developed a certain theory, we will only in the rarest cases have enough patience, time and interest to acquire the enormous amount of factual knowledge and methodical thoroughness that would enable us to follow the above indicated theoretical outline. Even in less consequential studies we may more easily become conscious of what our task *might* be and what we have *left out* if we keep the concept of central attitude in mind. The concept may help in developing a more conscious method and a greater capacity for the organization of studies [26].

Objections may be raised against my use of the term attitude (in the concepts of central attitude and typical central attitude, discussed later) because this concept claims a much more inclusive aspect of a personality and of a mental event than is customary in current sociological and psychological literature. I have, however, not been able to find a better term. "Position," which might be suggested, seems to point out a physical as well as deliberate characteristic. "Structure of assumptions" again seems to be limited to the sphere of the conscious, if not rational. I should be very grateful for suggestions of a better term.

Two remarks may broaden the aspect of the concept of central attitude.

1. If we keep in mind the concept of central attitude while trying to understand the behavior of a person (starting from his communicated mental event), we concentrate our efforts on becoming capable of forecasting attitudes that are not present in the communicated mental event in question. If, for example, we "know" a theory, we can forecast how it will deal with a subject matter not covered by it; or if we "know" an individual, we can forecast his behavior in situations still unobserved by us. The more factual knowledge about elements and attitudes we possess

and the more conscious a method we adopt, the more we are likely to attain such a degree of understanding, but the more shall we be unable to *formulate* the central attitude we are approaching because we are increasingly identifying ourselves with it. Somewhere along the line of this process of identification lies the scientific understanding that holds the balance between identification and distance through conceptual ties [27].

In our everyday social interactions we constantly practice the central-attitude approach without which we could not know how to behave toward other persons or how to read a book, to see a picture, or to play or listen to a piece of music (because we should not know what to expect of a person in any given situation or how to understand a book or a picture or a piece of music as a whole). An example of a certain type of social interaction which illustrates my point is offered in Ernest Hemingway's *For Whom the Bell Tolls*. Pilar, the Spanish woman, speaks of the "smell of death" and of her own capacity for perceiving it, hence foreseeing the death of the person that has that peculiar smell. She is describing to Robert Jordan, the American Republican soldier in the Spanish war, what nauseating things a person must do to acquire it.

> "But Pilar," Fernando said. "Surely you could not expect one of Don Roberto's education to do such vile things."—"No," Pilar agreed.—"You would not expect him actually to perform those degrading acts?"—"No," Pilar said [28].

Pilar (in spite of her vivid interest in telling her tale) knew that Jordan's attitude was too different from hers to expect him to accept her own central attitude which alone would enable him to accept also her belief in the "smell of death," which is an element in it. In everyday social interaction the case illustrated is less frequent than the case in which we perceive not differences in central attitudes (although likenesses are the exception) but differences in specific attitudes that can be overcome either by a discussion of the matter in question or by orienting our behavior toward individual attitudes of the other person. Differences in central attitudes probably become relevant to everyday social interaction in cases of greater cultural distance.

2. The particular relevance of the concept of central attitude for the sociology of knowledge lies in the possibility that this concept might displace the alternative between the immanent and the sociological interpretation of a communicated mental event, for both interpretations are contained in it. In order to understand an element in the sense of the central-attitude approach, I must be thoroughly acquainted with its intended

(immanent) sense; otherwise I shall have no clue to the understanding of its function within the whole of a mental event. Likewise, I must understand the immanent sense of a whole mental event in order to be able to understand its function in a still more comprehensive whole. (This logical order does not contradict the recipe of the chronological "Napoleonic" method in the quotation from Rosenzweig.) In our analysis we are always dealing, implicitly or explicitly, with the social units that condition or have conditioned a mental event.

If indeed further research should bring about the displacement of the immanent-sociological interpretation in favor of the central-attitude mode of understanding, we should have an example of how a new situation solves a problem (which development, in its turn, could be studied from the standpoint of the sociology of knowledge), how the chances of perception (immanent-sociological interpretation and its subject matter) can be changed (into the central-attitude approach and *its* subject matter), and why [29]. The consideration made in (2) holds true for studies in which the primary interest lies in *understanding* communicated mental events [30].

The scientist, in incorporating central attitudes into his universe of discourse and then in describing them, uses concepts that are current in, or that he must translate into, his public's universe of discourse. With these concepts he rationalizes his approach and his findings; therefore his interest in understanding communicated mental events is limited compared with the extreme of its possible attainment, which includes also nonscientific forms of understanding. This observation leads us to the concept of typical central attitude and to a tentative classification of typical central attitudes.

A typical central attitude (or, shorter, typical attitude) is a concept obtained by the reduction of an empirically traceable attitude to a defined type. This reduction is achieved by the elimination of empirical characteristics as deviations from the type [31]. This definition does not imply that the typical central attitude must necessarily be nonempirical, but it allows us to treat (empirically traceable) mixed attitudes as deviations of typical attitudes. Such concepts as "religious man," "scientist," "efficient business man," are ideal-typical structures of the same class as the structure of typical central attitude. In most empirical individuals whom we characterize as religious men, scientists, or efficient business men we can detect attitudes that are not religious, not scientific, not characteristic of an efficient business man, but which we treat as deviations from the ideal-typical structures. Likewise, when examining a communicated mental event, we facilitate our understanding by operating with typical attitudes [32].

Typical attitudes are autonomous insofar as they have to be understood according to their own structure [33]. At the present stage of methodological development I do not believe it is possible to determine the number of typical attitudes; the concept of typical central attitude itself must first be tested in research. We may assume that all attitudes have developed in historicosociological processes and that each pervades, as it were, all elements of the mental event that led us to become aware of it [34]. As sociologists of knowledge we may divide typical central attitudes into two main classes, the practical and the theoretical. A *practical* attitude is oriented toward concrete facts or conditions, in defense of, or adaptation or opposition to them. The criterion of a practical attitude is the very fact that there are always three possible attitudes toward one concrete condition, one defending it, the other opposing it, the third accepting it. Frequently, but not always, the representatives of the extreme (defending and opposing) attitudes are more easily identifiable with specific social groups than are those of the attitude of mere acceptance. Taking practical attitudes at random from our contemporary scene, I may mention the feudal attitude as adopted by the lord and the slave, the democratic versus the totalitarian, the imperialistic versus the anarchistic, and the capitalist versus the socialist or communist attitudes. A *theoretical* attitude is oriented toward the solution of a mental task, irrespective of the question of the cause, the use, and the effect of this solution in the practical sphere. The criterion of a theoretical attitude is that its corresponding attitudes of opposition and acceptance do not necessarily exist, but if they do they are likewise oriented toward a mental, not a practical task.

There are not only a great many typical attitudes but also an undefined number of empirical and typical combinations of theoretical, practical, and theoretical-practical attitudes (among them many in which the characterization as theoretical or practical may obstruct rather than facilitate understanding). Furthermore, the impact of emotion and mood is an element of first importance in understanding attitudes.

It must also be noted that attitudes determined by the application of theoretical solutions to practical tasks are practical attitudes (applied magic, applied science, etc.), but they may be considered identical with the social-activity attitude of those who represent them; thus we obtain the magician's attitude, the technologist's attitude, the priest's attitude, and so forth, as well as the corresponding attitudes that oppose or accept the concrete facts or conditions toward which they are oriented.

The most readily distinguishable among theoretical attitudes are the magical, the religious, the artistic, the philosophical, and the scientific. Although there are many practical typical attitudes, I cannot think of more than these five, or combinations among them, in which man can approach any mental task. As a tentative hypothesis we may therefore call them fundamental human (central) attitudes [35].

MAGICAL.   In attempting to define an attitude we observe or discuss we must try to avoid the confusion of our own interpretation with the feelings that the participants in the attitude may have themselves. Thus in the case of the magical attitude, which is usually far from our own, we must not confuse our interpretation of the magical performance with its meaning to the performer. The main emphasis in my listing typical central attitudes lies in their distinctness as autonomous frames of reference for our understanding of concrete communicated mental events. If we are excited, curious, scornful, or filled with dread when observing a magical performance, we must control our inclination to suppose that our feelings are shared by the performer; however, our emotional participation may be the basis of a successive understanding that can eventually be communicated to others in conceptualized form, whereas a mere analysis of the logical structure of magical performance—especially if referred to some system of our own—certainly neglects the emotional aspect of that performance. The investigation of magic through field work or field-work reports (mainly books by anthropologists and ethnologists), if undertaken with the intention of identifying ourselves with the magical attitude observed or described, will bring about a much more meaningful presentation than the one given by an attempt at defining it, for example, as "mistaking an ideal connection for a real one" [36], which definition is correct only from the standpoint of our own conception of reality and ideality. Probably one of the difficulties in understanding the magical attitude is that when magic has become the attitude of a minority, that is, in most civilized (as contrasted to preliterate) peoples, it becomes esoteric and disguises itself in opaque codelike formulas [37].

RELIGIOUS.   Having in mind the reservations that must be remembered when trying to define attitudes, I may attempt a hypothetical definition of the religious attitude (which is drawn from certain terms of Max Scheler): the nature or the fundamental assumption of the religious attitude is the attempt, or the success of this attempt, at getting in some kind of contact with some kind of a reality conceived of as powerful and sacred [38].

ARTISTIC.   To say that art (practice, enjoyment, and reproduction) is aesthetic and inspirational-intuitive is only expanding the term art, and conveys little to those who have not experienced the artistic attitude. This does not mean, of course, that certain concepts may not lead toward its understanding. The statement "To so enter into . . . [the object] in nature and in art that the enjoyed meanings of life may become a part of living is the attitude of aesthetic appreciation" [39], may well recall, in certain readers, recollections of their own experiences which greatly enhance the understanding of the autonomy of the artistic attitude. Hugo von Hofmannsthal may convey the specific character of the artistic, or of the romantic-artistic, attitude when he says, "The whole soul is never fully integrated (*beisammen*), except in rapture (*Entzückung*)" [40], or, "Where can thy self be found? Always in the deepest enchantment which thou hast undergone" [41]. According to my conception of the artistic attitude, knowledge exemplified in or knowledge about the nature of lyric, fiction, drama, fine arts, and music or of artistic techniques—literary, fine-arts, and musical productions—cannot be acquired or understood outside the artistic attitude.

PHILOSOPHICAL. Martin Heidegger's formulation of the fundamental metaphysical question seems to me a formula of the typical question of the philosophical attitude: "Why is there being (*Seiendes*) at all, and not rather nothing (*Nichts*)?" [42].

> Philosophy, according to Aristotle's striking remark, begins with . . . "wonder" that anything of "this" constant nature is there. . . . [It] *ultimately* drives at the question of how the ground and the cause of the world totality must be qualified so that "such a thing" . . . might be possible [43].

All metaphysical, ethical, logical, and aesthetic theories are ultimately conceived and understood in the philosophical attitude.

SCIENTIFIC. The most striking illustration I know of the scientific attitude is Galileo's *Eppur si muove!* Dewey thus circumscribes the scientific attitude:

> Scientific subject-matter and procedures grow out of the direct problems and methods of common sense . . . , and . . . react into the latter in a way that enormously refines, expands and liberates the contents and the agencies at the disposal of common sense. . . . Scientific subject-matter is intermediate, not final and complete in itself [44].

This statement leaves open the question whether the sociological function of science as indicated here is universally true or only in modern civilization. It may well be essential to science that its findings are being aimed at with the understanding of their accessibility and control through future research [45].

Although the concepts of central attitude and of typical central attitude belong to the methodology of understanding as it may be developed in research in the sociology of knowledge, I now wish to introduce briefly some tentative concepts that may eventually be of value in determining more accurately the notion of social setting.

Concepts Concerning the Relationship of the Author of a Mental Event to That Event. I wish to begin with the concept of distance and again to introduce it with a quotation.

> . . . it is to be observed that it is the same with time as it is with place; . . . as beyond a certain limit we can form no distinct imagination of distance—that is to say, as we usually imagine all objects to be equally distant from us, and as if they were on the same plane, if their distance from us exceeds 200 feet, or if their distance from the position we occupy is greater than we can distinctly imagine—so we imagine all objects to be equally distant from the present time, and refer them as if to one moment, if the period to which their existence belongs is separated from the present by a longer interval than we can usually imagine distinctly [46].

> . . . it follows that all objects which are separated from the present time by a longer interval than our imagination has any power to determine affect us equally slightly, although we know them to be separated from one another by a large space of time [47].

Here we are less interested in the element of distance as pertaining to human thinking than in its variability in different mental events. We may define distance as the intensity of participation of the author of a mental event in certain elements of that event. Because distance is a relative concept, we must have at our disposal at least two comparable examples in order to be able to discover it; these examples can be within the same communicated mental event or distributed among various events, or one of them may be theoretically constructed by the investigator for reasons of comparison. The nature of the participation of the author of a mental event in certain of its elements varies with the magical, religious, artistic, philosophical, and scientific attitudes. I should like to illustrate the case of the scientific attitude (thus myself offering an example of distance in that I am not illustrating other attitudes).

The participation of the scientist in his work takes the form of the conceptual penetration of and the selection of elements in his subject matter. The sociologist of knowledge can discover distance in scientific work by examining the definiteness of concepts in use, as well as aspects of certain elements in the subject matter covered by the scientist. I want to show the significance of the concept of distance by considering the phenomenon of conceptual penetration.

We must distinguish among three areas involved in any scientific work, namely, the area of the taken-for-granted, the area of distance, and the residual area. First, the *area of the taken-for-granted* includes the unwitting assumptions of the scientist, his and his groups' folkways, mores, laws, beliefs, preferences, and feelings, in short, his undiscussed or "natural" *Weltanschauung.* Here we cannot speak of distance, because the scientist identifies himself with it imaginatively. Second, the *area of distance* is of varying definiteness, of discussed concepts, of doubt, examination, penetration, definition, arrangement, rearrangement, illustration, and opinion. Here the outsider can discover distance by observing how the area of the taken-for-granted interferes with the interest in conceptual penetration, how personal experiences of the author, his scientific, logical, and specialized training, as well as circumstances of the publication of the work under examination (the author's mood, emotion, physical and psychic endurance, plus all kinds of conditions of the publication itself), and how specific attitudes or the central attitude of the author influence the degree of his conceptual penetration [48]. Third, the *residual area* [49], in which the concept of distance again cannot be applied, covers undiscussed aspects of the phenomena, concepts discussed by the scientist, or aspects that might be considered relevant but have been overlooked or deliberately omitted from discussion. The reasons why these unexamined aspects are considered relevant must be defined by the investigator in each case. It should be pointed out further that the failure of the scientist to consider some aspects of his subject matter is not to be attributed to his taking them for granted but rather to a conscious or unconscious refusal to bring them into the discussion. An illustration may be found in the current sociology of knowledge in general [50]—and particularly in the work of Mannheim—in which works of literature are discussed or mentioned without taking into account their aesthetic qualities. This procedure is quite distinct from taking aesthetic qualities for granted in that the question whether these qualities can be factors in certain situations involving works of literature does not even occur, nor is there any awareness of a significant omission among these factors. (In this example, of course, I intend only to give an illustration of the concept of residual area, but I can neither prove my statement regarding the lack of concern with aesthetic qualities in the current sociology of knowledge nor can I suggest reasons for this lack. All this, however, would have to be done if one tried to apply the concept of residual area in a concrete research case.)

With respect to types of knowledge, we may call the type we find in the area of the taken-for-granted naïve or practical; that within the area of discussion and of distance, reflective or theoretical; nonknowledge dominates the residual area. To summarize drastically the three concepts discussed, we might say that the area of the taken-for-granted covers things that are there, but the scientist does not know it; the area of distance covers things the scientist sees with varying clarity; and the residual area covers all that might be there but is not.

CONCLUSION

It might be permissible to call this paper the first outline of a new attitude if it were not for a possible objection to the term "new"—an objection that might be raised by pointing out that an empirical attitude is characteristic already of the French and some other studies in the sociology of knowledge. I am disregarding this possible objection for the moment in order to develop the following line of thought. By characterizing the attitude outlined as empirical (as contrasted to speculative) its place in the history of the sociology of knowledge may be located, but this location does not familiarize the reader with this attitude in a way that will enable him to identify himself with it and to forecast how it will deal with a subject matter not covered by it [51]. *This* is indeed the purpose of this chapter—In this sense it conveys a "single thought." If this attitude takes root and is shared by other students and taken as a basis for research, it may possibly be identified as an attitude characteristic of the sociology of knowledge. We must recognize that all sciences correspond to specific attitudes that are hardly accessible to outsiders. It may be that the peculiar viewpoint of the sociology of knowledge, which sees mental events in their relative social settings, has already enabled us to recognize the peculiarities of our own attitude at a stage of early development, whereas we deal with the attitudes of other sciences at a stage of relative stabilization (after they have shaped their outwardly accepted folkways) [52].

I conclude with two remarks. First, I propose that psychology and psychoanalysis should be considered with respect to concepts that might be of immediate use in research in the sociology of knowledge [53]. Furthermore, I wish to mention a few conceptual complexes (which only for the reason of their being mentioned are not residual in my paper); I think these complexes might be treated for the purpose of obtaining additional conceptual tools useful for research. One is the concept of the *literal versus the symbolic aspect* in mental events [54]. Another is that of *language*, both in specific slang and terminology, and in a more fundamental consideration of the significance of language as a medium of communicating mental events [55]. A further complex is the relation between the *purpose* (overt as well as latent) of the communication of a mental event and the purposes of the groups to which its author belongs and the effects of his communication on various groups, including the question whether a rule obtaining between these relations can be established. Finally we may investigate the relation of *logical contradictions* in communicated mental events to central attitudes, and it may be possible to treat these contradictions as indices of (typical) attitudes.

Second, I mention at random some projects, or rather complexes of projects, that may show the breadth of the field of research in the sociology of knowledge.

1. A study of the Nazi movement with emphasis on the question how knowledge, attitudes, beliefs, preferences, viewpoints, the areas of the taken-for-granted, the residual, and distances in the conceptual penetration exhibited by which people are influenced in what way, by which means, and with what effects; what the differences are in regard to the role knowledge in totalitarianism and in democracy; what suggestions for eventual educational and other social reforms in the American democracy can be made if and as they seem to be warranted on the basis of such a study. (This last point may fall under the name of applied sociology of knowledge.)

2. A biography of a sociologist, possibly a living man who could cooperate. The following points should be investigated in particular: approach to his central attitude; deviations (and their explanations) from the scientific character (to be defined) of his writings; investigation of his social setting through his work (including articles and reviews) and of its presence in his work and in his own statements in interviews, reports of conversations with him, diaries, letters, unpublished manuscripts; effect of his personality and his work on precisely defined individuals, groups, and institutions. Those sources that should have been used according to the scope of the study but were not accessible would have to be stated and the reasons for their inaccessibility explained. (This last remark applies to any research project in the sociology of knowledge.)

3. A preliminary typology of American sociologists with reference to their social backgrounds, their official and private research interests, their methods, their influences on defined individuals, groups, and institutions and through these—not directly—on sociological thought, or with reference to other viewpoints.

4. Who reads what, when, how, why, and with what effect on what and whom? (To be made specific as a sample study.)

5. Who sees which moving pictures, how often, when, why, and with what effect on what and whom? (To be made specific as a sample study.)

6. Propaganda, including commercial advertising, is a vast field for research in the sociology of knowledge. An arbitrary example: What are the processes of thought that lead a banker, a seamstress, a grade-school teacher, an army officer, a college professor, an unemployed Texan, or an unemployed European refugee to buy a certain type of clothes? What is the methodological significance —adequacy or insufficiency—of these occupational and national categories within this research?

7. Who spells "through" "thru," "though" "tho," "thought" "thot," etc.? For how long has he been doing it, under the influence of whom or what, for which reasons, under which circumstances, and to what extent has this usage become a habit or folkway (taken-for-granted) with him? Can we detect any influence of this orthographic custom on the thought of such a person?

8. How do (certain selected and defined) individuals write book reviews? For which papers? Why? Who determines the selection of the books and according to what principles? Is there something that might be called monopolization in connection with the reviewing of certain books for certain publications? How do these reviewers obtain their information about the books to be reviewed? How frequently and how intensively is a book read before it is reviewed? What influence has the reviewer's mood, the amount of time at his disposal, his expectation with regard to the printing of the review, and his relations with the publiher, the author, the newspaper or magazine owner, and certain readers on the nature of his review? What are the effects of his review on selected groups

with respect to their purchase, opinion, and recommendation of the book reviewed?

9. What differences are there in the roles played by material objects, folkways, institutions, emotions, metaphors, and symbols in the poetry of various contemporary poets or of selected poets of various defined epochs and cultures? Can any definable relation be established between these roles and the social backgrounds and central attitudes of these poets? Can any definable relation be established between these roles and certain epochs and cultures?

10. A parallel study with regard to musical forms; for example, what is the role of the triplet in selected pieces of Beethoven, Wagner, or Gershwin? [Questions corresponding to those in (9).]

11. What do selected individuals mean by "chair," "beauty," "nazism?" Which elements in their statements are stable, which vary? What are the relations between certain elements of these statements and various defined characteristics of the individuals who have made them?

12. A study of magical and religious texts and usages to determine the particular character of knowledge embodied in them. (To be made specific.)

13. A comparative study of translations by various persons into the same language or into different languages of an identical text, with special attention given to the relation between literalness and symbolic character determined by the interplay between the areas of the taken-for-granted observed in the translators (as expressed in terms of their respective individualities or cultures—both terms to be defined) and linguistic demands of the technical task (likewise a term to be defined), and, furthermore, with attention to the question of the selection of the elements in the original text which are transformed, preserved, and lost in the translation and to the effect of the translation on defined groups [56].

Such projects might contribute toward the demonstration of the usefulness or uselessness of concepts that are part of the theory of the sociology of knowledge. Studies of this kind will suggest not only other conceptual approaches in the field but also many other projects for further study so that eventually the objective, analytical methods developed by the sociology of knowledge may become a part of our more general thought and folkways.

NOTES

1. Part of this chapter was presented to the Sociology Section of the Southwestern Social Science Association, Dallas, Texas, April 11, 1941.

2. The most important works in this regard are those by Max Scheler, Karl Mannheim, Alexander von Schelting, and Ernst Grünwald. It would, however, be an immense task to collect all philosophical and other writing that, explicitly or implicitly, has some bearing on the sociology of knowledge and to build up a philosophical system of this discipline. Cf. Ernst Grünwald, *Das Problem der Soziologie des Wissens* (Wien: Braumüller, 1934), Chapter II, especially pp. 52–55.

3. Talcott Parsons, "The Role of Theory in Social Research," *American Sociological Review*, 2 (1938), 15; Robert S. Lynd, *Knowledge for What?* (Princeton, N.J.: Princeton University Press, 1939), especially Sections IV and V. Robert K. Merton, in his review of Znaniecki's *The Social Role of the Man of Knowledge, American Sociological Review*, 6 (1941), 112, distinguishes between sociology of knowledge and sociological theory of knowledge; cf. Arthur O. Lovejoy "Reflections on the History of Ideas," *Journal of the History of Ideas*, I (1940), 17–18 and Gerard De Gré, "The Sociology of Knowledge and the Problem of Truth," *ibid.*, 2 (1941), 115. Among empirical contributions, in addition to those listed in Karl Mannheim, *Ideology and Utopia* (New York: Harcourt, Brace, 1936), pp. 303–304, and, in addition to some of the well-known works of Durkheim, Lévy-Bruhl, Halbwachs, Granet, and others, Mannheim's own "Das konservative Denken. Soziologische Beiträge zum Werden des politisch-historischen Denkens in Deutschland," *Archiv für Sozialwissenschaft und Sozialpolitik*, 57 (1927), 68–142, 470–495, and Ernst Kohn-Bramstedt, *Aristocracy and the Middle-Classes in Germany: Social Types in German Literature, 1830–1900* (London: King, 1937) may be mentioned. Among works of the pre-*wissenssoziologischen* phase an outstanding approach to the sociology of knowledge which has decidedly influenced the entire discussion in the field is exemplified in Max Weber's *Gesammelte Aufsätze zur Religionssoziologie*, 3 vols. (Tübingen: Mohr, 1920, 1921, 1921), a famous part of which has been translated by Talcott Parsons as *The Protestant Ethic and the Spirit of Capitalism* (New York: Scribner, 1930). The listing of a large number of "implicit" American contributions would require a special study, for "what the sociology of knowledge deals with systematically and explicitly has been touched on only incidentally within the framework of the special discipline of social psychology or has been an unexploited by-product of empirical research." (Louis Wirth, Preface to Mannheim's *Ideology and Utopia, op. cit.*, pp. xx–xxi.)

4. Cf. Grünwald, *op. cit.*, pp. 1–51, especially 32–42, and 60–61; Mannheim, *Ideology and Utopia, op. cit.*, pp. 278–280; Gottfried Salomon, "Historischer Materialismus und Ideologienlehre," in *Jahrbuch für Soziologie*, Vol. II (Karlsruhe: Braun, 1926), pp. 386–423; Helmuth Plessner, "Abwandlungen des

Ideologiegedankens," *Kölner Vierteljahrshefte für Soziologie*, **10** (1931), 147–170.

5. Max Scheler, "Die Formen des Wissens und die Bildung," in *Philosophische Weltanschauung* (Bonn: Cohen, 1929), p. 113.

6. In regard to pre-Marxist thinkers who were expressly interested in the "social determination" of knowledge, see Hans Speier, "The Social Determination of Ideas," *Social Research*, **5** (1938), 203–205, 198; Hans Speier, "Militarism in the Eighteenth Century," *Social Research*, **3** (1936), 330; Grünwald, *op. cit.*, pp. 4 ff.; Mannheim, *op. cit.*, p. 55; Werner Sombart, "Die Anfänge der Soziologie," in Melchior Palyi, Ed., *Hauptprobleme der Soziologie: Erinnerungsgabe für Max Weber* (München: Duncker und Humblot, 1923), p. 15. I extend my thanks to Dr. Harry Estill Moore, University of Texas, for suggesting a study of the work of the English institutional historians such as Maine, Maitland, Harris, Hobhouse, Toynbee, and Tawney, with reference to their possible contributions to the sociology of knowledge.

7. Scheler, of course, must not be interpreted as a sociologist but as a philosopher. The controversy between Scheler and the Marxist Max Adler strikingly reveals the two contrasting positions of the metaphysical and the Marxist ideologist [*Verhandlungen des Vierten Deutschen Soziologentages* (Tübingen: Mohr, 1925), pp. 118–237].

8. Talcott Parsons, *The Structure of Social Action* (New York: McGraw-Hill, 1937), p. 14, n. 1. Hans Speier ("The Social Determination of Ideas," *loc. cit.*, *passim*) implies that his technical and promotive or theoretical ideas are rational and fully conscious. C. Wright Mills, "Methodological Consequences of the Sociology of Knowledge," *American Journal of Sociology*, **46** (1940), 316–330, speaks of inquiries (*passim*) as the subject matter of the sociology of knowledge but seems to imply also that certain types of language (p. 322) and, more generally, verbal components of actions (p. 329) are within its field. Alexander von Schelting, *Max Webers Wissenschaftslehre* (Tübingen: Mohr, 1934), p. 85, insists that the sociology of knowledge has to distinguish between two spheres: (1) knowledge of empirical data, epistemology, and methodology, and (2) "those structures of thought . . . in which this . . . empirical world . . . is transcended." He does not decide, however, whether one or both spheres are the subject matter of the sociology of knowledge; neither does he do so in his earlier article, "Zum Streit um die Wissenssoziologie," *Archiv für Sozialwissenschaft und Sozialpolitik*, **62** (1929), 1–65, in which he develops this distinction more extensively on the basis of the categories of Alfred Weber's *Kultursoziologie*.

9. With the exception of Scheler; cf. n. 5. This limitation of the sociology of knowledge has hardly been changed by the highly significant contributions of the French school (mainly Durkheim) or by the irrational-naturalistic thought of Nietzsche, Pareto, Sorel, probably Freud, and others. For an excellent general characterization of the German compared with the Anglo-French thinker type and the former's peculiar atmosphere see Ernst Troeltsch, *Der Historismus und seine Probleme* (Tübingen: Mohr, 1922), pp. 141–143 (Vol. III of *Gesammelte Schriften*); see also Pitirim A. Sorokin, "Some Contrasts of Contemporary European and American Sociology, *Social Forces*, **8** (1929), 57–62.

10. Max Scheler's term: "Probleme einer Soziologie des Wissens," in *Die Wissensformen und die Gesellschaft* (Leipzig: Neue-Geist, 1926), p. 59.

11. Cf. John Dewey, *Logic: The Theory of Inquiry* (New York: Holt, 1938), p. 66. My forthcoming attempt at a theory that could account for the interest in the sociology of knowledge and the role of this discipline—both lasting after and far more significant than its historical incipiency—cannot be outlined here; it has to do with the gradual breakdown of traditions and norms and the possibility of nihilism in the last hundred years in European development as typified in a psychologically accessible process I call labilization.

12. It is probably Mannheim whose theories have been most widely discussed, and he may therefore be taken as representative in indicating the ultimate inconclusiveness of attempts at a clear definition of the concepts of knowledge and social setting (or however else these phenomena may be designated) and their relation. Mannheim's own terms (cf. *Ideology and Utopia, op. cit.,* pp. 239–256) have received much criticism that has revealed their ambiguity and logical insufficiency; the most thorough analysis was made by von Schelting (*Max Webers Wissenschaftslehre, op. cit.,* pp. 94–167). This gist of the extensive discussion of the general problem of the sociology of knowledge (see bibliography in Mannheim, *op. cit.,* pp. 300–303) lies in the relation between the social process and knowledge and in the clarification of these two concepts; particularly, it lies in the determination of imputation, that is, in the question how a specific piece of knowledge can be ascribed to a specific group or class and what exactly is meant by such terms as imputation or ascription. Even the most recent treatment of this theme with which I am acquainted [Arthur Child, "The Problem of Imputation in the Sociology of Knowledge," *Ethics,* **51** (1941), 200–219] does not put the question generally, as the title of the article might suggest, but limits it to the internal criticism (p. 200) of Lukács, Grünwald, and Mannheim, thus remaining within the historical boundaries mentioned before in this paper.

13. Cf. Morris R. Cohen and Ernest Nagel, *An Introduction to Logic and Scientific Method* (New York: Harcourt, Brace, 1934), p. 217.

14. In the process of understanding relations may become psychological facts.

15. The only purpose of this terms is to serve as a one-word name for individuals, groups, and institutions.

16. Cf. von Schelting, *op. cit.,* pp. 78, 85–87. The most inclusive definition of knowing is, I think, that of Max Scheler. Knowing is "the participation of a being (*Seiendes*) in the existence (*Sosein*) of another being" ("Erkenntnis und Arbeit," in *Die Wissensformen und die Gesellschaft, op. cit.,* p. 247). If, however, we try to find the empirical phenomenon, or fact, corresponding to these metaphysical units mentioned, we again must stop at general mental events and investigate concrete problems in order to arrive not only at an empirically controllable definition of knowledge but also at the relations between knowledge and other mental processes and their results.

17. This list of phenomena accessible to sense perception (facts) about which

the sociologist of knowledge wants to find out something is, of course, not peculiar to this discipline; the specific character of the sociology of knowledge lies in its selection and its treatment of these facts.

18.   Among the social units listed only "individual" and "numerical aggregate" are capable of sense perception, and "social group" and "institution" are mental units that may be facts psychologically in the minds of the observers of and participants in them. See Eric Voegelin, "The Growth of the Race Idea," *The Review of Politics*, 2 (1940), 284. Almost no term used in sociology, and thus none of the abovementioned, has found a definition that is generally agreed on. My use of these terms is based on their current conception in American sociology, but this use must be specified in concrete research whenever any doubt occurs in the mind of the investigator about the unambiguosness of a term adopted.

19.   Cf. Karl Mannheim, "Ideologische und soziologische Interpretation der geistigen Gebilde" ["The Ideological and the Sociological Interpretation of Intellectual Phenomena"], in *Jahrbuch für Soziologie, op. cit.*, Vol. II, pp. 424 ff.

20.   My definition of the universe of discourse (of an individual or a group) is the totality of concepts used (by that individual or group) plus their implications.

21.   I have made no attempt at a definition of understanding; this would transcend the scope of this chapter. In accordance with the empirical attitude in the sociology of knowledge, I believe in the necessity of concrete research before a logical system (as evolved in such research) can be defined. I fully realize that in any such attempt the problem of understanding will be of the greatest importance.. The attack on it, I think, will be based largely on Max Weber's conception as contained, especially, in "Ueber einige Kategorien der verstehenden Soziologie" [1913], in *Gesammelte Aufsätze zur Wissenschaftslehre* (Tübingen: Mohr, 1922), pp. 403–450, and "Methodische Grundlagen der Soziologie" (1920), *ibid.*, pp. 503–523, and on its analyses by von Schelting, *loc. cit.*, and Talcott Parsons, *The Structure of Social Action, op. cit.*, pp. 610–639. Special attention is likely to be given to such concepts as causal reference, ideal-types, *aktuelles* and *motivationsmässiges Verstehen*, and acausal complexes of meaning. Strictly speaking, we must distinguish between the primary method of the sociology of knowledge—that of understanding—and various secondary methods whose use has the purpose of enhancing understanding and of checking the results reached in the process of understanding. The selection of these auxiliary methods is determined by the particular problem under examination. They may involve the use of statistical devices and various tests, scores, and scales. In the discussion of the chronological course of the process of understanding I proceed without regard to possible auxiliary methods.

22.   Cf. John Dewey, *op. cit.*, p. 67.

23.   Cf. a similar aspect of fact in Cohen and Nagel, *op. cit.*, p. 218.

24.   "This is the *fate*, more, this is the *sense* of scientific work . . . : every scientific 'fulfillment' means new 'questions' and *wants* to be 'surpassed' and

become obsolete . . . Fundamentally, this process is infinite." [Max Weber, "Wissenschaft als Beruf" (1918), in *Gesammelte Aufsätze zur Wissenschaftslehre, op. cit.,* pp. 534–535.] (Cf. "Science as a Vocation, in *From Max Weber, op. cit.,* p. 138.)

25. Franz Rosenzweig, "Das neue Denken" (1925), in *Kleinere Schriften* (Berlin: Schocken, 1937), pp. 375–376.

26. This presentation of the "central attitude" is itself an example of an attempt to convey a "single thought." The concept—still speaking by way of illustration—is an element that can be understood as a function of an attitude to be coordinated with other elements and attitudes. This process of understanding eventually leads the investigator to the central attitude of the concept's author which gave rise to his study.

27. See the discussion of a typical central attitude, pp. 115 ff.

28. Ernest Hemingway, *For Whom the Bell Tolls* (New York: Scribner, 1940), p. 257.

29. On chances of perception see n. 48.

30. Thus my general characterization of the process of understanding might become obsolete, but see my reference to scientific progress in n. 24.

31. Typical central attitude is an ideal-typical structure; on ideal type (Max Weber's term) see Max Weber, "Methodische Grundlagen der Soziologie," *op. cit.,* pp. 505–506; Talcott Parsons, *op. cit.,* pp. 653 ff., 716; von Schelting, *op. cit.,* pp. 329 ff.; Marcel Weinreich, *Max Weber, l'homme et le savant* (Paris: Vrin, 1938), pp. 96–113.

32. Typical central attitude—a concept—has nothing to do with a discussion of human nature which aims at establishing variable and invariable human properties.

33. This statement does not imply that we do not have to assume changeless components in mental processes, such as certain processes of thought or of feeling (a syllogism, the feeling of anxiety). The important problem of changeless versus changeable elements in mental processes has to my knowledge not yet found a detailed examination with respect to the establishment of a sociology of knowledge (in spite of the works of Durkheim, Lévy-Bruhl, and Granet). The most explicit statement about it has been made, I think, by von Schelting ("Zum Streit um die Wissenssoziologie," *op. cit,* p. 31). According to him, nobody has yet succeeded in proving "that the fundamental forms of apperception and categories and the basic forms of the contemplative, explicatory, concluding, and systematizing forms of the human intellect . . . have . . . changed." As a hypothesis I assume that there are certain logical and emotional processes whose function, rather than nature, changes with the typical central attitudes in which they appear. See also Francis M. Cornford, *The Laws of Motion in Ancient Thought* (Cambridge: University Press, 1931) and other works of his. Alvin P. Bradford's forthcoming thesis (University of Texas), "An Approach to the Philosophy of Adjustment: A Consideration of Organic Categories and the Sociology of Knowledge," should throw light on this problem.

34.   This hypothesis, of course, does not concern a fundamental assumption of the sociology of knowledge as well as of sociology and psychology, namely, the possibility of explaining how attitudes originate in a given case and, eventually, of establishing a typology of attitudes and coordinated causes. In attempting such an explanation and such a typology on the basis of research, however, the process of understanding the attitude itself comes first.

35.   Without daring to answer the question regarding human nature raised in n. 32. Of course, actions are performed in the spirit of these attitudes, but we can understand them, at least more easily, by understanding these attitudes. In many cases understanding may be attained by reference to the attitude of social activity (a practical attitude).

36.   E. B. Tylor, quoted in Sigmund Freud, "Totem and Taboo" (1913) in *The Basic Writings of Sigmund Freud* (New York: Modern Library) p. 868.

37.   See Eliphas Lévi, *Histoire de la magie* (Paris: Alcan, 1892), p. 1. This book, as well as Lévi's two others—*Dogme et rituel de la haute magie*, 2 vols. (Paris: Alcan, 1894), and *La clef des grands mystères* (Paris: Alcan, n.d.)—contains a multitude of descriptions of magical practices among civilized peoples. Being themselves magically biased, the three works are likely to familiarize the reader with the magical attitude.

38.   Cf. Max Scheler, "Probleme einer Soziologie des Wissens," *op. cit.*, p. 64.

39.   G. H. Mead, "The Nature of Aesthetic Experience," *International Journal of Ethics*, **36** (1926), 384.

40.   Hugo von Hofmannsthal, *Buch der Freunde*, 2nd ed. (Leipzig: Insel. 1929), p. 36.

41.   *Ibid.*, p. 39.

42.   Martin Heidegger, *Was ist Metaphysik?* [1929] (Bonn: Cohen, 1931), p. 28. Similarly Max Scheler, *Man's Place in Nature*, translated and with an introduction by Hans Meyerhoff (New York: Noonday Press, 1961) pp. 88–90. A position that stresses the constructive aspect of the philosophical shock is adopted by Karl Jaspers; see his *Existenzphilosophie* (Berlin: de Gruyter, 1938), p. 1, and his *Man in the Modern Age* (1931), translated by Eden and Cedar Paul (London: Routledge and Kegan Paul, 1933), p. 186.

43.   Max Scheler, "Erkenntnis und Arbeit," *op. cit.*, p. 253. It is obvious that these quotations and references refer to an attitude entirely different from that of American pragmatic philosophy, especially C. S. Peirce and John Dewey, which is determined in part by the emphasis on practice as against reflection; see John Dewey, *The Quest for Certainty: A Study of the Relation of Knowledge and Action* (New York: Putnam, 1929), p. 37. For a discussion of pragmatism, especially Peirce and William James, from the Schelerian position, see Max Scheler, *op. cit.*, pp. 259–324. The autonomy of the philosophical attitude is more evident in the former quotations (with their philosophy for philosophy's sake) than in the pragmatic, less self-sufficient position.

44.   John Dewey, *Logic, op. cit.*, p. 66.

45.   See the quotation from Max Weber in n. 24: it continues to discuss the

meaning of science in the light of occidental intellectualization and rationalization (*op. cit.*, pp. 535–536). For the development of science in the occident cf. Wilhelm Dilthey, *Einleitung in die Geisteswissenschaften* (1883), 3rd ed. (Leipzig: Teubner, 1933), pp. 150–386.

46.   Spinoza, *Ethic* [1677] (London: Frowde, 1910), p. 181.

47.   *Ibid.*, p. 188.

48.   It may be noted that sufficient research with respect to distance may enable us to find typical distances that may be ordered according to the degree of their frequency (with the possible result of finding relatively permanent and variable distances) within certain historical periods or according to types of scientist and science. The distance-taken-for-granted-residual approach seems to me more specific, that is, more easily verifiable by research, than Mills's utilization of G. H. Mead's concept of the generalized other ("Language, Logic, and Culture," *American Sociological Review*, **4** (1939), 672–676, or Mannheim's "chances of perception" (*Ideology and Utopia*, op cit., pp. 237–238, *passim*). I cannot, however, enter into an examination here of the relatedness of these concepts.

49.   I owe this expression to Talcott Parsons' term residual category (*op. cit.*, pp. 16–20); however, the meanings of residual category and residual area are different.

50.   Again with the exception of Scheler and certain scholars of the French school.

51.   Cf. the discussion of central attitude above.

52.   This consideration might be taken into account in an examination of the conditions that were necessary for the rise of the sociology of knowledge in addition to what Mannheim wrote about this question (in *Ideology and Utopia, op. cit.*, pp. 252–253, "The Acquisition of Perspective as a Pre-Condition for the Sociology of Knowledge").

53.   Perhaps similar to the way in which Harold D. Lasswell has utilized psychoanalysis in his consideration of politics.

54.   One suggestion how to develop this problem may be found in the distinction between symbolic and actual behavior as indicated in Richard T. LaPiere and Paul R. Farnsworth, *Social Psychology* (New York: McGraw-Hill, 1936), pp. 232–233.

55.   In the direction of such studies as Ogden and Richards, *The Meaning of Meaning*.

56.   It is obvious that much literature that is useful, directly or indirectly, already exists in connection with these projects or with certain of their aspects and should be consulted with respect to their eventual formulation and execution.

Reprinted from *Philosophy of Science,* **10** (1943), 104–123, by permission of the publisher. The essay has been edited and partially revised by the author.

6

THE UNIQUE
AND THE GENERAL:
Toward a Philosophy of Sociology. 1948

PHILOSOPHY OF SCIENCE

The term philosophy of science is used here to refer to the study of the approaches and methodologies of the sciences [1]. By approach is understood the totality of the *presuppositions* of a given science (body of sciences or scientific product): more precisely, both philosophical and scientific presuppositions, that is, categories, postulates, and premises as *conditions*, and existential presuppositions (organic, geographic, and sociocultural). By methodology is understood the *intellectual-emotional structure* of a given science; that is, its categories, postulates, and premises as *characteristics* and its concepts, methods, and techniques. Further, I advocate investigating a given science (body of sciences or scientific product) in a study of its approach and methodology. Finally, I submit that the best understanding of either of the two is impossible without the study of the other. More specifically, I advocate the interpretation of the intellectual structure or methodology of a particular science (body of sciences, e.g., the social sciences, or scientific product) (immanent interpretation [2]), followed by the study of its presuppositions or underlying approach (transcendent interpretation).

THE NATURAL-SCIENCE AND THE HUMAN-STUDIES
CONCEPTIONS OF SOCIOLOGY

Two conceptions of sociology have been in existence for some time. The first conceives of sociology as one among the natural sciences. The second sees considerable methodological implications in the fact that sociology, along with social psychology, cultural anthropology, political science, economics, and perhaps history, is a social science [3]. The difference between the two concepts lies not so much in research techniques (as part of methodology) as in approach. More particularly, it lies in the fact that each bases its methodology on a different premise regarding the nature of the subject matter of sociology (hence regarding its methodology other than research techniques). The only feature shared by the two concepts is precisely the conviction that sociological research should be executed by scientific methods. What research is to be carried on; why, and because of what nature of sociology? These and many other questions are answered differently by the two concepts and their schools.

It is hazardous and easily misleading to compress even the outstanding features of the approaches of these two concepts into formulas. Nevertheless, this is what we must attempt if we would carry the discussion further. To make this discussion possible is the only purpose of what at best is an oversimplified classification. Remembering this serious qualification, we characterize the two concepts as follows:

1. The *natural-science concept* postulates that sociology can and should study its subject matter as other natural sciences study other parts of nature which are *their* subject matters. However this subject matter is defined—as social relations, social processes, social interaction, group relations or processes, and the like—it exists outside the sociologist, is external to him, and he has but to discover, study, and learn about it [4]. Thus perhaps the most outstanding assumption of the natural-science approach, from which all its other assumptions and methodological tenets seem to derive, is the axiom that the subject matter of sociology, inasmuch as is natural or part of nature, is given and given alike to all investigators. It is this same assumption that is *not* shared but replaced by a very different one in the other concept of sociology.

2. This other concept may be called the *human* or the *human-studies concept*. Its postulate, which corresponds to that of the common-givenness of the natural-science concept, may be formulated by saying that the subject matter of sociology is given only in the sense that it emerges in the process of understanding, a process that (according to this concept) is, both individually and historically, never completed or completable.

Thus the human approach does not emphasize subject matter and given-
ness (in the methodology of science a correlate of subject matter) but
rather the investigator as an agent and his investigation as action, as
creative action. The fundamental methodological question of the human
approach is therefore to ask how we can investigate unilluminated aspects
of man and of men's living together.

The human approach is still reticent to delimit the area within which
the subject matter of sociology should be confined because it feels that it
has not itself been sufficiently exemplified or even articulated in theory
or research to outline a classification of the social sciences that would be
commensurate with it—that is, adequately independent of traditional historical classifications. This reticence, of course, is not in conflict with the
fact that the human concept of sociology could not have developed, nor
feel the sort of sophisticated reticence just alluded to, without the antecedent development of science, social and natural, by which it has been
stimulated. More specifically, it could not react against the natural-science
concept of sociology unless this concept itself existed [5].

In the natural-science approach [6] the role of scientific method is
pivotal; in the human approach it is taken for granted. As has been said
in a facetious manner, the former is interested in a refinement of scientific
techniques and procedures at the exepense of human relevance, whereas
the latter may pursue significant questions but cannot test what it is
doing; or the former gets remarkably wise to increasingly dull matters,
the latter knows less and less about more and more; and so on. Yet in
spite of the differences in the concepts of science and scientific method
that distinguish the two approaches, it must be emphasized that the
human approach, where it has not yet developed scientific methods, endeavors to do so; that in terms of creativity, that is, in terms of the perception of problems and methods for solving them and in the breadth of
its interests—hence in its function in the development of the study of
man—it is more scientific than the natural-science approach; that it thus
has at least equal claim to being scientific, particularly as an expression of
increasing secularization and an increasing secular attitude.

It is thus erroneous to maintain, as some seem to do, that anything but
the natural-science approach, and more specifically the human approach,
is unscientific or less scientific than itself. It is true, on the other hand,
that many among the antecedents of the human approach, and thus
Dilthey as well as much of the humanities, notably all that has to do
with interpretation (e.g., literary criticism), suffer from a lack of rigorous
method and systematicity in comparison with much of the natural sciences. This, I think, need not be so. I should regard it rather as an invitation to devise more scientific methods in the human studies (both in

the social sciences and in the humanities) than as a suggestion to abstain from investigating problems that by some at least are felt to be important, only because we have not yet developed scientific methods for investigating them.

Both the natural-science and the human-studies concepts of sociology, then, have a scientific character. Yet the problems to which identical or similar research techniques are applied and the role of these problems in the general approach vary with the approach itself: the approach at least codetermines the problem selection. The differential concept of scientific character and method is an element in the approach.

Regarding this differential concept I am able to make only fragmentary statements. I hope, however, that these statements will enlighten, and will be enlightened by, those already made on the two approaches to sociology themselves. It should also be noted that the partial analysis that I have tried to undertake will be implemented by examples discussed in a later section.

It is not necessary to offer a definition of science. For our purposes its customary conceptions are adequate. Rather, that aspect of science stressed in the human approach must be emphasized. This aspect has, I think, been unduly neglected, but perhaps it can, if appreciated, lead to a less one-sided, hence more fruitful and more economical, sociology than we have at present. This aspect, which may be called the human equation [7], refers to the continuous challenge to remain aware of the relation between scientific pursuit and spontaneous experience, and consequently it refers to the inclusion of this awareness in the definition of the scientist [8]. I am convinced that it is not only useful but necessary for the development of sociology to include this awareness in the definition of the sociologist. This conviction rests on a concept of man that stresses, more than American sociology does, his irrational as well as creative, hence inexhaustible [9], qualities. With Cassirer [10] it emphasizes man as a symbol- and myth-making animal or, with Durkheim [11], man as an ideal-making animal, both ethically and cognitively. In Western civilization this notion of man has informed the artist, the religious, and the philosopher more often and more typically than the scientist. Yet I consider its incorporation into his approach a challenge to the scientist at the same time that I regard the incorporation of science and of scientific method into the study of man's creative efforts—artistic, religious, philosophical (and scientific)—a challenge to their traditional disciplines, mainly the humanities.

The following discussion of some concerns that so far have not, or only scarcely, been studied sociologically or, for that matter, scientifically, will serve to implement the general outlines of the human concept of sociology. This discussion suggests how sociology can study three phenomena that are important on the basis of the concept of man sketched, that illustrate the notion of the human equation of science, and that have hitherto been the almost exclusive domain of the humanities. The three phenomena chosen are the study of the unique, of the meaning of history, and of aesthetic experience. I begin with a description of the unique, then consider its study, and finally, more specifically though much more briefly, deal with the sociology of the meaning of history and of aesthetic experience.

THE UNIQUE

The human concept of sociology here advocated and developed agrees with the well-known tenet of science according to which science aims at the establishment of uniformities—whether the avowed purpose of this establishment is to understand the structure of the universe, to make predictions, or both. The human conception of science, however, advocates greater scientific concern with the unique than is customary in order to enrich materials from which to hypothesize and eventually to establish uniformities.

After anticipating this emphasis of the human conception, it is necessary to explain it; that is, it is necessary to define or at least circumscribe "unique." In the first place unique is *not* a logical or ontological concept. Logically, there is either no unique, inasmuch as everything is homogeneous in some respect to everything else, or nothing but uniques exist, inasmuch as nothing is homogeneous in all respects or identical with anything but itself. Hence logically speaking, unique is better replaced by single, and single is *not* the referent of unique as used here. Ontologically, unique makes sense only in reference to something that is, on the basis of some concept of the nature of being, in fact, unique, that is, outstanding in a particular way in reality or value. This is a use of the term that points to a frame of reference outside any discussion in this paper.

In the second place, although unique is neither a logical nor an ontological concept, it is, positively speaking, a psychological (teleological, creative) concept. More specifically, the unique belongs to the process of understanding (see below). In the third place, the unique is suggested by such terms as empathy, intuition, insight, apprehension, grasp, mystical union, trance, identification, love (most obviously at first sight), vision, inspiration, flash, and revelation, all of which refer to experiences that to the experiencer are characterized, cognitively [12] by a sudden passive-creative incorporation of elements, which he believes to be important, into his universe of discourse. This is by no means to suggest that any of these terms is synonymous with understanding. Understanding, rather, is conceived here as a process that lies on a continuum extending between the two extremes. One is complete strangeness toward its object, the other, complete identification with it. The object changes with the process of its understanding and, in this sense, is the subject matter or given of understanding [13].

In the fourth place, most concrete understanding lies between the extremes indicated, and this is true also of scientific understanding. Scientific understanding may be defined more precisely as that in which identification with the unique is counterbalanced by testable communicability. If the scale is weighted in favor of identification, testability and even communicability suffer (as, characteristically, in studies done in the humanities); if it is weighted in favor of testable communicability, the grasp of the unique suffers (as in many studies by positivistic sociologists). Maximum understanding, a synonym for scientific understanding, is thus seen to result from the combination of a sense for the unique with scientific training. But what do grasp of the unique and sense for the unique refer to?

It is here that the experiences of empathy and intuition, may help to further the argument. The human concept advocates that its followers consider certain possible topics of understanding as uniques [14] by approaching them, actually or typologically (a question decided by the scientist's own psychological make-up), in such experiences as have been listed; that is, any student will entertain possible topics of understanding on the basis of his personality and the culture in which he lives. His culture, if he is a scientist, includes his scientific training, and his scientific training is particularly significant for his scientific pursuit, of which the selection of a topic of understanding and an approach toward such a topic are elements. More specifically, then, the human concept advocates that the scientist consider those possible topics of understanding as uniques about which he has doubts that the development of the methodology of his discipline has satisfactorily reduced to mere crosspoints of uniformities [15], and he must make explicit the reasons for his doubts. Even this statement, however, must be qualified, for if, as is held here with Pareto [16] and many others, science can be concerned only with successive approximation to reality (an ontological proposition), the degree of approximation held satisfactory at any given time is determined not only by the development of scientific techniques or methodology but also by extrascientific factors, such as the intellectual interests of a student or his time. Hence the above statement appeals to the whole personality of the scientist; at any rate, in the social sciences much less than in the natural sciences can he point to available objective criteria by which to justify his advocacy of the understanding of certain topics as uniques. Nevertheless he has more to go by than his feelings. It is my belief that at the present stage in the development of sociology three such possible topics—or complexes of topics—are culture, personality, and intellectual products. In the next section of this paper an outline of their study as uniques is given in an effort to justify my doubt, that is, to suggest the superiority of their study as uniques to other ways of studying them. This is done in a discussion of the study of the unique, with culture, personality, and intellectual products as examples, and is followed by an application of the method suggested to the more specific topics of the meaning of history and aesthetic experience.

In the fifth place, then, there is the question of what is to be considered as a unique. The scope of this paper allows no more than the suggestion of an answer. Moreover, this suggestion has already been implied in the preceding paragraph. Inasmuch as unique is a psychological concept, not everything can, for psychological reasons, be so considered: nobody can live without routine. Furthermore, what is to be so considered depends on the personality and the culture, general and scientific, of the student. We can now say that the unique emerges in such instances in which (for reasons he must endeavor to become aware of and state) the student stops taking his methodology for granted and begins to question his approach.

This more than commonly questioning attitude is one illustration of the greater scientific character in the sense of greater secularization which has been asserted as a characteristic of the human conception. To use a metaphor, when he studies the unique, the student drops as much of his scientific and general-cultural cloak as he can in order to expose himself to his subject matter. (He cannot drop it all inasmuch as he is a human being who by definition has culture.) To use Alfred Weber's terms, he realizes the civilizational character of his routine pursuits and enters the sphere of culture [17].

The introduction of the concept of the unique is thus seen to be an appeal to greater self-awareness and skepticism, or secularization, on the part of the scientist. The purpose of such appeal is, as has been anticipated, to enrich materials from which to hypothesize uniformities. It may be added that the human conception may also lead to the elimination of errors, factual as well as methodological. How this may be done, that is, what the scientist does after he emerges from the unique or how he studies it is our next concern.

The nature of the unique may be clarified further by contrasting it with the logical (rather than psychological) concept of ideal-type. (This is especially useful in view of the discussion of culture in the next section.) In speaking of Pareto's "abstract rationalistic type of society," Talcott Parsons [18] writes:

> . . . it is clearly understood that "integration" in this complete sense applies only to the abstract society; in‹ this as in other respects it is a limiting case. Certainly neither Pareto nor the present author means to imply that concrete societies are in general or even approximately perfectly integrated in this sense, or that their members are normally, the majority, conscious that there is any system of common ends. But whether this system be explicit or implicit, whether integration be closely or only very distantly approached, does not affect the theoretical importance of this theorem, any more than the fact that feathers fall slowly and irregularly affects the importance of the law governing the falling of bodies in a vacuum. A concrete example which comes relatively close to the experimental conditions of the theorem is that of the Calvinists of Geneva in Calvin's own time who might be said to be pursuing the common end of establishing the Kingdom of God on Earth.

Here, then, as in Tönnies's *Gemeinschaft and Gesellschaft* [19], in Max Weber's conception of ideal-type [20], in Redfield's folk and urban societies [21], or in Howard Becker's sacred and secular societies [22], we are dealing with ideal-types in the sense of constructs in terms of which elements of reality (here, specifically, actual societies) can be understood. This is all well known, but what must be pointed out is that when cultures are designated as uniques (as in the following section of this paper) it does not imply that they are conceived as completely integrated wholes and that the ideal-type method should not be considered applicable to the study under discussion when the student, following the human concept advocated, embarks on the elaboration of his materials. In other words, the ideal-type method is logically and psychologically irrelevant to, and thus compatible with, the human concept, inasmuch as it moves in the sphere of methodology, whereas concern with the unique is a concern with approach.

SCIENTIFIC STUDY OF THE UNIQUE:
THE SOCIOLOGY OF THE "MEANING OF HISTORY"
AND OF AESTHETIC EXPERIENCE

It should be remembered that naming is one phase of understanding and, further, that each culture possesses psychologically irreducible phenomena, or named uniques, which the individual in the culture usually takes for granted but which, as cultural anthropology has taught us, often strike the outsider precisely as uniques. Even if these uniques should occur in other cultures—and a variation of the question thus suggested will occupy us in the next section—their respective integrations in given cultures make them uniques. Hence each culture is unique, and for similar reasons and in a similar (always psychological, not ontological) sense each personality and each intellectual product is unique.

We are now in a position to suggest the basis of a methodology for the scientific study of the unique, a methodology I believe applicable to the study of cultures, personalities, and intellectual products, and perhaps to the study of other uniques. In the following discussion, at any rate, unique stands promiscuously for culture, personality, and intellectual product.

I submit that scientific understanding of the unique can be obtained by studing its central attitude. This term probably does not sound strange if the unique refers to a personality or even to an intellectual product, but it seems quite inappropriate if it refers to a culture. In the case of culture, therefore, such terms as pattern, configuration, and ethos, terms that are indeed closely related to central attitude, may be preferred to it and may be substituted for it in the following discussion, if this facilitates the argument.

The central attitude, then, refers to the attitude that reveals itself during the process of understanding a given unique as rendering understandable all single attitudes [23]. In order to show the relation of the unique to the general by way of the communicable—to call attention, that is, to the process of understanding as it overcomes the extremes of complete strangeness toward its object and of complete identification with it—I may be allowed to use my own statements as an example: obviously, on the basis of what has been said so far, the question is whether there is anything in what I am saying, whether there is anything in the concept of central attitude advocated. This question itself is one of the ways of introducing the understanding process—the most literal way but not the only one. Whether the process of understanding this (my) intellectual product is inaugurated in the manner indicated or in another manner, it is clear that the previously mentioned combination of a sense for the unique with scientific training produces maximum understanding of this intellectual product. It should be noted that both the inspector of an intellectual product and its (immediate) author enrich their respective universes of discourse with this product. They enrich it both additively and creatively: in the former sense the process involved is a relatively passive one of learning; in the latter sense it is a relatively active one of developing [24].

Does the concept of central attitude, then, give us the basis of a methodology for the scientific study of cultures, personalities, and intellectual products? I believe it does because it combines the highest degree of identification with the object of understanding which is compatible with testable communicability. This combination, it will be remembered, was posited as a necessity for maximum understanding.

It will probably be granted that the central-attitude method surpasses other methods of understanding in terms of intimacy (identification) with its object, but its testability and even its communicability will be considered with skepticism. It is true that its testability is precarious and its communicability probably limited to persons attitudinally predisposed toward it. This is not a condemning statement, for more than precariousness can be predicated of its testability, hence of its communicability. Positively, it can be stated that testability and therefore communicability obtain to the degree that the student of a unique making use of the central-attitude method is aware of, and makes explicit, the processes by which he arrives at the central attitude—a task for his mastery of the human equation of science, and that his approach incorporates into his and his public's universe of discourse (or explains) demonstrably *no fewer*, or demonstrably *more*, aspects of the phenomenon under study than does any other competing approach.

The second of these criteria of testability is one in all understanding, whether in its everyday or scientific forms. The first, reflecting the scientific tenet of public inspection, is usually replaced by the public inspection of the scientific method but, in keeping with our suggestions regarding the human concept of sociology, is extended here to include the approach inherent in a given investigation and not only its methodology. It is hoped and expected that as this human concept becomes more clearly developed (perhaps even formalized) it can be spotted at once, labeled, and taken for granted in future investigations, at which time public inspection may be limited to methodology. Such a situation is certainly far off, yet it can already be formulated as a development within science.

Let us now apply these general considerations of the study of the unique to the sociological study of the meaning of history and aesthetic experience. Two theses are submitted. The meaning of history, as an object of scientific understanding in the sense advocated here, can be one or both of two things. It can be a datum for scientific understanding, namely, some group's, some school's, or some culture's meaning of history, that is, as conceived by somebody, or it can be a concept emerging in the scientist himself, but as such it is scientific only in the measure in which the scientist developing it is aware of and makes explicit the processes by which he has arrived at it. It will be noted that I have just repeated one of the two criteria of testability and communicability (as among criteria of scientific procedure) mentioned in connection with the discussion of the scientific character of the central-attitude method. The explanation of this repetition is the hypothesis that to emphasize or make explicit this criterion of scientific procedure allows us to implement the extension of scientific procedure to the study of phenomena which, as has been pointed out, have hitherto been the exclusive domain of the humanities—at best, that is, of students deeply concerned with the identification of the unique but less so with testability. The same considerations apply to aesthetic experience: it, too, can be an object of scientific understanding either as a datum (somebody's aesthetic experience) or as a concept emerging in the scientist himself. Enough has been said concerning the second sense in which the meaning of history, aesthetic experience, and other uniques can become objects of scientific understanding, for this discussion was prepared for in the discussion of the study of the unique in general and the central attitude in particular. A second thesis dealing with the meaning of history and aesthetic experience as data [25] and. more precisely, as data for sociological rather than for generally scientific study remains to be stated.

At the present juncture of scientific development it is indispensable for the maximum understanding of the meaning of history, aesthetic experience, and other uniques that they be studied sociologically. Otherwise the fact that they are historical phenomena, that is, phenomena in a specific social time and space—a fact that we know or at least postulate and are therefore compelled to incorporate into our scientific universe of discourse—is left unanalyzed, hence uncontrolled by our understanding of them. This thesis calls for a discussion of the methodology of their sociological study. We may generalize and insist on a discussion of the methodology of the sociological study of intellectual products in general —intellectual products understood as a class of uniques. In other words, we are inquiring into the methodology of what has customarily gone under the name sociology of knowledge [26] and what may perhaps better be called the sociology of intellectual behavior.

Some elements of the *approach* of the sociology of knowledge have been indicated: it is sufficient to recall that this approach ought to be informed by the recognition of the importance of the unique or by the human equation of science. The fundamental problem, or at least one of the fundamental problems, of the *methodology* of the sociology of intellectual behavior is the interpretation and, more precisely, the sociological interpretation of its data. This problem has received a great deal of attention [27]. It is made more complex, however, by the approach suggested here. Yet before we come to this added difficulty we must briefly expound the difference between immanent and sociological [28] interpretation (the latter as one among possible transcendent interpretations). It should be noted that for the moment we must assume that the question of *what* is to be interpreted is settled, but this is a question to which we shall have to return presently in connection with the difficulty suggested above. At any rate, the immanent interpretation of an intellectual product uses as its source this product exclusively; transcendent interpretation uses other sources as well in order to throw light on the product, and, more specifically, sociocultural interpretation undertakes to explain the results of immanent interpretation in sociocultural terms [28].

The added difficulty becomes obvious when we ask what it is we want to interpret and beyond which we are not allowed to go if we would stay within the limits of immanent interpretation. The question, in the light of foregoing discussion, becomes synonymous with the question how something becomes a datum or given. The answer to it lies in the empirical study of the processes by which something does become a given, and this study is greatly facilitated by the scientist's report of these processes, a report to which he is committed by our first criterion of testability (applied to the central-attitude method and to the meaning of history and aesthetic experience as emergents). Thus, on the empirical level the question is answered [30], but it also has its epistemological implication, which, precisely, is the added difficulty that was anticipated, for we must also ask how it is *possible* that something becomes a given to be understood. This well-known question which, in another formulation, was one of the main concerns of Kant, cannot and need not be treated here. It should be remembered, however, that the unique by definition is incommunicable and that, on the other hand, it has in this paper been made the object of understanding. To remember this is to realize a contradiction that calls for a resolution, and it is this resolution that is an epistemological concern and to which we must now turn. This concern may also be formulated as the question how understanding and communication are possible in spite of unique experience, the postulate (leading to an answer) being that they are, in some sense, possible. In other words, what is it that all human beings have in common in spite of cultural differences? The very formulation of this question suggests the impossibility of absolute cultural relativism—epistemological, ethical, and aesthetic.

SOCIOLOGY AND CULTURAL RELATIVISM

It is submitted that for sociology, and what is particularly relevant here, for the sociology of intellectual behavior, to be possible as a discipline that understands something other than itself—in other words, it is not (culturally) solipsistic—it must accept as a hypothesis the epistemological postulate that human intellectual-affective behavior exhibits both cultural variability and biologically founded identity. Earlier students of this problem tended to overemphasize one or the other of these components [31], whereas the consensus in recent sociology-of-knowledge and related literature [32] seems to lie in the direction of the postulate stated. Yet a completely satisfactory formulation of the two components has to my knowledge not yet been attained.

Child's recent attempt [33], however, seems to me to have great promise. Child begins with an analysis of the question whether the categories of thought are universal or culturally relative. Neither alternative, he points out, can be answered unreservedly in the affirmative, for on the one hand the inherence of categories in the nature of man has not been demonstrated, inasmuch as allegedly universal and necessary categories have not been proved, but on the other hand we cannot conceive of categories arising from experience, because such a postulate implies the structuralization, that is, the categorization, of experience itself. Rather we must postulate two kinds of category: primal, or biotic or socially underived categories and supervenient, or sociotic or socially derived categories [34]. Categories, Child emphasizes, are forms "not of the mind but of the whole responding organism" [35]; and they are cognitive, emotive, or conative according to their orientation or preponderate intent.

> Cognitive predispositions are simply organic potencies of response as oriented toward knowledge of the world rather than toward some feeling of it or some action upon it [36].

More precisely, in regard to the distinction between categories and other elements of thought, hence in regard to universal identity against cultural relativity in human behavior, Child writes as follows:

> While the primal categories are presumably invariable in essence, the concepts correlated with them continue, when once formulated, to develop and to undergo theoretical formulation and concatenation. And the conceptual correlates of the primal predispositions react upon these predispositions in the sense, at least, of acquiring themselves predispositional correlates which cluster around the original primal predispositions and which, in consequence, affect the apprehension, as well as the understanding, which occurs in the sphere of the predispositions concerned. Indeed, *it is in and through this process of accretion that the primal categories exhibit their primordiality.* As example of the way in which the con-

cepts of the understanding may condition or provide the mode within which the primal categories operate, consider the fact that space and time may be differently felt in different cultures while the basic biotic forms of apprehension remain the same in the individuals of all different cultures. But, in so far as concepts function in this way, they do so as functionalized in supervenient categories. These categories, the *a priori* formalizing factors which do not inhere in men as animals, are those persistent and powerful tendencies to take the world as such-and-such which, under certain circumstances, in certain people or certain groups of people, have become compulsions. By becoming compulsions they become categories [37].

Although several questions can be raised in regard to this theory (the discussion of which, however, would far exceed the scope of this chapter). it seems to me that Child has made it exceedingly difficult to maintain absolute epistemological relativism and, because of his conception of the categories, has at the same time made it exceedingly difficult to maintain absolute ethical and aesthetic relativism.

If, then, we accept Child's distinction between primal and supervenient categories, we are able to resolve the seeming contradiction between the incommunicability of the unique, and the unique as the object of understanding. Now we can say that unique is a primal category that has been conceptualized and probably functionalized into a supervenient category on the basis of certain cultural circumstances and more precisely, even if still vaguely, on the basis of certain developments in philosophy and the social sciences, some elements of which have been alluded to in this paper [38]. If we accept these developments, what follows for the relation between epistemology and sociology or sociology of intellectual behavior?

To answer this question we would do well to act on the postulated principle of becoming aware of the processes by which we have arrived at our position, to the limited extent, at least, of retracing our major steps to this point. We began by distinguishing approach from methodology. We then sketched two concepts of sociology, the natural-science and the human-studies concepts, and in clarification and defense of the human concept we circumscribed a concept of science which is characterized by what was called the human equation. In this concept our attention was called to some phenomena—the unique, the meaning of history, and aesthetic experience—which we maintained were not studied as scientifically as our concept of scientific study would warrant. We gave a general description of the unique and indicated the outlines of the scientific study of the phenomena mentioned by introducing the notion of the central-attitude method. We suggested their study as both data and emergents and expanded on their study as data by requesting that it include their sociological investigation. This led us to one of the fundamental problems of the sociology of intellectual behavior, that of interpretation. The question of the object of interpretation itself, whether immanent or sociocultural, led further to the formulation of the contradiction between the incommunicable unique, and the unique as an object of understanding and to the resolution of this contradiction with the help of Child's statements regarding categories. The formulation of this contradiction and its resolution were recognized as an epistemological concern, but epistemological concerns, we now continue, are not sociological concerns, or, more generally, they are the business of the philosopher (particularly of the theorist of knowledge or epistemologist) not the scientist.

One can admit this and maintain [39] that whenever the behavior scientist deals with epistemological questions he no longer functions as a scientist but as an epistemologist. Yet the question may be raised whether we should stop at this recognition or rather consider the foregoing discussion of the philosophy of sociology as a challenge to undertake an even more radical reclassification of our intellectual efforts. This reclassification would be based on the twofold proposition, which is derived from the preceding discussion, that it requires the articulation of the relation between epistemology and intellectual efforts and that, inversely, the articulation of the relation between epistemology and intellectual efforts requires the classification of the latter. It is beyond the scope of this paper to undertake these articulations: here it must suffice to suggest their place and the need for them [40].

SUMMARY: IMPLICATIONS FOR SOCIOLOGICAL PRACTICE

In this last section an attempt is made to point out the implications of this chapter for the practice of sociological study. This is done in a two-fold application of the general concept presented. First I outline a specific research example that shows how the human concept of sociology, more particularly, the central-attitude method, applies to the study of a culture. Second, I make some general methodological observations that are primarily designed to dispel possible misconceptions of points raised in the present essay.

It has been suggested that in the study of a culture the aim of sociological understanding is terminologically more conveniently designated as culture pattern (or the like) than as central attitude. If the goal of the study is maximum understanding, the culture under examination must be conceived as a unique, even if its student (or other students) uses the results of the study of the culture as a unique as material from which to hypothesize and eventually to establish uniformities. In following the cultural approach—the variant, relevant to the study of cultures, of the more general human approach—the student is aware of the cultural equation. This awareness makes him suspicious of analyzing the culture in terms of contentual divisions such as child rearing, marriage, and death customs because he fears that they are naively, that is, relatively unaware, taken over from his own (general and special scientific) culture. He therefore discards this approach in favor of the pattern method, which he finds more in keeping with the study of the culture as a unique [41]. The two fundamental tasks of any scientific study of uniques—to grasp them to the highest degree compatible with testability and communicability—formulate themselves for the study of a culture as the question of ascertaining or selecting patterns to present a testable interpretation of the culture that is superior to all competing interpretations; that is, the student must present patterns and their interrelations in a manner that will enable him and his public to understand and predict the culture under study. The two criteria of understanding have been formulated as the demonstration of the degree to which the student is aware of the processes underlying his study and as the demonstration of the degree to which his study can compete with other studies. The criterion of prediction is the degree to which the propositions made in his study are confirmed in the future [42].

Similar remarks, as already suggested, could obviously be made in regard to the study of personalities and of intellectual products. It will also be recognized that they could generally be made concerning the investigation of any kind of human behavior. To recognize this amounts to admitting that this paper suggests the beginnings of a philosophy of the study of man as a sociocultural animal—a study to which social sciences other than sociology have made claims. It has been impossible to do more here than to show the relevance of this philosophy to sociology by taking examples from sociology and noting challenges to sociology rather than taking them from other social sciences and challenging them: sociology has not been defined nor has it been delimited in regard to other disciplines. To repeat, therefore [43], the next step is to develop the concept outlined by determining whether—and if so, how—it lends itself as an instrument for classifying subdivisions of the study of man. In line with this concept such a classification itself is seen as a vehicle toward a greater understanding of ourselves.

Fundamentally this paper advocates both the application of scientific method to topics traditionally outside the domain of sociology and a greater awareness in the scientific treatment of traditional topics (as here exemplified particularly by the topic culture). Furthermore, it suggests several tools designed to translate this advocacy into research practice. To avoid misunderstanding it is appropriate to conclude with a few clarifying remarks.

In the first place numerous questions dealt with in methodological literature have remained unanswered because they are irrelevant to the arguments expounded in this chapter. One is the applicability of the ideal-type method. Among many others, the following may be mentioned: what, in theory and in research, is the line between description and explanation, between idiographic and nomothetic study, between structure and content or structure and function? [44] All that can be said here in regard to these problems is that although they are irrelevant to the present discussion, inasmuch as they are methodological questions, they nevertheless require investigation in the framework of the approach presented and will, it is hoped, receive clarification from such discussion. The same goes for the various aspects of the relation between the unique and the general. Yet, in the latter case it must be noted that although the unique has been defined here according to its status both in the approach and in the methodology of sociology it is still necessary to define "general," at least in one of its various denotations, and more precisely in the denotation that supplements that of unique. The general, like the unique, is a psychological concept. Logical and ontological questions are as irrelevant to the concept of general as a concept within the approach of sociology as they are in regard to unique. More precisely, general refers to the methodologically *un*questioned, whereas (as stated earlier) the unique emerges exactly where methodology is questioned [45]. It becomes obvious that contemporary sociology (like any intellectual effort at any given time) is full of (conceptualized) generals, as well as of general areas, such as population, family, or "urban" [46]. This chapter, far from advocating the abandonment of these generals, merely urges an examination of the legitimacy with which their methodologies have been established; it urges a questioning of the division of sociology into these and similar branches, even as it urges, more articulately, that of our intellectual efforts in general [47].

In the second place a general placement of the conception of sociology advocated here ought to be worked out. It is enough to state that the one single concept to which it comes closest is that of Max Weber [48]. It is evident, however, that it would greatly benefit from a systematic investigation of similarities and differences between itself and Weber's concept, as well as those of Dilthey, Simmel, Znaniecki, Parsons, and of various recent cultural anthropologists.

It is hoped that the remarks in the last section place this paper within current problem complexes. Clearly, the paper entails two tasks. One is to solve the problems presented or merely mentioned in it theoretically. The other is to translate these problems into research as far as possible at present and to further their translation into research. It is in the hope that response to this paper will contribute to the solution of one or both of these tasks that it is submitted at this time.

NOTES

1. A first draft of this paper was presented early in 1947 in a Methodology of Science seminar conducted at Ohio State University by Dr. Virgil G. Hinshaw, Jr., to whom I am indebted for many stimulating and clarifying discussions. The revision of this essay (and its incorporation into a forthcoming monograph—cf. n. 42) was made possible by a grant from The Viking Fund, which is herewith gratefully acknowledged.

2. See (2).

3. For a recent convenient exhibition of the contrasts between the two conceptions see (17) and (34).

4. Cf. (29).

5. The claim to (as well as the exemplification of) some sort of human concept of sociology is, as has been suggested, well known: it goes back to the German controversy over *Naturwissenschaften* versus *Geisteswissenschaften*. Obviously the natural-science approach is related to the former, the human approach, to the latter. "Human studies" is a translation by H. A. Hodges (13), here adopted, of *Geisteswissenschaften*, particularly as used by Dilthey (13, p. 157). Moreover there seems to be evidence of a considerable approximation to the human approach, on the one hand, in the theoretical work of Znaciecki [see (33), (34), and (35)] and of some other contemporary American sociologists, particularly T. Parsons and R. M. MacIver, and, on the other, in certain recent anthropological literature; see (29), p. 175a, n. 2, for some references.

6. It will be noted that I have been using "approach" where I earlier used "concept" or "position." Approach, consistent with its definition given at the beginning of this chapter, is short for "approach characteristic of the (natural-science, or the human) conception of, or position in, sociology."

7. In parallel to the cultural equation pertinent to the study of cultures specifically; cf. (29).

8. The question whether it is useful to include this awareness in the definition of the natural scientist may be left unanalyzed here. An affirmative, though modified, answer would seem to be adequate in this case.

9. In the sense of the assumption that man can never be definitively defined.

10. Cf. (4) and (5). See also my review of the latter, *American Sociological Review*, 12 (June 1947), 372–373.

11. Cf. (9), especially pp. 139–140.

12. If they are, to the experiencer, cognitively relevant at all. At least, these experiences are not merely cognitive but involve affect and volition as well. This point is not important in the present context, however, inasmuch as at the moment we are concerned with developing the relevance of the unique in regard to the process of understanding. Although understanding, too, involves other than cognitive elements, it is nevertheless here (as is commonly done) regarded as a significantly cognitive process. The participation of affective and conative elements in understanding is not discussed in this chapter except that the question is touched on once again in connection with the discussion of categories (in the context of the discussion of cultural relativism).

13. Whether the unique is the predicate of the object of understanding or of the understander is an ontological question that is irrelevant here, inasmuch as the unique, as pointed out in the first instance, is a psychological concept.

14. Note the invitation to *consider* them as uniques, which consideration leaves the unique a psychological concept; that is, it does not make it ontological.

15. Cf. (22), paragraph 99.

16. *Ibid.*, paragraph 106.

17. Cf. (28), especially pp. 31–47; also (20) and (18), pp. 272–281. It should be noted that the use here of Weber's concepts as metaphors implies neither agreement nor disagreement with the conception underlying them.

18. Cf. (24), pp. 247–248.

19. Cf. (27).

20. The best succinct analysis of which is to be found in (23), pp. 12–15.

21. See, for example, (25).

22. See (2) and (3); also (1).

23. Cf. (32) [Chapter 5]. For the formulation of a further degree of awareness in appraising this concept, *ibid.*, n. 25 [Chapter 26, n. 26].

24. Thus in the example at hand the author of this intellectual product developed from the concept of central attitude that of typical central attitude (32) [Chapter 5]. For fuller presentations of central attitude and typical central attitude and for other concepts believed to be useful for the study of (certain) uniques, *ibid.*

25. It should not be forgotten that they become data or givens in the sense indicated earlier.

26. It is well known that this is a misnomer. See, for example, (21), 379–380.

27. For a good summary and analysis of relevant literature see (6), Chapter VII.

28. "Sociological interpretation" is used here synonymously with "sociocultural," "social," or "cultural interpretation." The differences among these various types are irrelevant to the present discussion and may therefore remain unanalyzed.

29. Cf. (30). Earlier in the present chapter "immanent interpretation" more specifically of a science was used to refer to the study of its intellectual structure or methodology as given and its "transcendent interpretation" to the study of its approach as not given with, but inferable from ("outside"), its methodology. On the two modes of interpretation in regard to culture patterns see (29). For a deliberate attempt at excluding all transcendent (and some elements of immanent) interpretation (an attempt that shows the striking paucity of the result in terms of the understanding of the object examined) see (31).

30. Cf. also (32) [Chapter 5].

31. The instinctivists, Freud, and the Kantians, in their stress of instincts, supposedly universal psychological complexes, and a priori categories of thought, respectively, neglected cultural relativity, whereas the modern discoverers of cultural relativity, particularly Sumner and Westermarck, failed to raise the question whether men had anything in common in spite of it.

32. See especially (26), (16), Chapter IV, (6), Chapter III, (15), and (14). For a more extensive treatment, see Chapter 7.

33. (7).

34. (7), 316–318.

35. *Ibid.*, 323.

36. *Ibid.*, 322.

37. *Ibid.*, 327–328. First italics added.

38. This concept of the unique not only allows us to resolve the contradiction just discussed but also throws light on our concept of understanding as an epistemological concept: epistemologically speaking, the aim of understanding is now seen to be the primal category of the unique by means of its culturally relative expressions, such as supervenient categories, concepts, and attitudes. The empirical vehicle of understanding is still the central-attitude method discussed earlier.

39. As has most explicitly been done by Virgil G. Hinshaw, Jr.: see (12) and (11).

40. It should be noted that lines of thought similar to those developed in regard to epistemology could (and should) also be articulated in respect to other traditional fields of philosophy such as logic, metaphysics, ethics, and aesthetics.

41. In a definition that is inadequate but sufficient for the present purpose "culture patterns" may be designated as *certain types* of uniformity of emotion, attitude, thought, knowledge, and overt action; in short, as *certain types* of uniformity of behavior.

42. For a considerably fuller presentation of the empirical establishment of culture patterns, see (29). (The application of the concept outlined here and in the paper cited is the topic of a monograph [in preparation] on the culture of a

small, relatively isolated, largely Spanish-speaking community in northern New Mexico.)

43. Cf. the end of the preceding section of this chapter in which (in the discussion of the relation between philosophy, particularly epistemology, and behavioral sciences, particularly sociology) some clues to such a classification are presented.

44. There is a similarity—which cannot be analyzed here—between the utilization of unique as emphasized and what Clerk Maxwell called the dynamical method. The following quotation (which I owe to Dr. J. N. Spuhler, Department of Sociology, The Ohio State University) may be reproduced as an example of the numerous passages found in methodological literature that need analysis in terms of the approach suggested. (This passage is especially noteworthy for coming from the pen of such an eminent natural scientist.) In the "statistical method of investigating social questions . . . [persons] are grouped according to some characteristic, and the number of persons forming the group is set down under that characteristic. This is the raw material from which the statist endeavours to deduce general theorems in sociology. Other students of human nature proceed on a different plan. They observe individual men, ascertain their history, analyse their motives, and compare their expectations of what they will do with their actual conduct. This may be called the dynamical method of study as applied to man. *However imperfect the dynamical study of man may be in practice, it evidently is the only perfect method in principle* . . . If we betake ourselves to the statistical method, we do so confessing that we are unable to follow details of each case and expecting that the effects of wide-spread causes, though different in each individual, will produce an average result on the whole nation, from a study of which we may estimate the character and propensities of an imaginary being called the Mean Man" (19), pp. 219–220. Italics added.

45. It may be said that structurally the two concepts belong in the same category, whereas contentually they are opposite and complementary.

46. It is interesting to note that Durkheim, both in (10) and again 13 years later in (8), p. 419, n. 1, suspects that the economic sphere—to use the terminology employed here—is the only one that sociology may have to leave unquestioned, whereas all other social spheres must be redefined (as religiously derived).

47. Cf. the end of the preceding section.

48. Cf. (23), especially "Weber's Methodology of Social Science," pp. 8–29.

REFERENCES

1. Howard Becker, "Constructive Typology in the Social Sciences," in Harry Elmer Barnes, Howard Becker, and Frances Bennett Becker, Eds., *Contemporary Social Theory* (New York: Appleton-Century, 1940), pp. 17–46.

2. Howard Becker, "Processes of Secularisation, An Ideal-Typical Analysis with Special Reference to Personality Change as Affected by Population Movement," *Sociological Review*, 24 (April–July 1932), 138–154; (October 1932), 266–286.

3. Howard Becker and Robert C. Myers, "Sacred and Secular Aspects of Human Sociation," *Sociometry*, 5 (August 1942), 207–229; (November 1942), 355–370.

4. Ernst Cassirer, *An Essay on Man* (New Haven: Yale University Press, 1944).

5. Ernst Cassirer, *Language and Myth* (New York: Harper, 1946).

6. Arthur Child, *The Problems of the Sociology of Knowledge* [Berkeley; University of California (unpublished Ph.D. thesis), 1938].

7. Arthur Child, "On the Theory of the Categories," *Philosophy and Phenomenological Research*, 7 (December 1946), 316–335.

8. Emile Durkheim, *The Elementary Forms of the Religious Life* (1912), translated by Joseph Ward Swain (London: Allen and Unwin; New York: Macmillan, 1915).

9. Emile Durkheim, "Jugements de valeur et jugements de réalité" (1911), in *Sociologie et philosophie* (Paris: Alcan, 1924), pp. 117–142.

10. Emile Durkheim, "Preface," *Année sociologique*, Vol. 2 (Paris: Alcan, 1899).

11. Virgil G. Hinshaw, Jr., "Epistemological Relativism and the Sociology of Knowledge," *Philosophy of Science*, 15 (January 1948), 4–10.

12. Virgil G. Hinshaw, Jr., "The Epistemological Relevance of Mannheim's Sociology of Knowledge," *Journal of Philosophy*, 40 (February 4, 1943), 57–72.

13. H. A. Hodges, *Wilhelm Dilthey: An Introduction* (New York: Oxford University Press, 1944).

14. Thelma Z. Lavine, "Naturalism and the Sociological Analysis of Knowledge," in Yervant H. Krikorian, Ed., *Naturalism and the Human Spirit* (New York: Columbia University Press, 1944), pp. 183–209.

15. Thelma Z. Lavine, "Sociological Analysis of Cognitive Norms," *Journal of Philosophy*, 39 (June 18, 1942), 342–356.

16. Clarence Irving Lewis, *Mind and the World-Order* (New York: Scribner, 1929).

17. George A. Lundberg, "The Proximate Future of American Sociology: The Growth of Scientific Method," *American Journal of Sociology*, 50 (May 1945), 502–513.

18. R. M. MacIver, *Society: A Textbook of Sociology* (New York: Farrar and Rinehart, 1937).

19. Appendix, Clerk Maxwell on Determinism and Free Will [1873], in Lawrence J. Henderson, *The Order of Nature* (Cambridge: Harvard University Press, 1917).

20. Robert K. Merton, "Civilization and Culture," *Sociology and Social Research*, 21 (November-December 1936), 103–113.

21. Robert K. Merton, "The Sociology of Knowledge," in Georges Gurvitch and Wilbert E. Moore, Eds., *Twentieth Century Sociology* (New York: Philosophical Library, 1945), pp. 366–405.

22. Vilfredo Pareto, *The Mind and Society*, translated by Andrew Bongiorno and Arthur Livingston (New York: Harcourt, Brace, 1935), 4 vols.

23. Talcott Parsons, Introduction to his and A. M. Henderson's translation of Max Weber, *The Theory of Social and Economic Organization* (New York: Oxford University Press, 1947).

24. Talcott Parsons, *The Structure of Social Action* (New York: McGraw-Hill, 1937).

25. Robert Redfield, "The Folk Society," *American Journal of Sociology*, **52** (January 1947), 293–308.

26. Alexander von Schelting, "Zum Streit um die Wissenssoziologie," *Archiv für Sozialwissenschaft und Sozialpolitik*, **57** (1929), especially 31–32.

27. Ferdinand Tönnies, *Gemeinschaft und Gesellschaft, Abhandlung des Communismus und des Socialismus als empirischer Culturformen* [1887], translated and supplemented by Charles P. Loomis: *Fundamental Concepts of Sociology (Gemeinschaft und Gesellschaft)* (New York: American Book, 1940).

28. Alfred Weber, *Ideen zur Staats-und Kultursoziologie* (Karlsruhe: Braun, 1927).

29. Kurt H. Wolff, "A Methodological Note on the Empirical Establishment of Culture Patterns," *American Sociological Review*, **10** (April 1945), 176-184.

30. Kurt H. Wolff, "Notes Toward A Sociocultural Interpretation of American Sociology," *American Sociological Review*, **11** (October 1946), 545-553.

31. Kurt H. Wolff, "A Partial Analysis of Student Reactions to President Roosevelt's Death," *Journal of Social Psychology*, **26** (August 1947), 35–53.

32. Kurt H. Wolff, "The Sociology of Knowledge: Emphasis on an Empirical Attitude," *Philosophy of Science*, **10** (April 1943), 104-123 [Chapter 5].

33. Florian Znaniecki, *The Method of Sociology* (New York: Farrar and Rinehart, 1934).

34. Florian Znaniecki, "The Proximate Future of Sociology: Controversies in Doctrine and Method," *American Journal of Sociology*, **50** (May 1945), 514–521.

35. Florian Znaniecki, "Social Organization and Institutions," in Georges Gurvitch and Wilbert E. Moore, Eds., *Twentieth Century Sociology* (New York: Philosophical Library, 1945), pp. 172–217.

Reprinted in modified form from *Philosophy of Science*, **15** (1948), 192–210, by permission of the publisher. The essay has been edited and partially revised by the author.

7

A PRELIMINARY INQUIRY INTO THE SOCIOLOGY OF KNOWLEDGE FROM THE STANDPOINT OF THE STUDY OF MAN.

1953, 1950

BACKGROUND MATERIALS

The sociology of knowledge [1] is usually considered the branch of sociology that studies relations between society and knowledge or knowledge in its social setting. The term itself, a translation of the German *Wissenssoziologie*, is widely recognized as a misnomer; actual contributions in the field have been concerned not so much with knowledge in the sense of scientific or positive knowledge as with ideologies, political doctrines, types or models of thought, and various other intellectual phenomena.

The two main antecedents of the sociology of knowledge are Marxism and Durkheimian sociology. Marxism (its vulgarized forms more notably than Marx's own writings) has tended to debunk intellectual behavior (except its own tenets) as ideological, that is, as rooted in the social, particularly the class, position of its exponents. Durkheimian sociology has concentrated on the relations between forms of society (chiefly primitive society) and forms or categories of thought. Neither Marx-Engels nor Durkheim and his followers used the term sociology of knowledge or its German or French equivalents. *Wissenssoziologie* itself, nourished by

Marxism more than by any other single source, flourished in Germany in the 1920s and, after the rise of Hitler, was transplanted mainly to the United States.

The two outstanding representatives of *Wissenssoziologie* were Max Scheler and Karl Mannheim. Scheler, a philosopher of phenomenologist inclination, tried to incorporate the sociology of knowledge into a system of philosophical anthropology, which, however, remained uncompleted. Mannheim formulated the difference between the sociology of knowledge and a sociological theory of knowledge but failed to solve the epistemological problems involved in this distinction. At the time that the sociology of knowledge was introduced in the United States, mainly through Wirth and Shils's translation of Mannheim's *Ideologie und Utopie*, closely related American efforts had been in existence for decades (and continue to exist, with little, though perhaps increasing, contact with the sociology of knowledge). These efforts are embodied, especially, in pragmatism and social behaviorism. Most American students interested in the field have based their labors on a combination of pragmatist and social-behaviorist ideas with German and, particularly, French ideas. In addition, the most systematic survey of the philosophical problems inherent in the sociology of knowledge, the most convenient summary of its sociological and research problems, and the most concise sketch of its background and its American relations stem from Americans—from Arthur Child, Robert K. Merton, and Louis Wirth, respectively [2].

The sociology of knowledge has been more speculative and theoretical than empirical, although it boasts some outstanding research. It has been both a scientific and a philosophical concern. Its heterogeneous antecedents and concepts have not been synthesized into a comprehensive theory designed to be tested empirically but instead, on the whole, have resulted in *more* (often polemic) formulations and conceptions. This state of affairs has discouraged acquaintance with the sociology of knowledge and its cultivation on the part of some students who are familiar with it. Its promise, as a scientific concern, would seem to lie in its liberation from those historical fetters that have kept it from developing into a general and systematic *sociology of intellectual-emotional behavior*.

If one were to undertake such a task, he would have to assemble the knowledge that has been gathered by a great many students in a great many fields, all of which bear on the central problem-complex of the sociology of knowledge—the relations between society and intellectual life. Obviously this applies to much work in the social sciences other than sociology and in the humanities but also in certain biological sciences. Overlooking all particular works and names, some of the most important areas of research and theory seem to be these: in the social sciences, in addition to general sociological findings and to more specialized findings (as in communication, public opinion, and propaganda), social psychology in a very broad sense (including child psychology, abnormal psychology and psychiatry, psychoanalysis and related movements, psychological testting, learning theory, and the study of social perception, attitudes, and social norms); cultural anthropology, particularly linguistics with its various subdivisions, the study of culture and personality, and the study of culture itself; in the humanities social and cultural history, literary criticism, historical linguistics, and the methodological and empirical aspects of philosophy—epistemology, semiotics, logic, metaphysics, ethics, and aesthetics; and, finally in the biological sciences, whatever throws light on the biological dimensions of intellectual behavior (i.e., especially the field of human genetics). All are sources of knowledge relevant to the problem of the relations between society and intellectual life. To assemble and dovetail them, obviously, is a tremendous task, but also, it would seem, a tremendous challenge.

What has just been presented is the kind of answer one might give to an outsider who asks: what is the sociology of knowledge? It is a commonsense description of it as a historical phenomenon. One might continue in a similar vein in reply to a closely related question: what has the sociology of knowledge given us by way of fruitful concepts or of scientific inquiries? Perhaps Mannheim's distinction between immanent (intrinsic) and transcendent (extrinsic) interpretation [3] or Znaniecki's typology of men of knowledge and of the social circle, self, social status, and social function of the man of knowledge [4] would be mentioned. Among scientific inquiries outstanding (but rather arbitrary) illustrations are Mannheim's earlier studies in historicism and conservative thought [5], Kohn-Bramstedt's work in the sociology of literature [6], Merton's investigation of seventeenth-century English science and technology [7], or Zilsel's explorations in the sociology of science [8]. Thus a vast and exciting panorama would be opened but to do so is not the purpose of this chapter. Its purpose is something I believe to be even more important. It is implied in the phrase "the study of man," from the standpoint of which the sociology of knowledge is to be considered.

THE STUDY OF MAN

The concept of social science that I call the study of man emerged chiefly out of the research done in Loma [9]. In this chapter I am trying to act on one of the tenets of this study by addressing myself to the sociology of knowledge. I do it by foresight, in the same way in which I found by hindsight that Loma was the occasion for the emergence and application of the study of man. This tenet is the need for emphasizing the interaction between the student of man and his subject matter—which in the present case is the sociology of knowledge— by which both become clarified and thus change. Put differently, I am now asking a question similar to the one or to the whole row of questions I found myself asking in Loma: What does it mean for me to study the sociology of knowledge? What is the nature of my research, of my contact with it? Who am I to approach the sociology of knowledge, what am I to do with it or to inquire into [10]? What is the sociology of knowledge as an interpretation of the world, its historical and symptomatic significance? What sort of a man is the man who invents it and is fascinated by it?

The first step toward answers to these questions, to this one question, is to define the sociology of knowledge operationally so that it is clear what I am inquiring into. To do this it is important to realize that the sociology of knowledge has been an enterprise that has not limited itself to scientific concerns but has also run into philosophical, especially epistemological, problems, and that this is most transparent in its philosophical assertions and claims—most pointedly when they were not meant to be but were held to be scientific or were not clearly distinguished from scientific statements. The best known case in point is Karl Mannheim [11].

I take Arthur Child's summary of the philosophical problems of the sociology of knoweldge [12] as the operational definition of my inquiry into this field. I am aware of the limitation imposed on my undertaking by this choice; most notably I shall not do full justice to Scheler, but I feel sure I catch significant aspects of the area and at least am able to show how I can apply an important tenet of the study of man. This is more pertinent at this time than to make the undertaking more comprehensive and definitive.

Thus I shall present the occasion of my inquiry by expounding and questioning as briefly as possible Child's conception with the sole purpose of equipping myself better for answers to the questions on my mind. Hence the elaboration of the problems posed by Child in the following section is only an incidental by-product of pursuing my principal quest.

ARTHUR CHILD'S SOCIOLOGY OF KNOWLEDGE

The basis of Child's studies in the sociology of knowledge is his doctoral dissertation [13], which is divided into eight chapters: Preliminary Approach, The Possibility of a Sociology of Knowledge, The Categorical Structure, The Relation Between Being and Thought, The Problem of

Imputation, The Problem of Truth, Immanent and Transcendent Interpretation, and Summary. Five of these chapters exist in revised form as published articles [14]. For convenience' sake, exposition and appraisal follow the chapter sequence of the dissertation.

Ideology. Child begins his dissertation with the "principal philosophical problems that arise out of a consideration of . . . [the] basic premises of the sociology of knowledge" *(Problems,* p. 1). After a brief discussion of the philosophical and historical origins of the field, the major portion of Chapter 1, Preliminary Approach, is devoted to a clarification of the concept of ideology. Two groups of theorists of ideology are distinguished. One holds that ideology is by its nature falsifying [15]; the other emphasizes the functional character of ideologies, and the function of an ideology may or may not be falsifying [16]. On the basis of the studies surveyed Child offers his own definition of ideology as

> a system of ideas which consciously or unconsciously tends to advance the interests—or reflect the class position—of some social class or section of such class *(Problems,* p. 22.)

Unfortunately, social class, one of the key terms in this definition is not defined.

Legitimacy of the Sociology of Knowledge. The title of the paper, which is a revision of the second dissertation chapter, «The Theoretical Possibility of the Sociology of Knowledge» [17], suggests a fundamental problem which, as Child points out, has been largely neglected.

> This problem may be formulated as follows: Is the sociology of knowledge, from a theoretical standpoint, even possible? And how, especially, can that possibility obtain a theoretical ground? . . . Unless one can establish the legitimacy of the sociology of knowledge, there would appear to be little reason in discussing the problems that can arise only on the presupposition of its legitimacy *(Possibility,* p. 392).

Child finds that the answers these and related questions have received in the extant literature are seldom explicit. Nevertheless he classifies their authors into three basic groups: those who altogether deny the possibility of the sociology of knowledge [18], those who deny its possibility as a science [19], and those who attempt a logical proof of the social determination of thought [20]. Yet the examination of these numerous efforts leads Child to make the statement

that if most of the refutations of the sociology of knowledge
depend on dogma and confusion, the sociologists of knowledge, on their side, have thus far advanced no coercive
ground for the objectivity of social determination (*ibid.*, p.
413).

To provide such ground is the task Child has set for himself. In this
undertaking, he starts from the premise that

no one with the slightest regard for the facts would deny that
to some extent, in some fashion or other, thought does exhibit
the influence of society. We shall therefore take this vague and
indefinite sort of social determination as admitted; it is at
least some kind of determination by a transcendent factor
(*ibid.*, p. 414).

By which factor or factors, and in which way, is social determination
effected? In answering these questions, three hypotheses may be entertained: thought is determined by one factor; it is determined by several
factors acting individually; it is determined by several factors acting
through one. Now, because it would appear that thought varies with
geography, nationality, and race, the first possibility—the one-factor
hypothesis—is ruled out, but so is the second alternative, for

it is within highly particularized social-historical contexts that
factors of geography and race, for instance, exert their hardly
deniable influence on mentality (*ibid.*, p. 415).

Hence, the third possibility is left, and this factor through which several
others act

could hardly be other than the social. . . . If the last alternative could receive an adequate ground, therefore, as specified
to the social, the arguments of postulational skepticism [21]
would be met, at last, in the measure and in the sense in
which it is at all possible to meet them (*ibid.*).

Thus Child arrives at his proper task—to advance a coercive ground
for the objectivity of social determination. The only way in which this
can be done, he writes, is to show that mind itself is social; and this, in
fact, *has* been shown by George H. Mead [22]:

If mind itself has a social origin . . . and if thinking consists
. . . in the manipulation of generalized attitudes . . . then

there can be no question of the social determination . . . of
knowledge and thought. And there can be no question, consequently, of the validity of the interpretation of thought from
a social standpoint. Furthermore, if thought is indeed a social
process, . . . then neither can there be any question that, whatever transcendent determinants may exist besides society, they
can determine mind only through the intermediation of social
reality *(ibid.,* p. 416).

Yet, even if Mead's theory were accepted, Child continues, three qualifications must be made. First; the theory may justify the social interpretation of thought, but it is insufficient to justify the sociology of
knowledge because to do so assumptions are required in addition to
those needed to establish social interpretation itself. Yet, although Child
differentiates [23] between the social interpretation of thought and the
sociology of knowledge, he does not define the difference. Nevertheless,
however we would define it—even if we followed the qualification just
mentioned—Child has failed in his undertaking to ground the sociology
of knowledge theoretically, as he himself explicitly admits *(Possibility,*
p. 417).

Second, Mead's theory may justify social interpretation, but it

leaves untouched the question of *the meaning and the extent*
of social determination, as well as the problem of the interaction between this objective determination, the inherent
logic of thought itself, and the spontaneous activity of the
organically individualized mind *(ibid.,* p. 417; italics added).

Inasmuch as these three interacting variables (social factors, logic, and
the individual) are neither defined nor shown to follow from Child's
preceding discussion, their interaction, indeed, calls for investigation, an
investigation that is not forthcoming in Child's work [24]. Third, Mead's
theory contains no research suggestions (cf. *Possibility,* p. 417). Nor
does Child stop his self-criticism at this point. He not only admits his
failure to demonstrate the theoretical possibility of the sociology of
knowledge but he also points out that Mead's theory itself (which would,
at least, demonstrate the possibility of social interpretation) has not been
proved:

. . . there is a last, unavoidable reckoning with postulational
skepticism—a reckoning, perhaps, which in a measure partakes of concession. For even if, in the view of social behaviorism, the theory of postulational skepticism has been

undermined, the invincible skeptic might retort that social behaviorism itself appears only on the assumption of the social postulate. But we can argue with the skeptic no further: here, it would seem, we have come to one of those ultimate philosophical oppositions beyond which no additional analysis can avail. At such a point, indeed, the thinker must make a decisive and unambiguous choice as to the postulates from which his constructive reasoning will flow, as to his final—and only in that sense metaphysical—assumptions (*ibid.*, p. 417).

In appraising Child's statements concerning the legitimacy of the sociology of knowledge, it must be pointed out that these statements suffer from the lack of a definition of legitimacy. This term may refer to the appropriateness of the sociology of knowledge as an instrument for ascertaining properties of knowledge (or intellectual behavior), society, and their relations. Such appropriateness can be established only on the basis of a metaphysical (more precisely, an ontological) theory [25]. Legitimacy may also refer to the appropriateness of the sociology of knowledge as an instrument for studying concrete phenomena that fall within its province, according to the definition of this field. Such appropriateness, by contrast to the former, can be established only through the empirical testing of a theory of the discipline [26].

Child fails to distinguish between these two referents of legitimacy—the metaphysical and the methodological. His admission that he has not demonstrated the legitimacy of the sociology of knowledge because he has not met Grünwald's objection actually refers only to his failure to demonstrate its metaphysical legitimacy, and he has failed to do so because he has not developed a metaphysic in which it alone could be grounded. His weakness thus is the same as Grünwald's. Unlike Grünwald, however, Child continues to examine problems of the sociology of knowledge as if he *had* established its legitimacy. The logical justification of this procedure lies in the fact that these problems are methodologically relevant irrespective of the question of ontological legitimacy. In other words, Child shifts from a failure in metaphysics to a heuristic approach in methodology.

Categories. Although Child has not established the (metaphysical) legitimacy of the sociology of knowledge and although (it will be remembered) he has said that without such legitimation "there would appear to be little reason to discuss the problems of the presupposition of its legitimacy," he does go on, as has just been anticipated, with this discussion. More precisely, in the next two chapters of his dissertation he undertakes to deal with the questions of what in thought is socially determined and what in society determines thought [27].

Child answers the first of these two questions by developing his concept of the categorical structure. This he conceives as intermediary between the substructure (a system of certain objective relationships at a specific time in history [*Problems*, pp. 85–86], that is, the economic-social-historical structure of a given period), and the superstructure, which is erected over the substructure [28]. The categorical structure, then, is the instrument with which the substructure determines the superstructure; it is the means for the transmission of social determination (*Problems*, p. 90).

This categorical structure—sometimes, in the terminology of other writers, called by such terms as standpoint, position, world view, attitude, and *Weltanschauung*—must be sharply distinguished from the Kantian categories of thought. Kant's categories, inherent in the mind, form all thought perpetually in the same way and in the same way for all men. By contrast, the categories, in the terminology of the sociology of knowledge, "are themselves formed by the substructure and therefore differ with different substructures and change as the substructure changes" (*ibid.*, p. 89). Despite the significance of the categorical structure, it has been explicitly considered (if not always by this name) by only three contributors to the sociology of knowledge—Scheler, Mannheim, and Grünwald. Their analyses, however, prove unsatisfactory to Child. He therefore turns elsewhere—again to Mead [29]—for a more satisfactory answer. Because, however, Child abandoned this Meadian elaboration in his later, more definitive, treatment of the question of the categories, it is not reviewed here.

This more definitive treatment [30] begins with the proposition that both types of theory dealing with the categories—those that posit the inherence of categories in human nature (e.g., Kant's) and those that, on the contrary, posit their social-experiential origin (e.g., Mead's)—must be rejected. For on the one hand Kant failed to establish the universality and necessity of his categories. On the other, it must be recognized that categories cannot develop from experience unless experience itself is structured, that is, categorized.

The way out of this dilemma is the postulation of two types of category—primal and supervenient. The primal categories are biotic, that is, socially underived; the supervenient categories are sociotic, "originating within a social context except insofar as they grow out of the experiential foundation provided by, or in the sense that they follow the guidance of, the primal categories" (*Categories*, p. 318).

In accounting for the existence of these two types of category, Child (thus deviating from Mead [31] and from his own earlier position) defines them, in act, "as formalizing intentions" (*ibid.*, p. 320) which, translated into concepts, appear "as some mode, manner, or order of being" (*ibid.*, p. 321), and, in potency, as predispositions.

> The term "predisposition" denotes any typified potency of response, any latent organization of organic processes with reference to a type of stimulus (*ibid.*).

By implication, this definition admits that inframental responses may possess categoriality; and far from denying this admission, Child writes,

> . . . we say that mind is simply a special range of organically unified organic response and that, while the categories become mental forms when they function within the response-range designated as mental, they are primarily forms not of the mind but of the whole responding organism (*ibid.*, pp. 322–323).

Nor is the notion of predisposition in conflict with a distinction between the cognitive, the emotive, and the conative: these three functions

> can be distinguished only by the criterion of orientation or of preponderate intent. Cognitive predispositions are simply organic potencies of response as oriented toward knowledge of the world rather than toward some feeling of it or some action upon it (*ibid.*, p. 322).

However, "predispositions . . . may actualize in non-categorical ways; and formalizing intentions . . . need not formalize categorically" (*ibid.*, p. 323). The specific characteristic of categories, as compared with noncategorical dispositions, is that they function apriorily [32]. More precisely, the primal categories possess both Kantian marks of apriority—universality and necessity, whereas the supervenient categories possess only necessity. Lest his discussion of apriority be misunderstood, Child points out that although it is commonly associated with concepts, a sharp distinction must nevertheless be made between categories and concepts, including aprioric concepts: "concepts can have categorical relevance only if they derive from, or become funded in, those predispositions toward the world which we distinguish as categorical" (*ibid.*, p. 326). Thus the nonconceptualization of a category does not prove its nonexistence, and neither does the assertion that a given concept is the translation of a category prove the existence of that category, for although the primal categories are presumably invariable in essence, the concepts correlated with them continue, when once formulated, to develop and to undergo theoretical elaboration and concatenation. And the conceptual correlates of the primal predispositions react upon those predispositions in the sense, at least, of acquiring themselves predispositional correlates which cluster around the original primal predispositions and which, in consequence, affect the apprehension, as well as the understanding, which occurs in the sphere of the predisposition concerned. Indeed, *it is in and through this process of accretion that the primal categories exhibit their primordiality.* As example of the way in which the concepts of the understanding may condition or provide the mode within which the primal categories operate, consider the fact that space and time may be differently felt in different cultures while the basic biotic forms of apprehension remain the same in the individuals of all different cultures. But, in so far as concepts function in this way, they do so as functionalized in supervenient categories. These categories, the *a priori* formalizing factors which do not inhere in men as animals, are those persistent and powerful tendencies to take the world as such-and-such which, under certain circumstances, in certain people or certain groups of people, have become compulsions. By becoming compulsions they become categories. And it is not at all surprising that these compulsions should sometimes originate in concepts, for it is clear that essence and existence stand, by and large, in a reciprocal relationship: we believe according to our responses and we respond according to our beliefs (*ibid.*, pp. 327–328; first italics added [in this connection, Child refers to Granet's work on Chinese thought]).

Although the question whether categories change has already been dealt with indirectly in Child's paper, the last part of it is devoted to an explicit discussion of that question. The crux of the answer is that biotic (primal) categories do not change but sociotic (supervenient) categories do—as well within an individual as interindividually, that is, both interculturally and interepochally (*ibid.*, pp. 330–335).

In a brief appraisal of Child's theory of the categories it should, above all, be pointed out that he has given us an entertainable description of the nature of human thought. If we accept his distinction between primal and supervenient categories, we can understand why the former should be universal (because biotic) and why the latter should be specific, particularistic, relative (because socially or culturally [33] conditioned). This concept throws considerable light on the difficult problem of understanding in the sociology of knowledge or intellectual behavior: it presents a constant challenge not to confuse primal with supervenient categories [34] and to distinguish, in analyzing any case of empirical validity (and of other, at least hypothetically, primal categories), what is primal and what is supervenient. More broadly speaking, Child's theory promises well for research to establish empirically where the line between primal and supervenient sources in categories must be drawn (both individually and typically).

Despite this great achievement, there are at least two areas, pertinent in this context, with respect to which some questions must be raised. In the first place, Child does not incorporate the postulated compulsory character of the categories into the rest of his theory. In the second place, and probably more important, Child fails to relate attitudes to categories, a relation of which he makes much in the first version of his treatment of the categories (in *Problems,* Chapter III). Although, for reasons stated, that version has not been summarized here, the chief questions it raises must now be recorded.

1. It is not clear in what sense implicit behavior patterns are identical with attitudinal structure (*Problems,* pp. 114–116).

2. Attitude itself is not defined. This lack is especially regrettable because it precludes the elucidation of attitudinal structure, a term that would seem to imply (cf. the reference to standpoint and world view in the third paragraph of this section) that it is not a mere sum of attitudes but rather a particular organization of them.

3. The arrangement of attitudes in the attitudinal structure is left un-analyzed. As just observed, both the term attitudinal structure and the general context in which its discussion occurs point to the assumption that attitudes are not homogeneous but distinct in terms of importance or in similar terms.

4. The merely psychological treatment of the question of the categories fails to meet the problems of validity and logic.

The first three of these questions, it will be seen, are not answered by Child's second version of his theory of the categories. The reason is, as has been suggested, that Child leaves an analysis of attitudes out of consideration. In other words, Child has given a highly suggestive answer to the problems of validity and logic but he has discussed neither the nature of attitudes nor their relations to categories [35].

Existential Determination of Thought. We saw how Child deals with the question of what element in thought is socially determined. After answering this question—in the dissertation, in the concept of attitudinal structure, and later in his theory of the categories—Child discusses the complementary question, namely, what element in society determines thought. He again begins with an examination of relevant theories [36] and then undertakes to develop his own.

An analysis of the notion that class interests determine thought leads him to point out the difficulties with which this notion is afflicted. These difficulties concern the nature of class, the character of the relations between class interests and individual interests, the conflict between the diversity of individual interests, on the one hand, and the postulated unity of class interests, on the other, and similar problems. Child asks why should social context be at all identified with class? Although the individual admittedly exists in some social context, class is only one among several conceptualizations of social contexts, only one element of the social situation.

After thus reducing the range of class, Child proceeds to narrow that of interests. It must be remembered, he tells us, that

> the social determination of thought involves much more than a mere conformity to interests. How, by the theory of interests, could one explain the fact that in certain periods virtually all theoretical fields . . . become permeated by some conception, some intellectual tendency, some style of thought, which manifestly possesses a social relevance but which cannot be derived, with any measure of conviction, from pure interests? [37]

In view of this consideration, Child subsumes the concept of interests— again following Mead—under that of "group attitudes as incorporated into the structure of the individual mind" (*Determination*, p. 182). More specifically, although interests, as Child admits, in some cases, at some time, determine group attitudes, there are other factors that determine these attitudes—factors such as social-historical tradition and social heredity,

> group emotion from whatever cause—whether from natural or social catastrophe, from movements of national aspiration, regeneration, triumph, from rivalry with other groups or co-operation with other groups (*ibid.*, p. 182),

and "the force of the individual genius" (*ibid.*, p. 183). Child emphasizes the advantages of elevating the concept of group attitudes (cf. *ibid.*, pp. 183–185) to the place often previously held by that of class interests.

In evaluating Child's notions concerning the existential determination of thought, it must be noted, in the first place, that although Child set out to ascertain what element in society determines thought, he again lands among the attitudes, that is, where he arrived when he discussed that other question [38], namely, what element in thought it is that is determined by society. In the second place, if group attitudes determine thought, the question of the precise relation between these two elements of intellectual-emotional behavior is not revealed by Child. In this connection Mead's identification of thinking with the taking of attitudes [39] is of no help: are logic and validity merely attitudes, and if so, how are they distinguished from others? If they are not attitudes, what are they? In other words, Child has failed to incorporate the concept of attitudes into his theory of the existential determination of thought—as he has failed to do so (it will be remembered) in regard to his theory of the categories. Finally, it is not shown that the disadvantages of the concepts of class and class interest necessarily result in the abandonment, for a theory of social determination, of any typical social context whatsoever. Do these disadvantages indeed lead to the thesis (which seems to be implied by Child's statements) that the conceptualization of particular social contexts must be undertaken merely in the course of research? In some of his statements on imputation, Child himself operates with typical uniformities in social contexts when he speaks of ruling class, and so on. One may well think that typical uniformities in social contexts lend themselves to heuristic hypotheses if one remembers only, for instance, the uniformities correlated with the distribution of power and with other aspects of stratification. Thus Child, even if indirectly, has formulated another problem for the theory of the sociology of intellectual behavior to resolve.

Imputation.   Among the various problems evolved in the literature of the sociology of knowledge imputation is noteworthy for three reasons. One is that it can be handled as a nonphilosophical problem: for the scientist its most relevant aspect is his understanding of it in regard to his research. Another reason follows from the first: it takes perhaps less effort to clarify the problem of imputation and thus to aid the scientist than is true of most other problems in the field. Finally, Child's treatment of imputation results from a critique of the major writers on the topic and can thus be taken as an authoritative and up-to-date statement. Its presentation and analysis, therefore, should yield relatively conclusive arguments.

Child has discussed the problem on three occasions [40]. In his earliest statement he clearly links the phenomenon of imputation to that of ideology; nor is this link repudiated subsequently. Despite this and despite the historical background of the linkage, it will be shown that the connection must be rejected.

> We can impute a given ideology to a definite class . . . by discriminating the attitudes that have produced it and by then assigning the ideology to the class to which the attitudes belong. That is the foundation of social behaviorist imputation (*Problems*, p. 190).

In order, however, for the imputer to know how to relate attitudes to classes, the concepts of attitudinal structure, simple and ideal, are needed.

> A simple attitudinal structure . . . is an implicit behavior pattern determined by the position of a class with relation to the total social process, by the interests resulting therefrom and by the natural drives as modified through social interaction (*ibid.*, p. 191).

The ideal attitudinal structure, on the other hand, is "*rationally suited to a definite, typical position in the process of production*"; it is "a situationally adequate behavior pattern" (*ibid.*) and

> is the structure that *would* prevail if the actual implicit behaviour pattern of the class in question *did* in fact correspond to the objective position of the class in reference to the totality of the social structure (*ibid.*, p. 192).

Hence one can speak of an ideological representative of a class other than his own as of a person whose actual attitudinal structure is identical with the ideal attitudinal structure of the class (cf. *ibid.*, p. 193).

The revision (*Imputation*) of Child's first inquiry into imputation is limited to an appraisal of Szende's, Mannheim's, Grünwald's, and Lukács's theories concerning the topic. The result is a convincing statement of their inadequacy, followed by an allusion to future analysis of the questions raised. This analysis is presented in Child's third study of imputation (*Resolved*).

The crux of the relevant literature, Child argues, is the assumption, shared by all contributors discussed in his second paper but not stated explicitly by any of them, that it is valid to impute ideas to socioeconomic classes. An investigation of this assumption is Child's prime motive, and from this investigation flow nine theses relative to imputation. These theses are not explicitly stated, but they may be construed profitably as such on the basis of a study of Child's propositions. They are briefly expounded here in the approximate order of their occurrence.

1. Imputation must be to "groups as they are rather than . . . to an ideal . . . class consciousness" (*Resolved*, p. 97). The reason, Child points out, is that ideal-typical class consciousness (Lukács's concept) is ideal not only in the traditional sense of being true to a type constructed as a limit of purity from atypical admixtures but also in the sense "of an end of personal or group desire" (*ibid.*) on the part of the imputer. In other words, despite the fact that ideal, as used in the term ideal type, customarily refers to empirically unattainable purity, Child suggests that the word, in this same concept, also partakes of the more colloquial referent of ideal—goal, aim, or challenge: the imputer vaguely entertains some such ideal and constructs his ideal type in conformance with it [41].

2. "The primary concern of imputation . . . lies . . . with the level of systematic theory"; for, in regard to perceptions they agree in general for practical purposes; and as for simple judgments they can be imputed only to some integral mode of interpretation as fragments thereof. In this case "the process of imputation would consist merely in the formation and verification of a hypothesis as to the implicit systematic relationship between simple judgments," (*ibid.*, p. 98).

3. Imputation is directed toward the constitutive function of the categories of thought; that is, it has as its subject matter different interpretations of approximately identical parts of reality. These interpretations are co-constituted by different categorical structures. Negatively, imputation is not concerned with the selective function of the categorical structure; it does not have as its subject matter interpretations of different parts of reality. The reason is that conflict occurs not among interpretations of different things but among different interpretations of the same thing. In practice, therefore, it is only in this second case that the need for (as well as the difficulties of) imputation develops (*ibid.*, pp. 98–99).

4. "For an idea to be imputable to any given class, sub-class, or stratum, it must so prevail among the members of that group . . . as recognizably to constitute the norm." Inversely, "the thought of any member of the group who does not have as his own that particular idea (or, more exactly, who does not think in such fashion that he has, or in principle could have, that particular idea as his own when the appropriate occasion arises) must . . . be recognizable as a deviation from the norm" (*ibid.*, p. 99). This is so because to be imputable to a group an idea must derive from "categories that are either peculiar to or primary to the given group" (*ibid.*).

5. Under normal conditions (i.e., under conditions not characterized by far-reaching changes in the power structure of the society under discussion) only a ruling class has "any considerable body of ideas—[that is, a] . . . more or less systematically articulated set of convictions, principles, beliefs, and opinions—of the nature which one terms 'ideological' " (*ibid.*). The question how one can determine whether a given ideology belongs to a given ruling class is answered as follows: "if the members of a ruling class reward the person who thinks in certain ways, if, that is, they encourage such thinking; if they themselves, insofar as they are themselves ideologically fertile, produce ideology of the type in question; if such ideology, by whomever produced, appears acceptable to, and vital in the lives of, the normal members of that class—then the imputation of the ideological tendency to the particular class in question seems quite justified" (*ibid.*).

6. Subordinate or nonruling classes have ideologies only in the midst of some great social crisis, especially in times of revolution. Although "the categories of critical or revolutionary periods may exist implicitly in, and develop from, earlier vague tendencies of thought," they "would not be systematically elaborated . . . into an integrated ideological structure; for the ideology actually prevalent in that class during a normal period would be the ideology of the dominant social class" (*ibid.*, p. 102).

7. "In a full and primary sense, the imputation of an integrated, systematically elaborated ideology can be made only to a group which is organized deliberately and ideologically . . . —not to the class or classes which that specialized group attempts to lead" (*ibid.*, p. 104), for, "because of its necessarily critical, expanded, additive, and organized nature" (*ibid.*, p. 103), an ideology is really possessed only by particular individuals making up an organization "which, while usually composed in the main by members of the class in question, is, nevertheless, an organization quite distinct from the class itself" (*ibid.*). This holds good for both normal and critical periods: in either case it is only an elite, not the mass of people making up a class, which can properly be said to have an ideology [42].

8. Although "in the case of a socioeconomic class, an ideology can legitimately be imputed only in the sense of prevailing among what appears to be the majority of the members of the class . . . , in the case of ideologically organized groups, . . . imputation proceeds on the basis of the acknowledged ideal of the members as organized" (*ibid.*, pp. 105–106).

9. According to G. H. Mead, all ideas have a group origin: even if an idea is developed by an individual, the mind of this individual is itself

the result of social interaction. Ideologies, as a particular kind of ideas, must therefore be shown to have a particular social origin. We have seen Child's early definition to ideology. Now he writes that "the individual origination of ideologies does seem to involve a quite explicit and conscious group reference" (*Resolved*, p. 106). An examination of this group reference shows that the ideologist refers in his ideology not necessarily to the group to which he belongs (in some one of the various senses of belonging), but to the group he represents. In consequence, imputation, too, is concerned only with the group a thinker represents, that is, with the group with which the thinker "actively identifies himself . . . , whose interests, whose aims, whose desires, whose ideals . . . he attempts to make his own" (*ibid.*, p. 107) and which, in addition, recognizes his leadership: representation refers to a reciprocal process. Further, "it is . . . the ideologically organized group alone of which the ideologist can be a representative; and it is only such an affiliational group . . . to which in general the ideas of the ideologist can legitimately be imputed" (*ibid.*, p. 108).

Child's linkage of imputation to ideology requires an appraisal of his concept of ideology before his statements on imputation can be appreciated. The definition of ideology recalled in connection with Thesis 9 suffers from relatively unanalyzed terms. Nor is this definition clarified when it is applied to other relevant passages in Child's writings on imputation. A comparison of these passages raises the questions whether any or only a ruling class can have an ideology; what unconscious ideology refers to; whether the ideas about a class's position in society which are taken for granted both by that class and by members of other classes are ideological (as they are according to the earlier definition of ideology) or not (as they seem to be according to several among the theses on imputation); whether, ideological or not, they can be imputed and, if so, how and to which class.

An inspection of Child's statements on imputation itself shows a shift of interest from methodology (cf. the emphasis on such concepts as simple attitudinal structure and ideal attitudinal structure) to social structure (cf. the discussion of class, affiliational group, and elite in regard to imputation). The chief unsolved problems of the earlier phase concern the interrelated conceptualizations and the operational definitions of class and of similar group (structural) terms, of simple and ideal attitudinal structure, and of class (etc.) with relation to the total social process or structure.

In the later phase these problems are omitted from consideration rather than solved. A study of this later phase—of *Resolved* or of its exposition in the form of the nine theses presented—shows that the range of imputation is ever more narrowed down in the course of the argument: ever more qualifications are admitted until at the end Child states: "The notion of imputation, indeed, perhaps obscures considerably more than it illuminates" (*Resolved*, p. 109). An examination of this skeptical statement may help to determine the sense in which the term imputation may legitimately be used at all.

Child employs this term in a number of ways. Thus a comparison of Theses 4, 7, and 8 shows that in Thesis 8 Child draws on the first two and distinguishes between their applications. Concretely, which of their applications are possible? They would seem to be as follows: An ideological statement (always provided a statement can be identified as ideological) can be imputed to a class (to that of the person making the statement or to some other class) if the statement made is subscribed to by the majority of the members of that class—regardless, it would appear, of whether the person making the statement is aware of its being subscribed to by those others. If he is aware, imputation becomes synonymous with the imputer's discovery of social solidarity, social cohesion, *esprit de corps*, or the like—but why should this discovery be called imputation? If the person making the statement is not aware of its being subscribed to by other members of that class, imputation becomes synonymous with enunciating a classificatory proposition, which is different in no way from other classificatory propositions; hence, again, there is no justification for applying the term imputation.

An ideological statement, however, can also be imputed to an ideologically organized group, provided the statement made is part of the ideology of that group. In this situation there would appear to be three possibilities.

1. The student may impute the statement to the group of which the person making it is a member or with which he otherwise identifies himself. In this case imputation becomes synonymous with the discovery of affiliation, membership, solidarity, or the like.

2. The student may impute the statement to a group of whose existence —or of his own relation to which—the person making the statement is not aware. In this case imputation becomes synonymous with enunciating a classificatory proposition.

3. The student may impute the statement to some group other than the group whose ideology the person making the statement erroneously believes himself to share. In this case, imputation becomes synonymous with the ascertainment of an error. In none of these cases, clearly, is the term imputation anything but misleading.

In accordance with Thesis 2, Child makes still another use of the concept of imputation: he uses it in the sense of Mannheim's *sinngemässe Zurechnung*. Is there, this time, any justification for using the term? The kind of inquiry within which such imputation has its place is the social interpretation (however this may be understood) of an intellectual product. While proceeding with a given social interpretation I am stimulated by certain elements, which I encounter in the intellectual product, to construct a *Weltanschauung* or attitudinal structure or similar construct and to test it by using it as a frame of reference for as many other elements (thoughts, concepts, etc.) as possible. In this procedure, according to the fate of my hypothesis, I find elements that explicitly contain their own relationship to the structure hypothesized. I find elements that can implicationally be related to this structure—which confirm, contradict, support, and qualify it (and the tracing of such implicational relations is part of "immanent interpretation" [43], or I find relations by analogy. Here again, and for reasons paralleling those mentioned in the preceding analysis of comparable cases, the concept of imputation has no specific referent.

It follows that imputation is not, hence should not be used as, a concept denoting fact. It is therefore proposed to use it only as a concept that refers to a heuristic-hypothetical relation between an element of thought, emotion, or volition, on the one hand, and a group, institution, time, *Weltanschauung*, or attitudinal structure, on the other. It will now be clear why it was anticipated that a concept of imputation is unrelated to that of ideology, for imputation, as understood here, applies equally well to all cognitive, affective, and conative phenomena and in no way preferentially, much less exclusively, to ideologies, however they may be defined.

In attempting to expound the Childian concept of imputation in its essentials (the nine theses), I did not comment on all of them, most notably parts of Thesis 2 and Thesis 3. The reason for this was implied earlier when it was suggested that for the practicing sociologist of intellectual behavior imputation need not be a philosophical problem (as largely implied in Theses 2 and 3).

In the Marxian tradition imputation has overwhelmingly had a polemic, debunking function for which there is no room in scientific procedure. This historical background suggests why the problem of imputation should have been tied up with such problems as the relativity of truth and validity and with other philosophical, especially epistemological, concerns. The present discussion, on the basis of Child's views, tries to separate it from such problems, which are not, of course, solved thereby. What, if any, is their scientific relevance?

It is submitted that their chief scientific relevance lies in the attention that such problems—as illustrated by the history of the concept of imputation and of its ramifications—have called to the existence of, and to the historical failure to distinguish between, the unavoidable scientific postulate of both fact (as the intended subject matter of the scientist) and interpretation (as his relation to fact). Here I have tried to show that imputation has been used as an untenable bridge between the two, and have advocated its use as a frankly interpretive concept. The same kind of confusion also besets, for example, the use of the concept of social class; it is not clear whether this concept is a factually vague term employed in the course of evincing an interpretation of social structure or of history (not only Marxian) or an interpretively barren exercise in statistics. Similar observations could be made in regard to ideology. Both facts and interpretation as well as an ever refined reflection on both these tools are needed for optimal science. I hope that this need has become plausible, in a preliminary form, through an appraisal of imputation.

Truth.   The discussion of Lukács's, Scheler's, Mannheim's, and Grünwald's treatments of truth [44] according to Child raises at least three questions regarding the concept of truth:

> First, there is the question of the sense in which, if at all, the concept of truth can apply to propositions assertive of concrete relationships between society and thought. With this question we shall not deal further, for our position . . . would follow, in any event, from our later discussion. There is the matter, second, of the relationship between the genesis of an idea and its truth; this question we shall presently take up with the idea of dismissing it. And then, third, there is the problem of the manner in which, the extent to which, and, perhaps, the social position from which, valid knowing can occur. The essence of the third problem, which we find the central and the only real problem, we prefer to re-formulate in its sharpest form as, namely, the problem of the possibility of a common and objective truth. To this we shall devote our attention as soon as we can dismiss the pseudo-problem of origin and validity (*Truth,* p. 22).

The origin-validity problem is a pseudo-problem because it can appear only if possible-accidental relations are confused with necessary-essential relations [45]. More particularly, if summarily,

> the relevance of origin to validity in this and only this: By investigating the origin of an idea, the student may be able to establish how it was, in some particular instance, that a spe-

cific ideologist, given his personal abilities and limitations, was socially enabled to develop an idea that was valid or was socially restricted to the development of an idea that was not valid. Or, conversely, departing from some social situation, the student may predict whether valid theories or invalid theories should be developed by the ideologists of the situation; and he may then proceed to test his prediction by the theories that actually were, or actually will be, developed. But in neither case does the genesis of an idea in any sense establish validity or invalidity; it can do no more than to explain the social possibility or to allow a prediction based on social probability. Always, therefore, *the validity* of an idea—*as well as its origin —is a matter for concrete and specific investigation; and the mere social derivation of an idea proves nothing whatsoever, one way or another, about its factual validity (ibid.,* p. 24; italics added).

The second question concerning truth, then, is how a common objective truth is possible. In answering this question, Child makes use of his conception of categories as predispositions and of his distinction between primal and supervenient categories. Error is possible only by social accretions (to the primal categories):

> . . . one of the chief causes of . . . error is . . . that the supervenient categories develop in part, too, under the influence of social determinants, the diversity of society being accompanied by a diversity in the interpretations of the same objective world. Still, these categories which yield error are also the only means to a more than primitive truth [i.e., to a truth other than that given by the primal categories]. Hence the problem of how a common objective truth . . . is possible in spite of, and yet through, the socially co-determined categories *(ibid.,* p. 32).

The resolution of this lies in the concept of creativity, of the independent directive power of mind, by virtue of which the individual "can and does criticize certain of his predispostions through the medium of others" *(ibid.).*

In an effort to appraise Child's concept of truth as related to the sociology of knowledge, several points must be made. Regarding the origin-validity problem, we noted that Child views it as a mere pseudo-problem, a problem that cannot and need not be solved on the basis of a theory of truth but only empirically from case to case. We can also formulate this view by saying that social origins and criteria of validity are two distinct classes of phenomena which, moreover, are related not logically but only empirically. It would seem, however, that one could, by empirical study, establish typical situations in which typical approximations to valid thought have a typical chance of occurring [46]. Although one must agree with Child's definition of the origin-validity problem as a theoretical pseudo-problem, it must be pointed out that empirical analysis could be carried considerably further than he has indicated. It must be added, also, that both in this context and in his inquiry into the problem of a common and objective truth Child has failed to define validity and, to relate specifically the problem of how universal validity is possible to the problem of how a common and objective truth is possible. (It is indicated above that his theory of primal and supervenient categories lends itself to a solution of the problem of universal validity but the theory does not explicitly offer this solution).

After anticipating so much of the problem of a common and objective truth it remains only to recall the relation between Child's distinction of primal from supervenient categories and truth. Primal categories, by their very definition, are incapable of error; error is due to the fact that we necessarily, because of our social heritage, operate with supervenient, socially codetermined categories. Hence we ask how we can correct error. The answer is the postulate of the creativity of mind [47]. Child, however, fails to analyze the normative concept of validity in relation to the other, structural, concepts. Does validity emerge from the interaction of primal and supervenient categories with the creativity and critical faculty of mind? Child's statements would seem to point to an affirmative answer but they do not give it explicitly.

Still another observation must be made. Child, without saying so, actually deals with only one type of truth—scientific truth [48]. It would appear, however, that there are other types of truth as well, types that must be accounted for by a theory of truth as needed by a sociology of knowledge and of intellectual behavior [49]. Such a theory will have to resolve the problems indicated here—categories and validity, validity and truth, types of truth—and it will probably do well to draw on Child's highly suggestive propositions.

Immanent and Transcendent Interpretation. The last problem taken up in Child's dissertation is that of the nature and relation of immanent and transcendent interpretation. To begin with, Child states that the sociology of knowledge, like the histories of science, literature, or philosophy, is knowledge about knowledge and, in that capacity, is bound to interpret its data. Further, the mode of interpretation of the sociology of knowledge is not immanent but transcendent and, more specifically, sociological [50].

The two explicit statements regarding interpretation come from Mannheim and Grünwald. Mannheim's weakness, Child points out, lies in his presentation of ideological and sociological interpretation as alternatives —to which, of course, other optional interpretations might be added. This fact opens Mannheim's position to Grünwald's skeptical strictures. To overcome the objections of Grünwald's postulational skepticism is, in Child's view, indeed the major problem of a theory of interpretation. In other words, it must be demonstrated that both types of interpretation—immanent and transcendent—are objectively warranted. Child's solution of the problem is the proposition of the objectively-real dual causation of thought. That is, thought is caused immanently and this warrants immanent interpretation. It is also caused socially (if one accepts Mead's theory of mind) and this warrants social or sociological interpretation. Hence the two interpretations are more than optional in Grünwalds' sense.

It remains only to show the nature of the relations between these two interpretations. This can be done by a closer analysis of the two aspects of thought. Immanent causation of thought refers to its immanent logic or implicational consistency, and this is what immanent interpretation examines. Social causation, or determination, of thought has in turn a dual aspect, selective and constitutive: social existence selects, but it also, through the medium of the attitudinal structure, coconstitutes what is selected. The implicit behavior patterns

> so select and so integrate that . . . the realized mental-structures . . . represent a perspectival apprehension of reality (*Problems*, p. 286).

> . . . social determination determines precisely what, out of the vast realm of objectivity, . . . [the thinking individual] does attempt to know. And various of the possible conceptual aggregates represent emphases—and often distorted and distorting emphases—upon certain isolated elements of the objective truth. It results, therefore, . . . that despite . . . [the] search for reality, the sociological determination of the thought of some particular group can inform the mental-structures of that group in a peculiar manner. And it is this ensuing characteristic tone of the thought of any group that signifies the constitutive relevance of social existence.

> Selective relevance is not incompatible, then, with constitutive relevance. And on the basis of the view of the sociology of

> knowledge here presented, they tend, indeed, to merge into
> one (*ibid.*, pp. 286–287).

This analysis leads Child back to the problem of truth and to a supplementation of the statements made earlier in his dissertation [51]. "We
noted," Child writes,

> that any thinker, no matter of what class, can think only
> with the aid of the already existing thought materials. He can
> rework them, he can modify them greatly, he can add to them;
> but use them he must: the sociology of knowledge is not
> needed to tell us this . . . Now the sociology of knowledge
> teaches that some position in society . . . possesses superior
> truth-capabilities; that social determination of a certain sort or
> sorts affords superior opportunities for the genuine cognition
> of reality. But consider this contention alongside of the unde-
> niable fact of the intellectual dependence of all thinkers upon
> the past. Do not these two propositions imply that no one
> position can stake out the exclusive potentialities for the cog-
> nition of truth? For the fact that elements not merely from
> the thought of the past, but also from the contemporaneous
> thought of other and even very antagonistic groups, become
> inextricably incorporated in the thought of that more favored
> social-historical position—this fact means that considerable
> sections of the thought of previous as well as of less favored
> contemporaneous groups must actually penetrate through the
> veil of class illusion and apprehend the structure of the objec-
> tive world. The possibility of truth, then, is not confined to
> any one class even at a particular period in the development
> of society (*ibid.*, pp. 288–289).

Child concludes his chapter [52] with an allocation of the two modes of
interpretation among the efforts of understanding human thought.

> If, as we have shown, the immanent and transcendent proc-
> esses [of thought] interact; if the search for reality (and the
> flight from reality) in which all men, in their various degrees
> and manners, are engaged, necessitates that interaction of
> both immanent and transcendent processes; if mental-struc-
> tures represent an amalgamation, through the selective and
> constitutive activities of the categorical apparatus, of both
> immanent and transcendent elements—then to split imma-
> nent and transcendent interpretation away from each other,
> and to forbid their cooperation in the momentous task of
> understanding the development of thought, constitutes a vi-

> cious bifurcation, an illegitimate dichotomy, a violation of
> that integral unity which reality itself has created (*ibid.*, p.
> 291).

This combination of the two interpretations, Child intimates, will not be easy; on the contrary, it will be more difficult than either interpretation alone, but the necessity of performing the twofold interpretation is the unavoidable consequence of the foregoing considerations. These considerations lead to one more conclusion, which Child states as follows:

> . . . a correct understanding of those basic concepts of the
> sociology of knowledge—immanent and transcendent inter-
> pretation—leads, when that understanding is carried to its
> limits, to the abolition of the sociology of knowledge itself and
> to its reconciliation with the historical school in opposition to
> which it arose.
>
> Standing before a higher synthesis, we must not regret the
> inevitable mortality of its partial and abstract moments (*ibid.*,
> p. 292).

Child has not incorporated his theory of interpretation into his later papers on categories and truth. Hence there is no statement from him concerning (above all) the connection between the categories and the dual nature and causation of thought, immanent and social. The tracing of this connection therefore appears as another task and as a task to be handled in the context of the closely related inquiry into the nature of interpretation itself. Such an inquiry, furthermore, will have to face and elucidate Child's conclusion that the correct understanding of the sociology of intellectual behavior, on his view of interpretation, leads to its own abolition and reconciliation with historicist immanent interpretation.

THE SOCIOLOGY OF KNOWLEDGE
FROM THE STANDPOINT OF THE STUDY OF MAN

In accordance with the intent of this paper, I now argue—instead of tackling any of the problems just mentioned—that we are ready to begin inquiring into the meaning of the sociology of knowledge as an interpretion of the world, as a way of looking at the world, into its historical significance and symptomatic character, and into the image of the man who has invented it and is fascinated by it.

Tasks Left by Child. My first step is to recapitulate the major tasks [53] that Child, explicitly or implicitly, has set for a concept, entailed by his own work, of the sociology of knowledge and of intellectual-emotional behavior in general:

1. Definition of ideology, in which terms themselves are defined (p. 159) [54].

2. Typology of intellectual-emotional products, with allocation of ideologies (p. 159).

3. Metaphysical theory in which to ground the appropriateness of the sociology of intellectual-emotional behavior as an instrument for ascertaining properties of intellectual-emotional behavior, including knowledge, of society, and of their interrelations (pp. 159-162).

4. Definitions of attitude, attitudinal structure, thought, and knowledge, and of their interrelations (pp. 162-166).

5. Elucidation of the compulsory character of the categories of thought (pp. 162-166).

6. Definition of "social" and "cultural" and elucidation of their interrelations (pp. 162-166).

7. Definition of (social) class (possibly in relation to 1 above) (pp. 166-168).

8. Definition of "interests" and elucidation of their relations to other types of intellectual-emotional behavior (pp. 166-168).

9. Typology of social contexts (pp. 166-168).

10. Typology of social positions in regard to accessibility (and to other relations) to truth (pp. 175-177).

11. An epistemology; particularly, a theory concerning the relations between categories, truth, and validity, and the social relations of all these (to be handled in relation to 3 above) (pp. 175-177).

12. Typology of knowledge (pp. 175-177).

13. Theory of interpretation as related to all preceding problems (pp. 177-179) [55].

This list contains several kinds of problem, among which are methodological and metaphysical. The various tasks regarding definitions and typologies belong to the former; certainly the task to develop a metaphysical theory in which to ground the appropriateness of the soci-

ology of knowledge and probably the task to articulate a theory concern-
.ing the relations between categories, truth, and validity, to the latter. By
a methodological problem I mean one that is concerned with procedure
of inquiry and to which statements on the nature of reality are irrelevant.
By a metaphysical problem I mean one that is concerned with the nature
of reality. The different purposes and subject matters of methodological
and metaphysical problems entail different criteria of confirmation. For
the former the criterion is pragmatic with reference to a given inquiry
or type of inquiry (e.g., scientific or philosophical): it is a means criterion. For the latter it is agreement with the result of the most rigorously
imaginable intrasubjective dialectical examination of one's most important experiences at one's most honest: it is an end criterion [56].

Methodological Premises of the Sociology of Knowledge. This is suggested in order to lend greater weight to the list of methodological premises of the sociology of knowledge as it is presented by Arthur Child
(and, although certainly not always in Childian terms, by most other
writers in the field), that is, to the list of propositions accepted as useful
guides in the pursuit of (scientific) research. In a roughly descending
order of certainty and clarity these premises appear to be the following:

1. The validity of thought has nothing to do with its origin.

2. There are logical and there are social aspects of thought; they can be
illuminated by immanent (intrinsic) and transcendent (extrinsic) interpretation, respectively.

3. Man's thought is in some sense determined by attitudes, which in turn
are incorporated into the structure of the individual mind. Further
methodological statements could be added with respect to the kinds of
group in which the individual develops his attitudes (family, play group,
etc.) and with respect to the relations between attitudes and thoughts
(cf. Pareto and Cooley).

4. There are primal and there are supervenient categories.

5. The social component in the supervenient categories accounts for the
possibility of (factual and/or logical?) error; and the creativity or independent directive power of mind accounts for the corrigibility of error.

It may be noted that a satisfactory definition of all these terms (and,
of course, of several others) will go a long way toward producing a
methodological framework of the sociology of knowledge; that is, it will

contribute much toward establishing the sociology of knowledge as a *science.*

Volitional Premises of the Sociology of Knowledge. I suggest that these methodological premises, these propositions accepted as useful guides in the pursuit of scientific research, are based on other premises, which are volitional. Both methodological and metaphysical concerns, I submit, are in the service of interpreting the world in which man (and society) engage in interpreting lives; and interpretation is both a cognitive and a volitional enterprise. In my interpretation I come to *know* something and to *want* something. The methodological premises of the sociology of knowledge which I have listed indicate some of the subject matter about which the sociologist of knowledge who acts on these premises expects to come to know something (scientifically). I suggest that it is what he *wants* that has led him to find these methodological premises and these subject matters. What do I, as a sociologist of knowledge, want? A list of my wishes might look like this:

1. Origin-Validity. I want social relevance, but I also want unimpeachable validity. I do not want absolute relativism.

2. Interpretation. I want maximum intrinsic interpretation and I want maximum extrinsic interpretation.

3. Thought-Attitude-Group. I want to see man as logical (rational) and emotional (irrational); hence I investigate the interaction of thought and attitude. I want to see man as a social being, whose even innermost thought is socially codetermined.

4. Categories. I want to understand as many different thoughts as I can, but in order to do so, I must postulate universal features of thought (the primal categories). At the same time I want to preserve the specificity of thought. I therefore seek to guarantee this specificity by raising it to categorical status (the supervenient categories).

5. Error. I want to account for error and its corrigibility—could I do so in terms of my notions about the categories?

6. Social Interpretation versus Sociology of Knowledge. Although social interpretation makes sense, I have not yet found grounds for institutionalizing the sociology of knowledge as a discipline. Might not the reason be that it is a latecomer and that (comparable to sociology itself) it thus does not have the tradition that would allocate a place for it among the disciplines? Might this not suggest a reconsideration of our whole classi-

fication of disciplines, with a view to revising it in terms of methodological considerations, not of historical contingencies, and (I add *as* a sociologist of knowledge, that is, a person who is aware of some of his metaphysical premises and abides by them) in terms of metaphysical considerations?

Metaphysical Premises of the Sociology of Knowledge.   I now go a step further and ask: What do I find out about the nature of reality, about my own reality, from an analysis of these wishes? I restate these wishes in fewer and more comprehensive terms:

1. I want social relatedness but I also want validity. I want to acknowledge the fact and to account for this fact, which is real to me, that matters are relative (socially, culturally, and biologically) and that they are true, irrespective of their relativity.

2. In slightly different terms: I want maximum intrinsic interpretation and I want maximum extrinsic interpretation. A poem is a poem, but it also has an origin, has come to be, and there is a relation between its origin and what it is. What is it? I want to push both intrinsic and extrinsic interpretation to the limit in order to find out.

3. A third variant: I want to understand phenomena in their own terms and I want to understand them as instances of laws. I want to carry each of these wishes to its extreme in order to do right by both.

I am discovering that these are indeed variations on two themes. I identify one of them by the form of these wish variations: the wishes are contrasting and complementary, based on the fact that matters are both relative and absolute—with the variations of this theme. The theme is dualism. I am discovering that I am espousing dualism, a metaphysical premise of the sociology of knowledge as an interpretation of the world, and this metaphysical premise is confirmed by the most rigorous examination of my most important experiences: as a student of man who wants to find out what the sociology of knowledge is and thus who *he* is, I find that I espouse dualism.

I identify the other theme by the content of my wish variations, which is the value placed on inquiry. I call this theme naturalism, in the sense of continuity of analysis [57]: I do not hesitate before an inquiry. On the contrary, I insist on investigating anything that may come to my attention as long as I have a hunch that it might be relevant to my inquiry. Furthermore, I try to enlist methodological aids that will make me more alert to investigable objects and to relevance [58].

Dualism and Naturalism as Metaphysical Premises. Once more I ask what it means to say that dualism and naturalism are *metaphysical* premises of the sociology of knowledge as I have come to recognize in my inquiry. A metaphysical problem, I said, is a problem concerned with the nature of reality, with ascertaining what is real; and the criterion for confirming a solution of a metaphysical problem is agreement with the result of the most rigorously imaginable intrasubjective dialectical examination of that solution in the light of one's most important experiences at his most honest. I must make the description of this criterion more exact and find that it is more accurate to say that the criterion of confirmation is the illumination and confirmation of one's experiences that one considers intrinsic to one's reality. What attainment of reality I have experienced tells me such and such—namely, a metaphysical statement— about reality. In the life of a person who has such a view of metaphysical statements these statements will never be static: the absolute is relative to his inquiry, which is life-long. And metaphysical statements can be discussed; the dialectical method for their examination can be applied intersubjectively.

I have said that this very continuity of inquiry, naturalism, is also a metaphysical premise. If my definition of a metaphysical statement holds, the metaphysical premise of continuity of inquiry is derived from some statement about the nature of reality, namely, that reality is investigable. This statement does not make investigation desirable. The desirability of investigation again follows from my experience: what attainment of reality I have experienced tells me that surrender [59] to reality is the method of attaining it and, furthermore, that inquiry into anything that comes to my attention, as long as I have a hunch that it might be relevant to it, is inseparable from the idea and practice of surrender. To say so is to articulate a valuation, which valuation, as this case clearly shows, is conducive to the investigation of reality. Both predications of reality and valuations of reality are thus metaphysical acts. The former may be called ontological, the latter, valuational.

Metaphysical statements, both ontological and valuational, are relatively absolute, that is, absolute relative to experience which, relative to a given stage of the individual's life, is absolute. This formulation allows us to distinguish valuational from volitional statements. I believe it is no accident that the list of volitional premises of the sociology of knowledge given above is longer and more particular than that of its metaphysical premises, which are three closely related statements that turned out to be variations on two themes. There is more to the difference between the two sets than is appreciated by calling the second, as I did, a restatement of the first in fewer and more comprehensive terms. The volitional prem-

ises of the sociology of knowledge, I suggested, lead the student to his
methodological premises, which in turn help him to learn something
about the subject matters he wants to know about. Why does he want to
know about these subject matters? Because of the time in which he lives.
His time is the occasion on which he develops wishes and methods, but
when he takes this occasion, in the form of his methodological and volitional premises, to attain reality which is not time-bound and historical,
he begins to make metaphysical statements, ontological and valuational.
The relation between both the methodological and volitional premises
of the sociology of knowledge and its metaphysical premises parallels
that between the historical occasion as a means and experience and
exemplification of man as an end.

Dualism and Naturalism and the Sociology of Knowledge.   It is the historical situation that must be envisaged to appreciate the specific function
of the metaphysical premises of dualism and naturalism in the sociology
of knowledge. Why is the sociologist of knowledge the man who is committed to dualism and naturalism and who has emerged at this time?
What is this time? This question about our time is indeed another occasion for surrender, but such surrender cannot be exemplified here (in the
way in which surrender to the sociology of knowledge has been exemplified, even though hardly more than didactically); instead, a tentative
result of surrender to our time must do if we would answer the first
question, thereby knitting together even more firmly the methodological-
volitional (historical) and metaphysical (human) premises of the sociology
of knowledge. As I took Child's treatment of the sociology of knowledge
as my occasion for inquiry into it, for surrender to it, so I now take "one
world and cultural relativism" as the occasion our time gives me, as my
operational definition of our time—except (to repeat) that this is an outcome rather than the beginning of a demonstration of my inquiry into
our time, of my surrender to it. "One world and cultural relativism"
is a fact that has never before in man's history been a fact. By it I refer to
the partly actual, partly potential fact that we now live in one world, in
which whatever matters anywhere matters everywhere, most obviously in
a political and economic sense but also, perhaps more dimly but yet
compellingly, in a moral and cognitive and metaphysical sense. This
extraordinary, hardly grasped fact of one world and cultural relativism
goes far to explain, I suggest, the sociologist of knowledge as the type of
man I have tried to identify.

By cultural relativism I mean the terrifying and confusing realization
that men everywhere have values, social orders, ways of life, of love and
hate, holiness and contempt, fear and trust, ignorance and knowledge,

and the questions resulting therefrom: what, if we realize this fact, are we to do with our own way of life, with our own values? I suggest that the immediate answers are methodological and volitional and the more indirect answers, ontological and valuational, the answers that emerged in the present inquiry as premises of the sociology of knowledge. In having and articulating these premises, the sociology of knowledge appears, indeed, as a revision of our way of life, of our way of looking at ourselves and the world, of our attitude toward the world, of our interpretation of it. It defines a new situation—one world and cultural relativism. Before this self-realization of the sociology of knowledge the situation was merely new, profoundly fascinating, and profoundly threatening. The sociology of knowledge therefore may be called an elucidation of a new experience man has had and is still having. Through it, man adapts himself to living in one world and transcends cultural relativism. This transcendence takes the direction of a view of himself as dual and forever challenging his own exploration.

NOTES

1. An earlier draft of parts of this paper was presented at the Annual Institute, Society for Social Research, The University of Chicago, August 5, 1949. I am indebted to Arthur Child, Virgil G. Hinshaw, Jr., Richard T. Morris, and Eliseo Vivas for their helpful criticisms of that draft.

2. For a selected Child bibliography sees ns. 13, 14, 32, and 42. Robert K. Merton, "The Sociology of Knowledge," in Georges Gurvitch and Wilbert S. Moore, Eds., *Twentieth Century Sociology* (New York: Philosophical Library, 1945); Louis Wirth, "Preface" to Karl Mannheim, *Ideology and Utopia* [1929], translated by Louis Wirth and Edward A. Shils (New York: Harcourt, Brace, 1936).

3. Karl Mannheim, "Ideologische und soziologische Interpretation der geistigen Gebilde," *Jahrbuch für Soziologie*, 2 (1926), pp. 424–440. [*From Karl Mannheim* (New York: Oxford University Press, 1971), pp. 116–131.]

4. Florian Znaniecki, *The Social Role of the Man of Knowledge* (New York: Columbia University Press, 1940).

5. Karl Mannheim, "Historismus," *Archiv für Sozialwissenschaft und Sozialpolitik*, 52 (1924), 1–60 ["Historicism," translated by Paul Kecskemeti, *Essays on the Sociology of Knowledge*, London: Routledge and Kegan Paul, 1952, pp. 84–133]: "Das konservative Denken; soziologische Beiträge zum Werden des politisch-historischen Denkens in Deutschland," *ibid.*, 57 (1927): 68–142, 470–495 ["Conservative Thought," translated by Ernest Mannheim and Paul Kecskemeti, *From Karl Mannheim, op. cit.*, pp. 132–222].

6. Ernst Kohn-Bramstedt, *Aristocracy and the Middle-Classes in Germany. Social Types in German Literature, 1830–1900* (London: King, 1937).

7. Robert K. Merton, "Science, Technology and Society in Seventeenth-Century England," *Osiris*, **4** (1938), 360–632.

8. As a summary see Edgar Zilsel, "The Sociological Roots of Science," *American Journal of Sociology*, **47** (1942), 544–562.

9. Kurt H. Wolff, *Loma Culture Change: A Contribution to the Study of Man* (Columbus, Ohio, 1952) [mimeographed].

10. *Ibid.*, p. 12.

11. Among the numerous critiques of Mannheim Child's work and Virgil G. Hinshaw, Jr., "The Epistemological Relevance of Mannheim's Sociology of Knowledge," *Journal of Philosophy*, **40** (1943), 57–72, are especially noteworthy.

12. In addition to giving us this summary of the problems, Child has offered answers to some of them and has astutely criticized many of the German sociologists of knowledge, particularly Ernst Grünwald, Georg Lukács, Karl Mannheim, Max Scheler, Alexander von Schelting, and Paul Szende.

13. Arthur Child, *The Problems of the Sociology of Knowledge: A Critical and Philosophical Study*, Ph.D. dissertation, unpublished (Berkeley; University of California, 1938). This work is henceforth referred to as *Problems*.

14. Four (of five articles) in *Ethics*: "The Theoretical Possibility of the Sociology of Knowledge," **51** (July 1941), 392–418 (Chapter II of the dissertation); "The Existential Determination of Thought," **52** (January 1942), 153–185 (Chapter IV); "The Problem of Imputation in the Sociology of Knowledge," **51** (January 1941), 200–219, and "The Problem of Imputation Resolved," **54** (January 1944), 96–109 (Chapter V); "The Problem of Truth in the Sociology of Knowledge, **58** (October 1947), 18–34 (Chapter VI); and "On the Theory of the Categories," *Philosophy and Phenomenological Research*, **7** (December 1946), 316–335 (Chapter III). When a revision (which is often fundamental) exists, we shall go by it rather than by the formulation presented in the dissertation.

15. Child discusses Scheler, von Scheling, Günther Stern, Mannheim, and Siegfried Marck.

16. Here Child appraises Heinz O. Ziegler, Hans Freyer, Hans Speier, and, again, Szende and Mannheim. (A feature common to the last three of these authors is the effort to develop a social theory of ideology rather than a biologistic one, as Ziegler and, to a certain extent, Scheler attempt to do.)

17. *Loc. cit.*, henceforth referred to as *Possibility*.

18. Julius Kraft, Ziegler, and Stern.

19. Grünwald and Helmuth Plessner.

20. Scheler, Mannheim, and Szende.

21. Among the thinkers discussed in the present context, Grünwald, to Child, is the most serious. Hence Child's constructive efforts are pointed toward a refutation of Grünwald's "postulational skepticism" (Child's coinage: *ibid.*, p. 404). Briefly, Grünwald's position is that the sociology of knowledge "is not a science whose propositions are unconditionally valid for any thinking individual, but only an optional scheme of interpretation" [Ernst Grünwald, *Das*

Problem der Soziologie des Wisses, Versuch einer kritischen Darstellung der wissenssoziologischen Theorien, Walther Eckstein, Ed. (Wien-Leipzig: Braumuller, 1934), p. 66]. "Postulational" refers to the many different postulates—determination by society, race, and climate—on each of which depends a different type of interpretation. "Skepticism" represents Child's judgment of Grünwald's claim that each interpretation, on the assumption of its basic postulate, has the same validity as every other; that is, in view of their incompatibility, the assertion of their equal validity amounts to skepticism of the validity of any of them. One might derive the term postulational skepticism by pointing out that Grünwald's position hides the skeptical postulate that there can be only one reality which must determine knowledge and intellectual behavior in general. [See also the quotation from Child (pp. 161-162) and Chapter 10].

22. G. H. Mead, *Mind, Self and Society,* Charles W. Morris, Ed. (Chicago: University of Chicago Press, 1934), especially pp. 6–8, 46–47, 90, 133–134, 155–158, 191–192, 270. (Cf. Child, *Problems,* p. 78.) Mead's concepts relevant to his theory of mind, are communication as conversation of meaningful gestures, significant symbol, generalized other. His crucial thesis: "Mind arises through communication by a conversation of gestures in a social process or context of experience—not communication through mind" (Mead, *op. cit.,* p. 50).

23. On two occasions, *Possibility,* pp. 392–393 and 417.

24. It may be noted that two of the three possible pairs in which these three variables can be arranged have received much attention in contemporary social-scientific literature, namely, social factors and logic (which involves basic epistemological problems of the sociology of knowledge) and social factors and the individual (which, under various labels, especially that of personality and culture, has aroused widespread discussion). The third possible pair—logic and the individual—has been dealt with mainly in connection with the other two complexes.

25. For the concept of "metaphysical" and "ontological" acted on in this paper, see below.

26. Cf. the indirectly relevant discussion of methodological premises of the sociology of knowledge; see pp. 182-183 and 184-187.

27. Inasmuch as both chapters have been published in considerably revised form, the original dissertation drafts are largely neglected here.

28. "We are well aware," Child writes, "that for Marx, the concept of the superstructure comprehends institutions—legal, political, religious—no less than the 'forms of consciousness' which 'correspond' to these superstructures built on the 'real foundation.' But in the sociology of knowledge, the term, 'superstructure,' apparently refers only to the ideologies; while institutions—as contrasted with their ideological expressions or reflections—seem to fall under the heading of the substructure or social-historical structure. If pursued far enough, this difference in the line of demarcation would perhaps reveal a basic difference in attitude between historical materialism and the sociology of

knowledge" (*Problems*, p. 87 n.). Aside from the value of the suggestion implied, this quotation also has the significance of showing that Child's main interest here is in the analysis of the categorical structure rather than in that of the other two structures: their vague definitions and the admitted indecision in their use in the sense of historical materialism or of the sociology of knowledge would indicate this. The same concentration of interest may also explain the lack of attention to still another concept, that of ideology. Child does not tell us whether he uses this term as previously defined or in a broader sense. Either use would have significant implications, also, for the definitions of the two concepts of structure.

29. Cf. Mead, *op. cit.*, pp. 125, 128, 129, 132, 156–157.

30. Arthur Child, "On the Theory of the Categories," *loc. cit.*, henceforth referred to as *Categories*.

31. *Categories*, pp. 319–320; Mead, *op. cit.*, p. 125.

32. Cf. Arthur Child, "Toward a Functional Definition of the 'a priori,'" *Journal of Philosophy*, 41 (March 16, 1944), 155–160.

33. Child, in common with most contributors to the sociology of knowledge, fails to distinguish between social and cultural. As a contrast to biotic he could have chosen, instead of sociotic, some term like culture-derived (culturotic); that is, he does not specifically define sociotic.

34. Cf. Arthur Child, "The Problem of Truth in the Sociology of Knowledge," *op. cit.*, p. 31.

35. For a briefer exposition of Child's conception of the categories in the context of the problem of sociology and cultural relativism and related problems, see Kurt H. Wolff, "The Unique and the General: Toward a Philosophy of Sociology," *Philosophy of Science*, 15 (July 1948), 203-205 [Chapter 6, pp. 144-146]. See also pp. 186-187.

36. Scheler's, Lukács's, and Grünwald's.

37. Arthur Child, "The Existential Determination of Thought," *op. cit.*, p. 181. This paper is henceforth referred to as *Determination*

38. Cf. "Problems," Chapter III, and the last paragraph in the preceding section.

39. Of which Child makes use in his dissertation; cf. *Problems*, p. 114.

40. *Problems*, Chapter V, "The Problem of Imputation"; "The Problem of Imputation in the Sociology of Knowledge," *loc. cit.* (henceforth referred to as *Imputation*, a revision of the former); and "The Problem of Imputation Resolved" (hereafter, *Resolved*).

41. It may be noted in passing that this notion, if applied to the history of the ideal-type concept, from Max Weber to Howard Becker and Robert Redfield, would probably yield significant insights.

42. Cf. Child's more casual use of the term imputation in a different content "One might select a group so large that the excessive breadth and pervasiveness, the excessive generality, of the esthetically relevant predispositions would exclude the legitimate imputation to them of any concrete and particular

esthetic response" [Arthur Child, "The Social-Historical Relativity of Esthetic Value," *Philosophical Review*, **53** (January 1944), 6]. Here Child seems to envisage, as prerequisites of imputing aesthetic matters, well-organized groups and well-organized aesthetic predispositions, paralleling the ideologically organized groups and the articulated ideologies in the case of imputing ideologies.

43. Cf. Kurt H. Wolff, "Notes toward a Sociocultural Interpretation of American Sociology," *American Sociological Review*, 11 (October 1946), 545.

44. Arthur Child, "The Problem of Truth in the Sociology of Knowledge," *op. cit.*, pp. 18–22. This paper is henceforth referred to as *Truth*.

45. Such an elementary confusion, Child maintains *(ibid.,* p. 23), characterizes the four types of erroneous theory dealing with origin-validity which he discusses, among them, Scheler's and Dewey's. Lukács is exculpated from any of these errors *(ibid.,* pp. 22–23).

46. Pareto's statements on nonlogical conduct, Max Weber's analyses of types of power and authority, and Znaniecki's theory of social actions and social types, especially social types of men of knowledge, contain rich suggestions for the typology envisaged.

47. The latter is a notion, evidently not taken from, but clearly inherent in, Dilthey's conception of understanding.

48. A common truth is defined by Child as "a socially agreed-upon proposition . . . which . . . does in fact reconstitute its object in mind in the measure and sense in which it claims to do so" *(Truth,* p. 25).

49. Note the relevance of the next section.

50. Child does not raise the question whether the sociology of knowledge shares transcendent interpretation with the related efforts just mentioned.

51. It will be recalled that Child's concept of truth, as presented in his dissertation, was superseded by his later *Truth*, which has been discussed here. The supplementation presently reported on, however, is not invalidated by this subsequent development.

52. And thus the dissertation, for the last chapter is merely a summary of the findings arrived at throughout the work.

53. Only the most important problems mentioned in the summary are listed here. Even this limited list, however, shows the scope of a theory of the sociology of intellectual-emotional behavior that can be envisaged on the basis of Child's work.

54. Page numbers in parentheses following the items in this list refer to the preceding part on Child. It is obvious that all these tasks are more or less intimately interrelated, but these interrelations have been indicated in only three instances.

55. Since the Spring of 1951 experiments in interpretation have been in progress at Ohio State University (so far three: Leo Spitzer's "American Adver-

tising Explained as Popular Art," a cartoon by Saul Steinberg, and "The Stranger" by Georg Simmel). They are promising as a basis on which to build a theory.

56. Cf. Wolff, *Loma Culture Change, op cit.,* "Introduction." Sections 12, 13, and 15, on respectively, scientific, philosophical, and religious elements in the study of man. This is an apodictic and elliptic formulation, an elaboration of which would exceed the scope of this chapter. It is designed merely to make what follows plausible.

57. In John Dewey's sense, as developed by Thelma Z. Lavine in her "Naturalism and the Sociological Analysis of Knowledge," in Yervant H. Krikorian, Ed., *Naturalism and the Human Spirit* (New York: Columbia University Press, 1944), p. 184.

58. I am not asserting that the metaphysical premises of dualism and naturalism, as defined here, are not found outside the sociology of knowledge, in other types of man, or in other enterprises, but I do suggest that their specific combination, as indicated, is an essential feature of the sociology of knowledge.

59. Wolff, *Loma Culture Change, op. cit.,* "Introduction," pp. 11–12 and Sections 5–7.

Reprinted in modified form from *Scritti di sociologia e politica in onore di Luigi Sturzo,* Vol. III (Bologna: Nicola Zanichelli, 1953), pp. 583–625, and *Ethics,* **61** (1950), 69–73, published by The University of Chicago, by permission of the publishers. The essay has been edited and partially revised by the author.

8

PRESUPPOSITIONS OF
THE SOCIOLOGY OF KNOWLEDGE
AND A TASK FOR IT. 1967, 1971

To begin the discussion of this topic, the presuppositions of the sociology of knowledge (and a task for it) [1], I shall try to show how it has come up for me. I found myself impressed by the fact that if one asks about the sociology of knowledge—for instance, what it is, where it comes from, who its main representatives are—the one who asks is a wholly unanalyzed subject. Possibly, or probably, it is the neutral *Man* of Heidegger [2], or it represents the public interpretation—Mannheim's term, taken over from Heidegger [3]—or Scheler's relatively natural *Weltanschauung* [4]. Let us imagine what would happen if we were not to ask in this fashion, if we did not take for granted the *Man*, the public interpretation, the relatively natural world view, with which in our uncritical unawareness we make common cause, but instead called them into question, neither denying or rejecting nor affirming or accepting but suspending or bracketing them? Would we then not come closer to what we are after than if we were separated from it by the opacity of the unidentified subject who does the asking, that is to say, if we were not separated from it by the veil of tradition? Can we lift this veil? How can we become conscious of the tradition, which we shared by our acceptance of the unanalyzed nature of that anonymous *Man*—by our identification with it? We must, of course, *wish* to lift the veil, a wish that may have various sources. To simplify the argument let us suppose that the source is our feeling of dissatisfaction with tradition, our feeling that there is something more

real than what we have inherited in tradition: our wish is to come closer
to that reality. How do we proceed if we call into question the only guide
we were taught and were convinced we had, that is to say, tradition?
If our wish to come closer to the reality we anticipate behind what tradition has taught us is strong enough, this wish will give us a new courage
for our inquiry. It will give us the strength required of human beings
who would face this time in which tradition has weakened and become
problematic. We may realize that between this process of self-enlighten-
ment, which is commensurate with the present time, and the sociology of
knowledge there is a specific affinity, for the sociology of knowledge, too,
especially as it was conceived by Karl Mannheim, calls into question,
relativizes, particularizes, and transcends.

This act or state which comes out of our time and in which whatever
emerges is questioned as thoroughly as a person engaged in such inquiry
can bear I call *surrender*, and the structure that emerges from it I call
catch, for it is a new, more trustworthy, more believable, more warranted
catching or conceiving than could even be expected before the experience
of surrender or the desire for it. The idea of surrender and catch itself
comes out of our time; it is diagnostic; it has a not yet foreseeable area
of meaning and application. So far I have tried to outline its relation to
religion, the crisis of mankind today, to aesthetic experience, community
study and social science in general, to rebellion, autonomy, to "beginning"
as meant in Hegel and what it may mean today, to Hegel's "cunning of
reason," and aspects of phenomenology [5]. Almost every one of these
efforts has been a new beginning, and the more so, the more efforts it
followed.

At this time, then, I shall try to clarify the relation between surrender
and the sociology of knowledge or rather to develop a previous attempt
[6], for early in the course of my preoccupation with the idea of surrender I tried to demonstrate it on the occasion of the sociology of
knowledge itself. The occasion of that surrender, in turn, was the analysis
of Arthur Child's presentation of the philosophic problems he found in
the sociology of knowledge [7]. I now present in incomplete form the
catch of that surrender.

In the first place Child—implicitly rather than explicitly—sets *tasks* [8]
that must be met before a sociology of knowledge or of intellectual-
affective life more generally, entailed by his study, can be worked out.
Among these tasks are at least two different kinds: methodological and
metaphysical. The methodological include demands for typologies; the
metaphysical, for metaphysical and epistemological theories. The criterion for testing the solution of methodological problems is pragmatic,

a means criterion; that for testing the solution of metaphysical problems is an end criterion, namely, the examination of the catch of the student's surrender.

I then moved on from tasks to premises from which the tasks can be shown to derive: methodological, volitional, and metaphysical. The latter I discovered to be *dualism* and *naturalism*, that is, I insist on investigating anything within the range of my attention that I feel, no matter how vaguely, might be relevant to my inquiry and try to be alert to whatever may make me more sensitive to the range of attention pertinent to an inquiry, to what is relevant within that range, and to the relevancies of the inquiry itself. In short, I found that I espoused surrender [9].

The relation between the methodological and volitional premises of the sociology of knowledge and its metaphysical premises parallels the relation between the means, the historical occasion of inquiry, and its end, the experience and exemplification of man as the being capable of surrender and catch. From the point of view of the inquirer the "world" [10] in which he focuses on methodological or volitional premises (and other methodological or volitional matters) is the mundane or everyday world; when he focuses on metaphysical premises, he has bracketed the world of everyday life and entered that of surrender, of "being" [11]. In the first he seeks scientific, in the second, existential truth [12]. In our own investigation we ourselves have moved from the first to the second, from the everyday world into the world of being: surrendering.

We may say, quite simply, that this world of being is not the world of everyday, but we may also do more than distinguish between the two, more than observe that moments of being are comparatively rare. We may express regret and pain, bewail the fate of man but bless those individuals, who, aware or not of their rootedness in being in whatever way, also lead their lives more nobly [13]. To advocate the experience of being or surrender is to espouse an image of man; that of the being who is capable of surrender and catch. It is an image of essential man, as he is revealed if he suspends as best he can his received notions, affirming only those he *can* affirm, that is, those that withstand the test of such surrender. It also follows from this image of man that these notions, which are the catch of surrender, are as truly and universally human as is possible within the unalterable limits of man's historicity, but these limits to universal truth are widened by surrender, for in surrender, man, whoever he may be, is thrown back on what he really is, which is what he shares with mankind [14].

To call this image of man an image of essential man means the postulation of a transcultural and transhistorical human nature and, at the same time, the invitation not only to support this image but to emulate it, that is, to lead lives that will do right by it [15]. What this entails is something every one of us must come to know. This question may well be an occasion for surrender. It might be to make music, as Pablo Casals did all his life, for peace, against totalitarianism; to put one's body on the line against oppression as Jean-Paul Sartre would like to do; to persevere in the pursuit of science on the faith in knowledge [16]; or many other things, including the study of the sociology of knowledge. I conclude by suggesting a direction in which research in the sociology of knowledge might go if it would translate what precedes into a concrete inquiry.

It would be an effort to increase our knowledge of people's desires, aspirations, fears, indifference, and ignorance in the hope of learning what social, political, and economic conditions would be favorable or unfavorable to the rise, development, decline, and other changes in their concerns. The purpose of this research would be to heighten our understanding of what we can do to bring about a society more conducive to a better life for more kinds of people and to a more widely diffused aspiration for being, as against leading a life, than are the societies in which we live. This goal is so ambitious that it may sound dreamy, frivolous, pious, or really irrelevant. I therefore add that the expectation on which the inquiry proposed is based is that in order to come closer to realizing the purpose in the service of which it is undertaken the world, the world of everyday, must be changed, an expectation that results from the critical nature of the idea of surrender [17]. The inquiry would focus not so much on the identification of desirable changes—a better distribution of wealth, health, education, and justice—on which research is hardly needed, as on the identification of the justifiable local or situational modes of these changes and above all the ways of bringing them about.

NOTES

1. In this chapter I modify and develop "Über die Voraussetzungen der Wissenssoziologie," *Praxis*, **1967**, 3, 373–384, which is based on my earlier writing, mainly, "A Preliminary Inquiry into the Sociology of Knowledge from the Standpoint of the Study of Man," *Scritti di sociologia e politica in onore di Luigi Sturzo*, Vol. III (Bologna: Zanichelli, 1953), pp. 583–623 [Chapter 28].

2. Martin Heidegger, *Sein und Zeit* (1927) (Tübingen: Niemeyer, 1963), especially paragraph 27, p. 126.

3. Karl Mannheim, "Competition as a Cultural Phenomenon" (1928), translated by Paul Kecskemeti, in *From Karl Mannheim*, edited and with an introduction by Kurt H. Wolff (New York: Oxford University Press, 1971), p. 228.

4. Max Scheler, "The Sociology of Knowledge: Formal Problems" (1926), translated by Rainer Koehne, in James E. Curtis and John W. Petras, Eds., *The Sociology of Knowledge: A Reader* (New York: Praeger, 1970), p. 177.

5. "Surrender and Religion," *Journal for the Scientific Study of Religion,* **2** (1962), 36–50; "Surrender as a Response to Our Crisis," *Journal of Humanistic Psychology,* **2** (1962), 16–30; "Surrender and Aesthetic Experience," *Review of Existential Psychology and Psychiatry,* **3** (1963), 209–226; "Surrender and Community Study: The Study of Loma," in Arthur J. Vidich, Joseph Bensman, and Maurice R. Stein, Eds., *Reflections on Community Studies* (New York: Wiley, 1964), pp. 233–263; "Surrender and Autonomy and Community," *Humanitas,* **1** (1965),173–181; "Beginning: In Hegel and Today," in Kurt H. Wolff and Barrington Moore, Jr., with the assistance of Heinz Lubasz, Maurice R. Stein, and E. V. Walter, Eds., *The Critical Spirit: Essays in Honor of Herbert Marcuse* (Boston: Beacon, 1967), pp. 72–103; "Surrender and Rebellion: A Reading of Camus' *The Rebel,*" *Indian Journal of Social Research,* **11** (1970). 167–184; "On the Cunning of Reason in our Time," *Praxis,* **1971,** 1–2, 129–137; "Sociology, Phenomenology, and Surrender-and-Catch," *Synthese,* **24** (1972), 439–471; *Surrender and Catch: A Palimpsest Story* (Sorokin Lectures, No. 3, Saskatoon: University of Saskatchewan, 1972). Also *Hingebung und Begriff* (Neuwied: Luchterhand, 1968). [Almost all these papers are part of *S&C.*]

6. "A Preliminary Inquiry into the Sociology of Knowledge from the Standpoint of the Study of Man" [Chapter 7]; see also "The Sociology of Knowledge and Sociological Theory," in Llewellyn Gross, Ed., *Symposium on Sociological Theory* (Evanston, Ill.: Row, Peterson, 1959), pp. 567-602 [Chapter 9].

7. [Chapter 7, n. 14.]

8. One of them, it may be recalled from Chapter 7, is a theory of interpretation that Child wrote himself, but he did so much later than his major work on the sociology of knowledge and hardly with reference to it, as suggested here. Arthur Child, *Interpretation: A General Theory* (Berkeley: University of California Press, 1965).

9. Neither dualism nor naturalism-surrender as a metaphysical premise but their combination [described in Chapter 7] defines the sociology of knowledge at this time in history. Metaphysical statements can be (rationally) discussed and the method of their intrasubjective examination, mentioned above, can be modified for intersubjective application. Cf. "Beginning: In Hegel and Today," *op. cit.,* pp. 91–95 ("The possibility of intersubjective existential truth").

10. Cf. Alfred Schutz, "On Multiple Realities" (1945), in *Collected Papers, Vol. I, The Problem of Social Reality,* edited and with an introduction by Maurice Natanson (The Hague: Nijhoff, 1962), pp. 207–259.

11. Cf. "Beginning: In Hegel and Today," *op. cit.,* pp. 85–90 ("Beginning and experience of being"), and "Sociology, Phenomenology, and Surrender-and-Catch," *op. cit.,* paragraphs 16–22 and 27.

12. Cf. "The Sociology of Knowledge and Sociological Theory" [Chapter 9], pp. 579–580; "Beginning: In Hegel and Today," *op. cit.,* pp. 99–102 ("Truth:

existential, everyday, scientific"). Scientific truth is more closely related to theoretical and everyday or "commonsensical" truth and existential truth is more closely related to practical and philosophical truth than the first group (or typology) is to the second, despite important differences within each of them (each of which also contains additional types).

13.   Cf. "Beginning: In Hegel and Today," *op. cit.,* pp. 88–90; "Sociology, Phenomenology, and Surrender-and-Catch," paragraphs 22 and 27.

14.   "Surrender and Religion," *op. cit.,* p. 40.

15.   Cf. "Beginning: In Hegel and Today," *op. cit.,* p. 94 (paragraph 39).

16.   It happens that a recent issue of *The New York Times Magazine* (October 17, 1971) contains relevant material on these last two options (hence my mentioning them here): an interview of Sartre by John Gerassi and an article on René Dubos by John Culhane.

17.   On which see "Surrender and Rebellion," *loc. cit.,* above all.

This is Chapter 28 (Supplement) of *Trying Sociology, op. cit.*

9

THE SOCIOLOGY
OF KNOWLEDGE
AND SOCIOLOGICAL
THEORY. 1959

In memory of Karl Mannheim

The chapter that follows is a very personal paper [1]. It is, however, neither private nor idiosyncratic but, on the contrary, an experiment in communication--with myself and with those whom I hope to draw into it. You and I will be participating in a joint venture. We shall start in an expository mood, but as we proceed we shall find ourselves in a more pleading mood, and there will be points in our journey at which we may attain unexpected balances between exposition and rhetoric.

We shall visit much longer with the sociology of knowledge and sociology than with sociological theory, to which we shall come only at the end of our journey. When we look back then, our itinerary should lie clearly traced on the map that we shall realize we have used for our trip.

We start, naturally, from home, with the familiar. We begin with a standard review of the sociology of knowledge. We ask for information and receive it.

"WHAT IS THE SOCIOLOGY OF KNOWLEDGE?"

We are told, or we remember, that it takes only a slight acquaintance with the subject to suspect or know that the term sociology of knowledge is a misnomer, namely, a translation of the German *Wissenssoziologie*. *Wissen*, however, is broader than "knowledge" [1]. Knowledge usually refers to scientific or positive knowledge. *Wissen*, on the other hand, is at least noncommittal on the inclusion of other kinds of knowledge. *Soziologie* is closer to social philosophy and thus broader than "sociology," which, particularly in its American usage, is more closely linked to a natural-science model. Indeed, efforts carried on in the name of the sociology of knowledge, no matter in what language, have been concerned less with scientific knowledge than with outlooks, world views, concepts, and categories of thought. Furthermore, these efforts have been made less in a self-conscious sociological perspective than in the moods of philosophy of history, epistemology, or philosophical anthropology.

The two immediate antecedents of the sociology of knowledge are Marxism [2] and Durkheimian sociology. What is usually referred to as sociology of knowledge, however, is the *Wissenssoziologie* [3] that flourished in Germany in the 1920s and was predominantly Marxist or anti-Marxist. Since 1933 it has led a precarious, transplanted existence, mainly in the United States, although since the end of World War II it has also been revived in Germany [4]. Its two outstanding representatives were Max Scheler (1874–1928) and Karl Mannheim (1893–1947), its two signal publications, Scheler's "Problems of a Sociology of Knowledge" (1924) and Mannheim's *Ideology and Utopia* (1929) [5]. Durkheim has had his greatest effect, outside France, in the United States, where the sociology of knowledge, nevertheless, was introduced chiefly by the English edition of Mannheim's book (1936) [6].

In the United States movements theoretically similar to the sociology of knowledge had existed for roughly half a century. Historically, however, and thus in their general intellectual significance, these movements [7] were different. Pragmatism, social behaviorism, and instrumentalism are, among other things, distillates of a more general and pervasive American outlook: practical, amelioristic, and future-oriented [8]. American students of the sociology of knowledge have combined these American orientations with the German and French. Among the results of their efforts are the most orderly survey of important philosophical problems of the field yet achieved (Arthur Child's [9]), the most succinct summary of its sociological research problems (Robert K. Merton's [10]), and the most concise sketch of its background and its American relations (Louis Wirth's [11]).

One way of characterizing the writings that have been produced in the name of the sociology of knowledge in general and of *Wissenssoziologie* in particular is to call them more speculative and theoretical than empirical and to consider them in need of systematization into a general sociology of intellectual-emotional behavior [12], intellectual life [13], mental productions [14], the mind [15], or gnosio-sociology [16] (to mention some of the few attempts at improving on the term sociology of knowledge). Such systematizing, however, would have to be preceded by inventories of considerable bodies of knowledge and theory, which, though accumulated outside the sociology of knowledge, nevertheless bear on its central problem, the relations between society and intellectual life. They lie scattered in the social sciences, the humanities, and certain biological sciences [17].

We might add to the answer to our question, "What is the sociology of knowledge?," some observations, such as these: despite its predominantly speculative and theoretical character, the sociology of knowledge has produced some outstanding empirical investigations [18]. It has given us useful (though not too widely used) concepts—for example, Mannheim's typology of interpretations [19] or Znaniecki's of men of knowledge [20]. It has had a continuing effect as a latent frame of reference [21] in other disciplines. Some of its American students, both sociologists [22] and philosophers [23], have later in their careers turned to work in other areas; the selection of this work, however, or the approaches to it, have probably been influenced by their previous preoccupation with the sociology of knowledge, and they may yet return to such preoccupation, for their careers are still going on.

The foregoing answer to our question, "What is the sociology of knowledge?," is what we referred to as a standard review of the field. Now we are going a step further. We shall take such a step when we realize, first, that in our question and in the answer to it we paid no attention to the persons who did the asking and answering; second, that not to have done so is a serious omission, which we must now try to make good. Let us attempt to identify these persons—first as types of men and then historically, that is, in respect to place and time.

OUTSIDERS AND PARTICIPANTS

We did say something about the types of men who inquired into the sociology of knowledge and who expounded it by referring to them as seeking and receiving information. They were outsiders to the sociology of knowledge. They talked from the standpoint of some unarticulated version of the contemporary academic tradition in social science. Not only were they not among the developers of the sociology of knowledge, they betrayed no awareness that to ask and be given information about an intellectual endeavor is one thing but that to develop it and participate in it is quite another. It involves a much greater risk.

In our asking and answering there was no risk. There was no risk of participation in which the two activities of asking and answering and the two roles of asker and answerer might have fused and been transformed into one joint venture. The outcome would not have been certain—the kind of outcome, in fact, quite unforeseeable. Yet the sociology of knowledge, like any intellectual endeavor worth its salt, has had its participants; it could not have come into being without them. Unlike the asker and answerer of the question with which we started on our journey, these participants were startled, puzzled, bewildered, and troubled by novel problems. Among them, Karl Mannheim perhaps took the greatest chances of becoming confused and stymied, accepted the fewest among the received notions at his disposal, and staked the most of himself: he was the most unconditional participant. This may be gathered, even more palpably perhaps than from his published writings, from a letter written (April 15, 1946) to me in response to a critical analysis of Mannheim's work by members of a seminar on the sociology of knowledge. Mannheim wrote:

> . . . If there are contradictions and inconsistencies in my paper this is, I think, not so much due to the fact that I overlooked them but because I make a point of developing a theme to its end even if it contradicts some other statements. I use this method because I think that in this marginal field of human knowledge we should not conceal inconsistencies, so to speak covering up the wounds, but our duty is to show the sore spots in human thinking at its present stage.
>
> In a simple empirical investigation or straightforward logical argument, contradictions are mistakes; but when the task is to show that our whole thought system in its various parts leads to inconsistencies, these inconsistencies are the thorn in the flesh from which we have to start.
>
> The inconsistencies in our whole outlook, which in my presentation only become more visible, are due to the fact that we have two approaches which move on a different plane [*sic*].
>
> On the one hand, our most advanced empirical investigations, especially those which come from history, psychology, and sociology, show that the human mind with its whole categorical apparatus is a dynamic entity. Whereas our predominant

epistemology derives from an age, the hidden desire and ideal of which was stability, the traditional epistemology still thinks of concepts as reflecting eternal ideas. The premium is put on absoluteness and supertemporaneousness and accordingly, no other knowledge and truth can be conceived . . . [than] the static one. . . .

Now, whereas one part of our progressive insight convinces us that language and logic are also a part of culture which, in its turn—most people will agree on that—is different with different tribes and in different epochs and therefore nothing can be stated but in relation to a frame of reference; the other part of our intellectual orientation through its traditional epistemology cannot put up with this insight. The latter is reluctant to accept this because it failed to build into its theory the fact of the essential perspectivism of human knowledge.

To use a simple analogy, what happens is that in our empirical investigation we become aware of the fact that we are observing the world from a moving staircase, from a dynamic platform, and, therefore, the image of the world changes with the changing frames of reference which various cultures create. On the other hand, epistemology still only knows of a static platform where one doesn't become aware of the possibility of various perspectives and, from this angle, it tries to deny the existence and the right of such dynamic thinking. There is a culture lag between our empirical insight into the nature of knowing and the premises upon which the traditional idealist epistemology is built. Instead of perspectivism, the out-of-date epistemology wants to set up a veto against the emerging new insights, according to which man can only see the world in perspective, and there is no view which is absolute in the sense that it represents the thing in itself beyond perspective.

In the world of visual objects, we acknowledge that completely. That you can only see various perspectives of a house and there is no view among them which is absolutely the house and in spite of that there is knowing because the various perspectives are not arbitrary. The one can be understood from the other. What we, without any difficulty, admit for the apperception of the visual world, we ought to admit for knowledge in general.

I hope this is intelligible and it at least convinces you and your seminar that if there are contradictions they are not due to my shortsightedness but to the fact that I want to break through the old epistemology radically but have not succeeded yet fully. But the latter is not one man's work. I think our whole generation will have to work on it as nothing is more obvious than that we transcended in every field the idea that man's mind is equal to an absolute Ratio in favour of a theory that we think on the basis of changing frames of reference, the elaboration of which is one of the most exciting tasks of the near future. . . [24].

Mannheim's letter has been quoted exclusively as the document of an insider and is commented on in this respect alone. It suggests that, for the insider, problems of the sociology of knowledge—leading toward it or issuing from it—are more or less faithful formulations of his craving for an ordered world: they are existential problems for him. In the case of Mannheim, in particular, most of the work he did (not only that explicitly devoted to the sociology of knowledge) could be characterized as a diagnosis of our time (the title he gave one of his books): for him, existential problems were above all historical problems. They were the questions: "Where have we come from?" "Where are we?" "What, therefore, must we do?" Though never as clear on the matter as some might have desired him to be, Mannheim appears to have held that if we know who we are we know what we must do.

This is an old proposition. We do well to realize, however, that it is incompatible with the much newer, though almost all-pervasive, total separation between the Is and the Ought. For more than two millennia men had been saying that our existence itself, our "Is," is normative, that it includes the "Ought"; hence that if we recognize ourselves we know what we must do. What is new, now, about this Socratic position is the place and time of its rediscovery—of, perhaps, its fermenting.

We have touched only lightly on the place and time of the outsider who inquires into the sociology of knowledge. All we have said is that he seeks information, raising his question on the basis of some unarticulated version of the contemporary academic tradition in social science in which he has grown up but has hardly examined. Mannheim's example suggests an additional distinction between outsider and insider. It is that, unlike the outsider, the insider finds that he cannot inquire into the sociology of knowledge short of examining this tradition and that examining this tradition includes exploring his place and time. We shall now attempt to visualize such an exploration.

ON OUR PLACE AND TIME

We begin with the place and the time: the West, now. This includes something on Western tradition, and later we shall examine some features of our tradition in sociology in particular. In our inspection of place and time we limit ourselves to three interrelated aspects: the administered nature of our lives, the world as underdeveloped; and one-world-and-cultural-relativism.

1. The part of the social structure that administers our lives is bureaucracy, "the type of organization designed to accomplish large-scale administrative tasks by systematically co-ordinating the work of many individuals" [25]. This part is so important that much of our outlook and conduct is the outlook and conduct of the administered life: not spontaneous interaction, but control, and the fear of its failing. If this is so, the reason may be that we have not come to terms with secularization and rationalization [26], but that we are ambivalent toward them. On this we shall have more to say below. Now, we put the matter by stating that we find ourselves having to pay for the recession of objective reason [27]. What do we mean by this?

Objective must be distinguished from subjective reason. Subjective reason is part of our mental equipment. It is our faculty of thinking, notably that of adapting means to ends [28]. Objective reason is the rational order of the cosmos (nature, society, history), which also contains *us*. This order is normative, teleological; it includes ends. Yet when we employ our subjective reason in a manner that lets us forget objective reason we lose our very capacity to assess ends. One effect of this forgetting and this loss is that ends turn sour, and we may declare them to be matters of taste, irrational [29]. Is and Ought have become divorced. Once this divorce has occurred, all our efforts to derive Ought from Is are vain [30].

The last sentence expresses a logically correct proposition. Its empirical applications, however—such as doubt and worry over the Ought or attempts at obtaining it from the Is—are so frequent that they may be said to characterize our contemporary consciousness [31]. To recognize the recession of objective reason may help us understand another phenomenon of our time, the simultaneous spurt in science and technology and the emergence of totalitarianism. It may come to appear less paradoxical that this period of unprecedented rise in the standard of living, of democratization, of decreasing superstition, of proliferating options should also be the period, not only of totalitarianism, but also of Western feelings that traditional ideals have lost significance, and the goal of a higher standard of living has become a barren one.

The administered nature of our lives has been hinted at in many expressions—for example, "brave new world," "1984," "other-directedness" (David Riesman), "escape from freedom" (Erich Fromm), but it could be that the contrasts or solutions, such as Riesman's "autonomy" or Fromm's "productive personality" [32], will be confined to the status of options in addition to those already available, thus contributing to their proliferation. As long as ninety years ago, Dostoyevsky wrote:

> In those days people seem to have been animated by one idea, but now they are much more nervous, more developed, more sensitive—they seem to be animated by two or three ideas at a time—modern man is more diffuse and, I assure you, it is this that prevents him from being such a complete human being as they were in those days [33].

2. We in the West have not, perhaps not yet, recognized the objectively rational status of man's desire to be free from hunger, sickness, fear, and ignorance. We have not recognized that from this desire we might develop the world. Instead, we tend to single out some areas of it as needing a push in the direction of Western development. On this view, the current notion of underdeveloped peoples or countries appears as a distortion of what should read "the world as underdeveloped" [34]. It is a corrupted text, the corrupting element being a Western projection. *We* are underdeveloped, as witness our helpless, administered lives, our helplessness in front of totalitarianism, the climax of administeredness, of derationalization and, at the same time, detraditionalization, of ahistoricity and, at the same time, amorality.

No matter how much our projectionism is attenuated—not least by the spontaneous understanding and puzzlement of social scientists, among them some of those active in underdeveloped countries [35]—we are glad, nevertheless, and understandably so, to repress our own dilemma. We tend to hold on to the essentially nineteenth-century dichotomies of sacred, folk, traditional versus secular, urban, rational societies, believing ourselves to belong to the latter, with which we want to dominate the nascent one world. Instead, we might cling to such nonprojective ideas as that the science and technology we have mastered under the very guide of subjective reason and its stubborn insistence on control (and in only precarious relation with objective reason), if deliberately applied to our economies, can reduce hunger and sickness faster than they have been; that return to trust in objective reason can increase knowledge and alleviate fear [36], and that, acting on these insights, we may help reason in its "cunning," recognizing in our very befuddlement a reminder of objective reason and of the relation of objective to subjective reason.

3. Such help to reason may be help to us at this time when one of the most palpable meanings of one world is the feeling of global claustro-

phobia. On the one hand, our science and technology have made our destruction feasible and thus a possibility. On the other, our social science in particular (especially cultural anthropology) has so overwhelmed us with a range of cultures that are strange, yet human—and, being human, ours—that we are terrified and confused. We may feel relief when we can transcend our terror and confusion by transforming them into questions such as these: What can we do with our own ways of life? How can we reinterpret our traditions so that we can all live together not by compromise but by being truer to ourselves? In the light or mood of such questions the idea of one world and cultural relativism may impress us as a democratized version of the idea of the brotherhood of man and the immortality of the soul. If developments under the sway of subjective reason have disenchanted us to the point of being haunted by our own disappearance, we may revive by insisting that these developments, despite world wars, death camps, atom bombs, genocide, and the administered life, are a phase of secularization and rationalization whose enchantment we have yet to discover. We may revive if we realize that this phase challenges us to reinvent ourselves so that we may learn how we can *live* in one world. We must get hold of our *trans*cultural selves after we have been so fascinated by cultural relativism, by our cultural unselves.

Without postulating a transcultural human nature, we could not account for the possibility of understanding between two persons of different cultures [37]—but this means between any two persons, even myself today and yesterday, here and in another place. The pursuit of understanding others and ourselves evinces faith in their dignity and our own, in the dignity of man. It is incompatible with condescension, toward underdeveloped man and ourselves alike and perpetually challenges us to keep to the fine line between the belief of being in grace and the sin of pride. In the pursuit of understanding it is of secondary importance whether by our "transcultural selves" we mean a supracultural core or residue, biological or spiritual, and whether, accordingly, we engage in the investigation of the physiological processes of thought, of intellectual history, or of the sociology of knowledge. In all these endeavors we further our understanding by the awareness that we are embracing both transcultural human nature and human culture, both man, or human nature, and unique cultures, and must be wary lest we confuse the first with the second or the second with the first—learning with biology, acquired with innate traits, nurture with nature, environment with heredity, or supervenient with primal categories [38].

METHODOLOGICAL, VOLITIONAL, AND METAPHYSICAL
PREMISES OF THE SOCIOLOGY OF KNOWLEDGE:
ITS DUALISM AND NATURALISM

We may seem to have strayed from the sociology of knowledge. Actually, we are in the process of becoming insiders, of participating in it. For that matter it has come up in the course of reflections on our time as one among various endeavors in the pursuit of understanding; it was also referred to, by implication, in the warning not to take supervenient for primal categories (and vice versa): we may recall this distinction as Arthur Child's attempt to solve one of the crucial philosophical problems of the sociology of knowledge, precisely that of the categories of thought. It is now necessary to show that the connection between the sociology of knowledge and our time is not casual, that it can be analyzed, and that it can be argued to be of a determinable kind and importance.

In his first explicit paper on the subject (1925) [39] Karl Mannheim examined four ultimate, fundamental factors which constitute the problem constellation of the sociology of knowledge. These are (1) the "self-transcendence" or "self-relativization of thought," that is, the possibility of not taking thought at its face value; (2) "the emergence of the 'unmasking' turn of mind" (or debunking); (3) the transcendence of thought toward the historical and social sphere, which is hypostatized as the ontological absolute or emerges as a new system of reference; in other words, the understanding of thought as the expression of or in relation to history and society; and (4) the social relativization of the totality of the mental world, not only of *some* thoughts. Without these four factors, Mannheim held, the historical emergence of the sociology of knowledge is unthinkable, but once in existence these factors make for a constellation which necessarily gives "rise to [its] problems" [40]. More succinctly, the sociology of knowledge tackles the question of what happens if intellectual processes and products are unmasked as the expression of, or in relation to, social-historical circumstance—if intellectual life as such is so unmasked. The sociology of knowledge must come to terms with this question because this is precisely what has actually happened. It has to come to terms with what it realizes has happened in the modern world. It must transform a new and shattering experience into a problem.

This does not mean that the theoretical distillate of this historical experience depends for its emergence exclusively on that experience. Theoretical preoccupations with the sociology of knowledge are at least as old as Xenophanes of Colophon (sixth century B.C.) and Sextus Empiricus (A.D. third century), to mention only two [41] of many theoretically relevant writers throughout the ages, but, as in the case of the American predecessors, their general intellectual significance is different from that of the historically conscious sociology of knowledge.

Mannheim's previously quoted letter, written more than twenty years after the paper referred to, shows that even then he was still struggling with the problem of intellectual life unmasked; that problem had not lost its humbling magnitude. Already the early source presents him engaged in a diagnosis of our time: he asks where we have come from, where we are, what, therefore, we must do, and he looks for an answer in the exploration of the modern (Western) consciousness.

Such a concept of consciousness is Hegelian-Marxian. Possibly for this reason it is absent from American preoccupations with the sociology of knowledge. Even the few American comments on the time and place in which the sociology of knowledge originated do not imply it, let alone explicitly use it. Those by Louis Wirth and Robert K. Merton may serve as illustrations.

Wirth describes that time and place, our period, as one of increasing secularization. As such, it has come to question "norms and truths which were once believed to be absolute," and to recognize that thought itself is disturbing because it is "capable of unsettling routines, disorganizing habits, breaking up customs, undermining faiths, and generating skepticism." Certain "facts" of the social life may not be investigated because this would impinge on vested interests. Mannheim, says Wirth, has gone beyond this insight into the reflection of interest "in all thought, including that part of it which is called science." Mannheim has tried "to trace out the specific connection between actual interest groups in society and the ideas and modes of thought which they espoused" [42].

Thus Wirth, in his attempt to locate our time historically, in effect praises Mannheim as a modern representative of the Enlightenment, particularly of the Enlightenment theory of interests. We saw, however, that Mannheim himself, even before publishing the book to which Wirth wrote the introduction just quoted, had no longer operated with such a theory but with the social relativization of the totality of the mental world. As to the Enlightenment itself, Mannheim argued, in the earlier paper, that it was a phase in the development of the modern consciousness we have left far behind. It was a phase endowing Reason with autonomy and thus "least likely to effect a relativization of thought." Rather it pointed "in the opposite direction, that is, toward an absolute self-hypostatization of Reason" [43].

Merton remarks that in an era of increasing social conflict and distrust, inquiry into the validity of ideas tends to shift toward preoccupation with their origin. "Thought becomes functionalized; it is interpreted in terms

of its psychological or economic or social or racial sources and functions":
witness not only the sociology of knowledge but also "psycho-analysis,
Marxism, semanticism, propaganda analysis, Paretanism, and, to some
extent, functional analysis" [44]. Merton no more than Wirth operates
with a conception of history in which the notion of a consciousness either
commensurate with or reflective of a period is a constitutive element.

The exploration of our time and place undertaken in the preceding
section suggests the hope of an understanding that presupposes the acceptance of the dualism of man and his unique cultures. An analysis of recur-
ring problems of the sociology of knowledge undertaken elsewhere [45]
has shown the same dualism as one of the metaphysical premises of the
sociology of knowledge—and naturalism as the other. As this is explained,
it will become evident that naturalism, too, is a presupposition of the
understanding in which we have found the hope of transcending our time.

Besides metaphysical, there are two other kinds of premise: methodological and volitional. The distinctions among the three may be made
as follows: A *methodological premise* is a proposition accepted because of
its usefulness as a guide to inquiry. A *volitional premise* is an affect or
desire that animates the researcher. A *metaphysical premise* is a proposition concerning the nature of reality.

Among the methodological premises of the sociology of knowledge are
the propositions that the scientific validity of intellectual phenomena has
nothing to do with their origin, that intellectual phenomena have logical
as well as social aspects. The corresponding volitional premises of the
sociology of knowledge are the desires for unimpeachable validity, on the
one hand, and social relevance, on the other. They are the desires for
maximum intrinsic interpretation, which illuminates the logical aspects
of intellectual phenomena, and for maximum extrinsic interpretation,
which illuminates their social aspects. The nature of these wishes presupposes a certain conception of reality, which is expressed in the metaphysical premises of the sociology of knowledge. Accordingly, reality is both
relative (socially, culturally, historically, and biologically) and absolute,
that is, itself, true, irrespective of relativity. It follows that the appropriate approach to reality likewise is dual: both the most thorough extrinsic
interpretation of phenomena (as instances of laws) and their most thorough intrinsic interpretation (in their own terms) which are possible on
any given occasion at any time.

The first of these metaphysical premises (concerning reality) predicates
ontological dualism; the second (concerning the interpretation of this
reality) espouses naturalism, understood as continuity of analysis [46].
It should now be clear (as has been anticipated) that naturalism, in this
sense, also is a metaphysical premise of the understanding which resulted

as a hope from the analysis of our time and place. This analysis implied that the inquiry into the nature of man and culture and into their mutual relations and boundaries would never be completed.

SCIENTIFIC VERSUS EXISTENTIAL TRUTH

It is important to realize that methodological problems, including those of testing methodological premises, and volitional and metaphysical problems, have different criteria of confirmation or truth. For methodological problems the criterion of truth is pragmatic in relation to a given inquiry or type of inquiry; in this sense it is a means criterion. For volitional and metaphysical problems the criterion is agreement with the result of the most rigorously imaginable intrasubjective dialectical examination of one's most important experiences: it is an end criterion [47].

The truth sought in the solution of methodological problems may be called *stipulative* in the sense that the predicate "true" is stipulated as suitable to the investigatory purpose in hand (or to the class of investigatory purposes of which the one in hand is an example). It may also be called *hypothetical* in the sense that it is contingent on the validation of a given hypothesis being examined in respect to its truth or in the more compelling sense that, even if validated, hypotheses remain hypotheses, namely propositions that can be validated only within the hypothetical methodological, pragmatic, scientific attitude—that attitude for which metaphysical propositions (concerning the nature of reality) are irrelevant. Finally, this truth may be called *propositional*, in the sense that it is predicated only (or predominantly [48]) of propositions. It is clear that this stipulative, hypothetical, propositional truth, which is the truth sought in the solution of methodological problems, is also the truth sought in the solution of scientific problems. This is widely, if not generally, recognized by philosophers of science and of value. It implies that science makes no claims about the nature of (ultimate) reality; it is not concerned with this reality. We refer to this stipulative, hypothetical, propositional truth as *scientific* truth.

The truth sought in the solution of volitional and metaphysical problems may, in accordance with the definition given above, be called experiential or *existential*. From a sociological standpoint the seeker after scientific truth who commits an error risks his technical well-being, including, if he is a scientist, his professional reputation. By contrast, the seeker after existential truth risks his life and the world. Concerning both he may die in greater error than he would if he had "surrendered" [49] more fully, consciously, and intelligently to them.

Paul Kecskemeti has illuminated the nature of Mannheim's sociology of knowledge by arguing that Mannheim in effect distinguished between two kinds of truth, which are closely related to scientific and existential truth. These are the "Aristotelian concept of truth as 'speaking the truth,'" or "the truth of propositions..."; and truth as "one's response to reality," "the existential concept of truth as 'being in truth.'" We should remember, Kecskemeti writes, that truth has been conceived in these two ways throughout the history of philosophy. For the first, truth is predicative of sentences; it

> has nothing to do with the things of the world as they exist in themselves. According to the other definition, 'truth' is first and foremost an attribute of *existence*, and only secondarily of *discourse*. One *is* or *is not* in the Truth; and one's possession of Truth depends on being in communion with a reality which 'is' or embodies truth [50].

SOCIAL NOMINALISM VERSUS SOCIAL REALISM

This reality, for Mannheim (for the early Mannheim, as we shall see later in this section), was history. The positing of history, or of anything else, as real is not for the scientist to do. He pursues scientific truth and in so doing ignores metaphysical questions. In other words, the scientific attitude "brackets"—to use the language of phenomenology—the ontological quest. To the extent, however, that a given science or scientist deviates from the type, there may be metaphysical premises that have their influence on the selection and formulation of problems, on the interpretation of findings, and so on. Mannheim is by no means alone, or even an exception, in such deviation. Thus it has been said of American sociology as a whole that it is characterized by "voluntaristic nominalism"; that is, by

> the assumption that the structure of all social groups is the consequence of the aggregate of its separate, component individuals and that social phenomena ultimately derive from the motivations of these knowing, feeling, and willing individuals.

American sociology, therefore, is unsympathetic to any social determinism.

> A sociology of knowledge, for instance, which maintains a strict causal relationship between a specific form of social existence or class position and knowledge is unlikely to gain

> many adherents among American sociologists. . . . neither Durkheim's notion of society as an entity *sui generis* nor Marx's interpretation of social stratification in terms of economic relations and consequent class consciousness has been accepted in American sociology in spite of widespread familiarity with these ideas [51].

Not being pure, that is, self-conscious, self-critical, self-correcting, neither American nor European sociology wholly rejects its own metaphysical inclinations. As sciences, they should withhold an accent of reality, whereas, in fact, they bestow it, although each of them bestows it on a different sphere. American sociology places it on the individual, withdrawing it from society. We may refer to this by saying that American sociology represents individual realism (and social nominalism, to paraphrase the term voluntaristic nominalism). European sociology places it on society or history, withdrawing it from the individual. It represents social realism (individual nominalism).

Social realism is related to historical realism. This relation has been shown by Ernest Manheim in respect to Karl Mannheim's career. The later stages of this career, Manheim observes, show increasing interest in psychology, which "is inherent in Mannheim's adoption of the nominalist theory of groups, the view that groups have no reality of their own beyond the existence of their individual members." (This is, of course, the characteristically American conception of sociology.) This turning toward social nominalism also explains Mannheim's "*abandonment of the doctrine which asserts the primacy of the historical frame of reference.*" As Ernest Manheim points out, it is only in what has been called individual realism, that is,

> when the individual becomes the ultimate term of reference of sociological constructs (as is typically the case in American sociology) that questions of motivation can have meaning for the analysis of social action. Sociological concepts formed on the level of the group are impervious to psychology [52].

Thus we can formulate a further contrast: American sociology is characterized by psychological realism (social nominalism); European sociology, by social realism (psychological nominalism).

It is perhaps unnecessary to point out that these are no more than broad characterizations. For a fuller description (surely not to be undertaken here) qualifications must be entered; for instance, much recent American work in bureaucracy and social stratification leans more toward social realism; on the other hand, there is a strong interest in psychology, verging on psychological realism, in European writers as different as Tarde, LeBon, and some writings by Simmel. It is also possible to make relevant distinctions on the American scene according to individual and typical sociologists, institutions, and levels (e.g., textbook versus monograph). On the whole, nevertheless, American sociology has almost from the beginning been more deeply involved with (social) psychology (interests, social forces, instincts, needs, and attitudes) than with society or history, whereas the opposite tends to describe European sociology.

Ernst Grünwald's distinction of the psychological and historical theories as the roots or forerunners of the sociology of knowledge suggests the pertinence of this discussion for the sociology of knowledge. The psychological theory, includinig its conceptions of truth and falsehood, is based on a theory of human nature; the historical theory, with the same inclusion, on a theory of history [53]. Without detailing names, tendencies, and movements, it is clear that the sociology of knowledge, although the German variant more than the French, is in the historical rather than the psychological tradition. Along with much European sociology—to add a last generalization—the sociology of knowledge operates with a concept of existential truth, sometimes at the cost of inadequate attention to the concept of scientific truth. This last contrast gives credence to the often-heard derogatory designation of European sociology in general as philosophical, metaphysical, speculative, or armchair, and to the European comments that in American sociology "reliability has been won by surrendering theoretic relevance" [54].

A summary presentation of suggested characteristics of American and European sociology may be useful (Table 1):

Table 1.   *Metaphysical Tendencies of American and European Sociology*

American Sociology	European Sociology (and Sociology of Knowledge)
Scientific Truth	Existential Truth
Individual-Psychological Realism	Social-Historical Realism
Social-Historical Nominalism	Individual-Psychological Nominalism

CONNECTIONS BETWEEN THE SOCIOLOGY OF KNOWLEDGE AND OUR TIME

At the beginning of our inquiry into the premises of the sociology of knowledge we spoke of the need for showing the nature of the connection between it and our time. The intervening discussion was necessary before we could hope to meet this need. Here we try to do so. It may help to recall the course of our argument. In recalling it, we rephrase it in the light of the gains we have made.

We began by asking, "What is the sociology of knowledge?"—a question raised and answered by an outsider in search of scientific knowledge. The central concern of the insider, who was then introduced, emerged as the need to recognize himself and his fellowmen in their common time and place in order to know what to do. This—our—time and place appeared to us to be characterized by the administered nature of our lives, by the world as underdeveloped, and by one-world-and-cultural-relativism, with understanding as the hope of transcending this time, and dualism—and naturalism—as the metaphysical premises of such understanding. These were also seen as the metaphysical premises, related to its methodological and volitional premises, of the sociology of knowledge. We may now make explicit those implications of the subsequent steps of our inquiry that are relevant to the task of showing that the connection between the sociology of knowledge and our time can be analyzed and can be argued to be of a determinable kind and importance.

These steps dealt with the distinction between scientific and existential truth and with the preponderant association of the former with individual-psychological realism (social nominalism) and of the latter with social-historical realism (individual nominalism). Social-historical realism and existential truth, we suggested, characterize the sociology of knowledge, and one indication is its notion of historical consciousness. We had remarked earlier on the absence of this notion from the American preoccupation with the sociology of knowledge and had illustrated this absence with Wirth's and Merton's observations on the time in which the sociology of knowledge originated.

The connection between the sociology of knowledge and our time thus appears to be the following:

1. To speak of this connection makes sense only if the concept "our time" itself makes sense, and it does this only on a historical (social-historical-realist) rather than a psychological (individual-psychological-realist) view.

2. Once such a view is adopted, the sociology of knowledge can be seen as one of several articulations [55] of the consciousness of our time, an articulation which, as it becomes conscious of being such, contributes to the transcendence of this consciousness. The sociology of knowledge thus emerges as the reaffirmation or, better, reinvention of the Socratic position, on the occasion of its insight into its own time and place.

3. In becoming conscious of its methodological, volitional, and meta-

physical premises in their historical relevance, the sociology of knowledge appears "as a revision of our way of . . . looking at ourselves and the world, . . . an elucidation of a new experience man has had and is still having" [56].

In words used earlier, the sociology of knowledge transforms a new and shattering experience into a problem.

NINETEENTH- AND TWENTIETH-CENTURY CIVILIZATIONAL-HISTORICAL DICHOTOMIES, MODERN AMERICAN SOCIOLOGY, AND THE SOCIOLOGY OF KNOWLEDGE

In the exploration of our time and place the world as underdeveloped appeared as a correction of the notion of underdeveloped countries, that is, of the tendency to project our own underdevelopment on non-Western peoples. In that connection we commented on some civilizational-historical dichotomies as attempts at coming to terms with the emerging one world. We now wish to apply our subsequent distinction between scientific and existential truth to a reinterpretation of these dichotomies so that differences and relations between the sociology of knowledge and American sociology may be brought out further.

Henry Maine's contrast between societies based on status and societies based on contract, Herbert Spencer's military and industrial societies, Ferdinand Tönnies' *Gemeinschaft* and *Gesellschaft*, Emile Durkheim's societies characterized by mechanical and organic solidarity, Max Weber's distinction between traditionalism and rationalism, Howard Becker's sacred and secular societies, Ralph Linton's ascribed and achieved status (and universals and alternatives), Robert Redfield's folk and urban societies, and Godfrey and Monica Wilson's primitive and civilized [57], to mention only some of the dichotomies articulated during the last hundred years, are not only what they were predominantly intended by their authors to be, namely scientific hypotheses submitted for confirmation or falsification by subsequent research, they also claim existential truth:

> For decades, the pictures of primitive character brought back
> by anthropologists, no matter how well intended, were used
> by the denizens of Western industrialized civilization, either
> to preen themselves on their progress or to damn their cities,
> machines, or customs by reference to a constructed preliterate
> Eden—all, of course, under the guidance of such supposedly
> scientific terms as "folk society," "*Gemeinschaft*," "sacred
> society," and other such phrases [58].

In our words the existential element in these dichotomies is the mixture of faith and doubt that liberalism, increasing rationalization, reasonableness, and progress are indeed true. The faith probably is more plausible than the doubt, but we must recall that some of the dichotomists·did express their worries. Thus Durkheim was disturbed by anomie, Weber by bureaucratization, Mannheim by the preponderance of functional over substantial rationality, and Durkheim looked to social reorganization through professional groups. Weber expressed his belief in prophecy, Mannheim, in ecstasy [59]. The appearance of these dichotomies and their authors' attitudes toward them thus tell the later story of liberalism (more spontaneously or, one might say, in a more clinical sense than do Nietzsche, Spengler, or Toynbee) as the doubt concerning the existential truth of the liberal historical interpretation and the scientific truth of its historical account [60]. The dichotomists (or other Westerners) have not succeeded either in writing a scientifically more accurate history or in revising liberalism toward greater historical adequacy. Instead we have been overwhelmed by totalitarianism—among other things an alternative, antiliberal interpretation of the historical moment—and have experienced and witnessed the helplessness of liberalism confronted with it [61].

Reinhard Bendix has shown that certain trends in the development of the Western image of man from Bacon through the Enlightenment to Marx, Nietzsche, and Freud represent an increasing "distrust of reason" [62]. The last four centuries, especially the last hundred years, have thrown man ever more back on himself, unmasking ideas, beliefs, customs, and traditions as unreliable and unworthy crutches, as ideologies (Marx) or sublimations (Freud).

Therefore the question, "what, then, is man?" was raised. It was being asked by the same analysts who had stripped man to the necessity of (again) asking it, as well as by many others, from Descartes through Kierkegaard to the contemporary existentialists, phenomenologists, and various theologians. This question intruded during the same period in which science and technology developed and (especially in its later phases) the standard of living rose to levels never reached before. There was a temptation, therefore, to take these developments themselves as the answer to the question, "What is man?" This question had to be asked in a whisper, in an embarrassed whisper—as a lover asks his beloved in the din of a factory, a cafeteria, a movie house, and (particularly in the twentieth century) the roar of a world war or a concentration camp. Science, technology, prosperity, and disaster seem to have kept our self-inspection in a balance between the desire for it and its postponement as long as the automobile and the screen were there as an escape, and as long as the war, which had to be fought, urged us to tell who we are by asking science and ignoring history. Witness scientism, infatuation with methodology in general, and more particularly such phenomena as formal literary criticism, philosophical analysis, structural linguistics, and the strong ritualistic element in social relations [63].

These are some historical problems to which modern sociology, specifically, might address itself. Instead, it appears to be preoccupied, in America possibly more than elsewhere, with rather ahistorical, formal structural relations and processes and with improving itself as a specialty in such preoccupation. To say this is not to suggest that sociology should not be a generalizing science. Rather it is to argue that sociology would facilitate its task of being a generalizing science if it recognized its need for a historical theory of society, no matter how crude it might be to begin with [64]. If sociology wants to be historically relevant, it cannot reject its commitment to historical realism and abide its psychological realism which no longer is historically adequate, for even a generalizing science, *if it is a social science*, starts with the historical situation. It may deny it but it cannot escape it. In this respect social science cannot be entirely true to the pure type of science which brackets the ontological quest [65].

The sociology of knowledge escapes this difficulty of modern American sociology by its historical realism and its much more openly recognized connection with the quest for existential truth. It is alien to the formalism of our time and in this sense, and by contrast, substantive [66]; it is applied theory, in the service of changing the world, whether according to Marx (specifically the *Theses on Feuerbach*) or Durkheim. Both Marx and Durkheim preceded the modern bifurcation of the world into Is and Ought, a bifurcation that has been shared and pushed by contemporary social science. Marx, much more than Durkheim, was one of the strippers of modern man, but his historical focus kept Is and Ought together. Durkheim, like Max Weber, is a figure of transition in the sense that in their actual researches both keep Is and Ought together, whereas in their explicit methodological writings they separate them (Weber more pointedly and passionately than Durkheim) [67]. In the United States the form secularization took in Marx (by way of Hegel and Feuerbach) appears to be an unmanageable alternative to American liberalism [68]. The other, the separation of Is and Ought, is intimately connected with the phenomena discussed in our exploration of the contemporary Western scene and with those mentioned above. In American sociology this separation is of recent date, probably the 1920s. It had not yet appeared in Cooley's *Social Process* (1918); Lundberg-Anderson-Bain's *Trends in American Sociology* (1929) was a milestone in its articulation and acceptance.

Already ten years later, Robert S. Lynd manifested discontent with it in
Knowledge for What?

MERTON'S COMPARISON BETWEEN
THE SOCIOLOGY OF KNOWLEDGE
AND MASS COMMUNICATIONS

Now let us consider the comparison between European and American
sociology that is most pertinent here: Merton's juxtaposition of the European sociology of knowledge and the recent branch of American sociology,
research into mass communications, that seems most closely related to it.

Although the sociology of knowledge and mass communications, Merton
observes, have on the whole developed independently from one another,
they may be regarded "as two species of that genus of research which is
concerned with the interplay between social structure and communications" [69]. The numerous contrasting aspects of these two "species" may
be presented in tabular form (Table 2):

*Table 2. Merton's Comparison Between the Sociology of Knowledge
and Mass Communications*

Aspects	Sociology of Knowledge (European)	Mass Communications (American)
Subject matter and definition of problems	Knowledge Bodies of systematically connected facts or ideas Total structure of knowledge available to a few	Information Isolated fragments of information available to masses of people
Data and facts	Historical Long-range Impressions of mass opinion set down by a few observers as facts	Contemporary Short-range Collection of facts
	Chief question: "why" Chief concern: problem, even if specula-tion is the best that can be done	Chief question: "what" Chief concern: securing adequate empirical da-ta, even if the problem gets lost
	Studies and findings are important, even if em-pirically questionable	Studies and findings may be trivial but are empirically rigorous

Table 2. Merton's Comparison Between the Sociology of Knowledge
and Mass Communications (contd.)

Aspects	Sociology of Knowledge (European)	Mass Communications (American)
Research techniques and procedures	Limited to the authentication of documents	A considerable array of various techniques
	Reliability is no problem	Reliability is an important problem
	A tradition in and from the history of different interpretations of the same data; a humanities background	No such tradition and background
	Cumulative nature of findings not stressed	Cumulative nature of findings is stressed
	No audience research because the chief question is the "why" or "how come" of the intellectual phenomena investigated	Emphasis on audience research because the chief question is the "what" or "what impact" of the intellectual phenomena investigated
	Impetus behind the studies is academic	Impetus behind the studies is practical (market and military research, propaganda, etc.) [70]
Social organization of research	Lone wolf	Team
	No organizational pressure toward reliability	Organizational pressure toward reliability
Social origins of investigators (tentative)	Investigators are marginal to different social systems and perceive diverse intellectual perspectives of different groups	Investigators are mobile within an economic or social system and get data needed by those who operate organizations, seek markets, and control many people

It is hardly necessary to insist that Merton's comparison of the sociology of knowledge and the study of mass communications largely agrees with that of the sociology of knowledge and American sociology, presented in this chapter. (It is true, of course, that each of the two efforts has commented on aspects ignored by the other; most obviously, the present essay has left out of consideration the last two of Merton's five categories, the social organization of research and the social origins of investigators.) Translating Merton's characterizations which touch most closely on our enterprise into the language of the latter, we obtain the following propositions:

1. According to subject matter and definition of problems, the sociology of knowledge examines intellectual life as a whole, whereas mass communications takes it for granted as it finds it and explores features that unexamined traditions have made problematical (cf. the last entry under "Research techniques and procedures" in the "Mass Communications" column of Table 2); the former is practiced in a philosophical-anthropological and historical sense, the latter is unsystematically contemporary.

2. For its data and facts the sociology of knowledge is guided by history, existential truth, causality, the nature of knowledge and of intersubjectivity itself, whereas mass communications strives to register the pulse of opinion with scientifically unimpeachable methods.

3. Research techniques and procedures for the sociology of knowledge are secondary, whereas for mass communications they tend to be primary, self-consummatory, and self-proliferating; the former is in the service of culture, the latter, of civilization [71].

Aside from these all too abbreviated comments on the content of these and Merton's characterizations, a word must be said about the difference between their volitional premises and criteria of truth. Merton wishes to establish true propositions concerning similarities and differences between the sociology of knowledge and communications research. He operates with the scientific conception of truth in line with the scientific approach and, more specifically, with his effort to codify extant theory and research. By contrast, what has been said in the preceding pages has affirmed the historical perspective in which it was stated as well as the effort to arrive at existential truth. To put it differently, Merton's chief concern is "what" (a characteristic of the right-hand column in Table 2); mine is "why" or "how come" (a characteristic of the left-hand column). Merton's analysis, and the translation of some of his own hopes stated in the text on which Table 2 is based, shows us gaps in the attention to scientific problems to be filled by scientific propositions, whereas the European column shows gaps in the attention to existential problems to be filled by existentially true propositions.

It should be noted, however, that what has just been said claims to be true in the scientific sense of the term. Its attitude is the same as that of Merton's analysis. What it talks about, however, is different, namely existential truth, on which Merton is silent. To discuss the nature of truth, as is widely recognized, is not the scientist's but the philosopher's concern. It is also widely recognized that it is important to distinguish between talking about one's own views of truth, which is considered a philosophical enterprise, and about somebody else's, which is accepted as a legitimate scientific enterprise. In expounding my own views of truth in this chapter, I have sometimes talked as a philosopher (in the philosophical attitude); in commenting on Merton's, I have talked as a scientist. Social science, in contrast to natural science, is concerned, no matter how indirectly, with human beings, that is, fellow men. At least *at this time* (which I have tried to characterize)—and we have no other—social science has to start, I have argued, with this time, with the historical situation. To grasp the historical situation and communicate the process of grasping it, as this process has been going on in the making of this chapter, I had to suspend (bracket) the safety that comes from limitation to scientific truth and open myself (surrender) to existential truth. On the occasion of commenting on Merton's paradigm I have returned to the scientific attitude.

THE SOCIOLOGY OF KNOWLEDGE
AND SOCIOLOGICAL THEORY

By now the reader may have long forgotten the title of this chapter. Actually, however, this entire chapter has dealt with the relation between the sociology of knowledge and sociological theory, as a concluding summary of what it has to say about this shows.

First, let us list some of the things it has nothing to say about.

1. It has nothing to say about the relation between the sociology of knowledge and sociological theory that might be disclosed by an analysis of the work of sociologists of knowledge and sociological theorists.

2. It has no recommendation to make concerning the way in which a scientific study is carried out.

3. It offers no list of scientific problems to be investigated under the program of a sociology of knowledge it conceives of; in the present context this is too large a topic [72].

4. It urges no particular definition of sociological theory.

At this point we must make an observation about sociological theory that will lead us to the more positive statements we have to submit. It is that, with only one exception that I know of [73], the relatively few extant definitions of the term sociological theory—to the extent that they go beyond elevating a casual collection of colloquial referents to definitional status—are much more specific about its formal features [74]—what its structure is like or how it is constructed—than about its content or what it is *about*. It is almost as if sociology, in relation to which they try to define theory, had no specific content. This suggests that these conceptions of theory do not regard human beings, the subject matter of sociology, of sufficient theoretical dignity to incorporate them into a definition of sociological theory. It is a further indication of their corresponding concepts of sociology.

This observation concerning sociological theory is the major reason why this chapter has proceeded as it has. Thus it has had to say much more about modern American sociology in general than about sociological theory or particular theories. Modern sociology and sociological theory are so intimately connected that a historical analysis has appeared to be a more adequate tool for identifying them than a systematic analysis would have been. A systematic analysis could easily fall prey to the temptation to take sociology and sociological theory at their face value. It is hoped, however, that this chapter may help clear the ground for such an analysis.

If we put positively what the last three paragraphs have said in the negative, we can formulate what this chapter has to say about the relations between the sociology of knowledge and sociological theory.

1. The analysis of the sociology of knowledge in the context of our time appears to make it incumbent on sociological theory to define itself, either in a way that is adequate to the subject matter of sociology and to the historical occasion of the definition, or to disprove the relevance of this double requirement of adequacy.

2. The existing, overwhelmingly social-historically nominalistic sociological theory appears to make it incumbent on the sociology of knowledge (reinspect the unfavorable items in the left-hand column of Table 2) to clarify its status in reference to scientific versus existential truth, science versus history, and science versus philosophy. As it is, the sociology of knowledge is two things. One, particularly in America, is dead. The other is not yet—it is a heap of fragments and shoots waiting to be given form and life. Dead is the excitement attendant on the appearance of Mannheim's *Ideology and Utopia*. It would be good if this chapter had managed to show that the excitement had a greater claim than that of a fad, and that there is hope of recalling its origin in a confrontation of sociology with history, existential truth, and philosophy. Not yet alive are two potentialities of the sociology of knowledge. The first is the codification

of the great mass of relevant research into a more viable sociology of intellectual life. The other, different, even though causally related, is the injection of more self-conscious humanness and historicity, and thus greater scientific relevance, into contemporary sociology.

Acknowledgment. I am deeply indebted to John W. Bennett and Llewellyn Gross, and also to Aron Gurwitsch, Paul Kecskemeti, Anthony Nemetz, Talcott Parsons, Alfred Schutz, and Melvin Seeman for critical readings of earlier drafts of this paper and for their pertinent comments. Unfortunately I have not been able to act on all of them.

NOTES

1. Jacques J. Maquet *(Sociologie de la connaissance: sa structure et ses rapports avec la philosophie de la connaissance; étude critique des systèmes de Karl Mannheim et de Pitirim A. Sorokin* [Louvain: Institut de Recherches Economiques et Sociales; E. Nauwalaerts, Ed., 1949], p. 19; *The Sociology of Knowledge: Its Structure and Its Relation to the Philosophy of Knowledge: A Critical Analysis of the Systems of Karl Mannheim and Pitirim A. Sorokin,* translated by John F. Locke [Boston: Beacon, 1951], p. 3) claims that "knowledge" in "sociology of knowledge" has greater denotations than *wissen,* which, "taken as a whole, means science, whereas 'knowledge' includes at the same time the simple act of presenting an object to the mind . . . and the act of thinking which reaches a complete understanding of this object." This greater denotation means that the German term connotes a higher claim to certainty than the French and English terms (to the latter of which corresponds the German *kennen,* not *erkennen,* as Maquet writes). By the criterion of the relation of knower to known, however, *wissen* is broader than knowledge, inasmuch as it refers not only to the scientist and his scientific knowledge but also to philosopher, artist, mystic, and religious person and their respective kinds of knowledge. For common-sense questions concerning the meanings of these terms this is the more expected criterion. It thus appears to be less misleading to say that *wissen* has a broader meaning than knowledge.

2. Along with historicism [cf. T. B. Bottomore, "Some Reflections on the Sociology of Knowledge," *British Journal of Sociology,* 7 (March 1956), 52–58, especially 52] and Nietzsche, leading to Freud and Pareto and the related current of positivism (Ratzenhofer, Gumplowicz, Oppenheimer, and Jerusalem: cf.

Karl Mannheim, "The Sociology of Knowledge" (1931), *Ideology and Utopia, op. cit.,* pp. 278–279). For the history of the sociology of knowledge and a critique of the major ideas advanced by its various factions, see Ernst Grünwald, *Das Problem der Soziologie des Wissens* (Wien-Leipzig: Braumüller, 1934). For the significance of Marxism see Robert K. Merton, "The Sociology of Knowledge," in Georges Gurvitch and Wilbert E. Moore, Eds., *Twentieth Century Sociology* (New York: Philosophical Library, 1945), Chapter XIII, *passim* [reprinted in Merton, *Social Theory and Social Structure: Toward the Codification of Theory and Research* (Glencoe, Ill.: Free Press, 1949), Chapter VIII; revised and enlarged edition (*ibid.,* 1957), Chapter XII]. For a collection of relevant texts by Marx himself, some of them previously untranslated, see Karl Marx, *Selected Writings in Sociology and Social Philosophy*, edited and with an introduction and notes by T. B. Bottomore and Maximilien Rubel (London: Watts, 1956), including the editors' introduction.

3. This term was coined in the early 1920s. It was subsequently taken over in translation. For French, Dutch, and Italian versions see Maquet, *The Sociology of Knowledge, op. cit.,* p. 261, n. 1.

4. Hans-Joachim Lieber, *Wissen und Gesellschaft: Die Probleme der Wissenssoziologie* (Tübingen: Max Niemeyer, 1952): Mannheim, *Ideologie und Utopie,* 3rd ed. (Frankfurt/Main: G. Schulte-Bulmke, 1952).

5. Max Scheler, "Probleme einer Soziologie des Wissens," in Scheler, Ed., *Versuche zu einer Soziologie des Wissens* (München: Duncker und Humblot, 1924), pp. 5–146; enlarged under the same title in Scheler, *Die Wissensformen und die Gesellschaft* (Leipzig: Der neue Geist Verlag, 1926), pp. 1–229; Mannheim, *Ideologie und Utopie* (Bonn: Friedrich Cohen, 1929).

6. Mannheim, *Ideology and Utopia, loc. cit.*

7. Louis Wirth, Preface to Mannheim, *op. cit.,* pp. xvii-xxiii [reprinted in Wirth, *Community Life and Social Policy*, Elizabeth Wirth Marvick and Albert J. Reiss, Jr., Eds. (Chicago: University of Chicago Press, 1956), especially pp. 40–45].

8. On the other hand, there probably is an affinity between the sociology of knowledge and a European outlook. A good deal of what I have to say later in this chapter bears on this affinity, although I do not analyze it explicitly.

9. [See Chapter 7, n. 14.]

10. Merton, "The Sociology of Knowledge," *loc. cit.*

11. Wirth, *op. cit.* See also Franz Adler, "The Sociology of Knowledge Since 1918," *Midwest Sociologist,* **17** (Spring 1955), 3 ff.

12. Kurt H. Wolff, "A Preliminary Inquiry into the Sociology of Knowledge from the Standpoint of the Study of Man," *op. cit.* p. 586 (henceforth *Inquiry*). [Chapter 7].

13. Louis Wirth, quoted in Howard W. Odum, *American Sociology: The Story of Sociology in the United States through 1950* (New York: Longmans, Green, 1951), p. 231.

14.   In his "Paradigm for the Sociology of Knowledge," Merton (*op. cit.*, p. 372, reprinted, *op. cit.*, pp. 221–222; rev. ed., pp. 460–461) uses "mental productions" without, however, advocating their sociology as a substitute for sociology of knowledge.

15.   Karl Mannheim, *Essays on the Sociology of Culture*, edited by Ernest Manheim in cooperation with Paul Kecskemeti (New York: Oxford University Press, 1956), Part 1, "Towards the Sociology of the Mind: an Introduction."

16.   Gerard DeGré, "The Sociology of Knowledge and the Problem of Truth," *Journal of the History of Ideas*, 2 (January 1941), 110.

17.   Wolff, *Inquiry*, p. 587 [Chapter 7]. See also Franz Adler, "The Range of Sociology of Knowledge," in Howard Becker and Alvin Boskoff, Eds., *Modern Sociological Theory in Continuity and Change* (New York: Dryden Press, 1957), Chapter 13. An attempt at assembling relevant materials, though in a rather haphazard and exceedingly incomplete manner, is my *The Sociology of Knowledge: A Preliminary Bibliography* [Columbus: Ohio State University, Department of Sociology and Anthropology, 1945 (mimeographed); "Additions," 1951]. Despite its serious shortcomings and its preliminary character, it is more comprehensive than others, among which Mannheim's (*Ideology and Utopia, op. cit.*, pp. 281–304, augmented in the 1952 German edition of *Ideologie und Utopie, op. cit.*, pp. 269–291) is the most important. For a comprehensive, indispensable, and only slightly overlapping bibliography on the sociology of literature see Hugh Dalziel Duncan, *Language and Literature in Society: A Sociological Essay on Theory and Method in the Interpretation of Linguistic Symbols, with a Bibliographical Guide to the Sociology of Literature* (Chicago: University of Chicago Press, 1953), pp. 143–214.

18.   [Chapter 7, ns. 5-8.]

19.   [Chapter 7, n. 3.]

20.   [Chapter 7, n. 4.]

21.   Leo P. Chall, "The Sociology of Knowledge," in Joseph S. Roucek, Ed., *Contemporary Sociology* (New York: Philosophical Library, 1958), p. 284.

22.   For Robert K. Merton, see his chronological bibliography in *Social Theory and Social Structure, op. cit.*, pp. 409–412. In regard to C. Wright Mills, compare his early work in the sociology of knowledge [e.g., "Methodological Consequences of the Sociology of Knowledge" *American Journal of Sociology*, 46 (November 1940), 316–330] with his later books on labor leaders, white-collar workers, and the power elite. Gerard DeGré [*op. cit.*, and *Society and Ideology: An Inquiry into the Sociology of Science* (Garden City, N.Y.: Doubleday, 1955); this study, however, shows that DeGré has not abandoned his interest in the sociology of knowledge proper; see especially pp. 34–37]. Frank E. Hartung, on the other hnd, has continued to publish from time to time in the field since 1944 [e.g., "The Sociology of Positivism," *Science and Society*, 8 (Fall 1944), 328–341; "Problems of the Sociology of Knowledge," *Philosophy of Science*, 19 (January 1952), 17–32]. For Howard Becker and Pitirim A. Sorokin the sociology of knowledge has never been central; cf. Becker and Helmut Otto Dahlke,

"Max Scheler's Sociology of Knowledge," *Philosophy and Phenomenological Research*, **2** (March 1942), 309–322; Sorokin, *Social and Cultural Dynamics*, Vol. II, *Fluctuation of Systems of Truth, Ethics, and Law* (New York: American Book, 1937), "a treatise in *Wissenssoziologie*, considered in its basic forms and principles" (*ibid.*, p. vii); Sorokin has been treated as a sociologist of knowledge by Merton, "The Sociology and Knowledge," *op. cit.*, and Maquet, *op. cit.*

23. Arthur Child, following his extended work in the sociology of knowledge, has turned to problems of philosophy of history; his "Moral Judgment in History," *Ethics*, **51** (July 1951), 297–308, is a connecting link. Virgil G. Hinshaw, Jr., has moved from the sociology of knowledge, especially the critique of Mannheim's epistemological claims ["The Epistemological Relevance of Mannheim's Sociology of Knowledge," *Journal of Philosophy*, **40** (February 4, 1943), 57–72 *(Relevance)*], to epistemology ["Basic Propositions in Lewis's Analysis of Knowledge," *ibid.*, **46** (March 31, 1949), 176–184] and philosophy of science ["Levels of Analysis," *Philosophy and Phenomenological Research*, **11** (December 1950), 213–220]. Thelma Z. Lavine ["Sociological Analysis of Cognitive Norms," *Journal of Philosophy*, **39** (June 18, 1942), 342–356] has subsequently undertaken studies in the history of epistemology ["Knowledge as Interpretation: An Historical Survey," *Philosophy and Phenomenological Research*, **10** (June 1950), 526–540, and **11** (September 1950), 88–103].

24. The purpose of this essay is not, of course, a critique of Mannheim's concepts. They have received abundant and incisive examination. To mention only the more painstaking analyses in English (except for the first) in chronological order, Alexander von Schelting, *Max Weber's Wissenschaftslehre; das logische Problem der historischen Kulturerkenntnis; die Grenzen der Soziologie des Wissens* (Tübingen: Mohr, 1934), pp. 94–100, 117–167, and his review of Mannheim's *Ideologie und Utopie*, *American Sociological Review*, **1** (August 1936), 664–674; Hans Speier, review of Mannheim's *Ideology and Utopia*, *American Journal of Sociology*, **43** (July 1937), 155–166; Maurice Mandelbaum, *The Problem of Historical Knowledge: An Answer to Relativism* (New York: Liveright, 1938), pp. 67–82; Child, *Imputation*, 204–207, *Possibility*, 410–411, *Truth*, 20–21; Robert K. Merton, "Karl Mannheim and the Sociology of Knowledge," *Journal of Liberal Religion*, **2** (Winter 1941), 125–147 (reprinted in *Social Theory and Social Structure*, *op. cit.*, Chapter IX; rev. ed., Chapter XIII); Hinshaw, *Relevance*; Maquet, *op. cit.*, especially Chapters 3 and 5.

25. Peter M. Blau, *Bureaucracy in Modern Society* (New York: Random House, 1956), p. 14.

26. On secularization see Max Weber, "The Protestant Sects and the Spirit of Capitalism" (1906) in *From Max Weber: Essays in Sociology*, translated, edited, and with an introduction by H. H. Gerth and C. Wright Mills (New York: Oxford University Press, 1946), p. 307; Talcott Parsons, *The Structure of Social Action* (New York: McGraw-Hill, 1937), pp. 685–686; and, one of the most searching recent analyses, Hannah Arendt, "History and Immortality," *Partisan Review*, **24** (Winter 1957), especially 16–22. On rationalization see *From Max Weber, op. cit.*, "Introduction," pp. 51–52.

27. Max Horkheimer, *Eclipse of Reason* (New York: Oxford University Press, 1947), pp. 3–4, *passim*. Here the discussion of value judgments in social science is relevant. See especially Max Weber, *On the Methodology of the Social Sciences*, translated and edited by Edward A. Shils and Henry A. Finch (Glencoe, Ill.: Free Press, 1949); Felix Kaufmann, *Methodology of the Social Sciences* (New York: Oxford University Press, 1944), Chapters IX and XV; Leo Strauss, *Natural Right and History* (Chicago: University of Chicago Press, 1953), Chapter II; Dwight Macdonald, *The Root Is Man: Two Essays in Politics* (Alhambra, Calif.: Cunningham, 1953), "Scientific Method and Value Judgment," pp. 36–39; Joseph Wood Krutch, *The Measure of Man* (1953, 1954) (New York: Grosset and Dunlap, n.d.), especially Chapter 4.

28. Despite terminological appearance possibly to the contrary, subjective reason is much closer to Mannheim's functional than to his substantial rationality (the unclarity in which he left the latter concept itself shows the loss of objective rationality): Karl Mannheim, *Man and Society in an Age of Reconstruction* (1935) (New York: Harcourt, Brace, 1940), pp. 52–60.

29. This experience is probably exhibited more poignantly by Max Weber than by any other social scientist. See Weber, "'Objectivity' in Social Science and Social Policy" (1904), *On the Methodology of the Social Sciences, op. cit.*, pp. 52–57; "The Meaning of 'Ethical Neutrality' in Sociology and Economics" (1913, 1917), *ibid.*, pp. 11–15, 18–21; "Science as a Vocation" (1918), *From Max Weber, op. cit.*, pp. 148, 152–153. Leo Strauss, *op. cit.*, has clearly described and criticized Weber's position.

30. On futile attempts at deriving Ought from Is, that is, on the naturalistic fallacy, see Eliseo Vivas, *The Moral Life and the Ethical Life* (Chicago: University of Chicago Press, 1950), Part I, "Animadversions upon Naturalistic Moral Philosophies," *passim,* especially pp. 81–82.

31. In an important if not the essential respect Erich Kahler's *The Tower and the Abyss: An Inquiry into the Transformation of the Individual* (New York: Braziller, 1957) is a history of contemporary consciousness.

32. David Riesman, in collaboration with Reuel Denney and Nathan Glazer, *The Lonely Crowd: A Study of the Changing American Character* (New Haven: Yale University Press, 1950), Part III, "Autonomy," especially pp. 287–288 (Anchor edition, 1953, p. 278); Erich Fromm, *Man for Himself: An Inquiry into the Psychology of Ethics* (New York: Rinehart, 1947), pp. 82–107.

33. Fedor Dostoevsky, *The Idiot* (1869), translated with an introduction by David Magarshack (Penguin, 1955), p. 563.

34. Cf. my "The World as Underdeveloped," *Atti del Congresso internazionale di studio sul problema delle aree arretrate* (Milan: Giuffre, 1955), Vol. III, *Communicazioni*, pp. 505–508.

35. The literary record of these social scientists is impressive and important. Cf. Edward H. Spicer, Ed., *Human Problems in Technological Change: A Case Book* (New York: Russell Sage, 1952), *Human Organization*, official journal of the Society for Applied Anthropology; the increasing attention to relevant

problems in several social-scientific periodicals, especially in anthropology and sociology, including certain issues of the *Annals of the American Academy of Political and Social Science,* such as Vol. 305, "Agrarian Societies in Transition" (May 1956). For representative statements on problems of applied anthropology see *Anthropology Today: An Encyclopedic Inventory,* prepared under the chairmanship of A. L. Kroeber (Chicago: University of Chicago Press, 1953), "Problems of Application," pp. 741–894; Sol Tax, Loren C. Eisely, Irving Rouse, and Carl F. Voeglin, Eds., *An Appraisal of Anthropology Today (ibid.),* Chapters X and XI; William L. Thomas, Jr., Ed., *Yearbook of Anthropology—1955* (New York: Wenner-Gren Foundation for Anthropological Research, 1955), Parts 4 and 5, *passim;* the symposium on applied anthropology at the 1957 meetings of the American Anthropological Association [*Human Organization,* **17** 1 (Spring 1958), "Values in Action: A Symposium, 2–26]. Note also the recent collaboration of several social sciences, including history and economics, on common problems (in contrast to the more accustomed interdisciplinary work among sociologists, anthropologists, psychologists, psychiatrists, and psychoanalysts); see especially Mirra Komarovsky, Ed., *Common Frontiers of the Social Sciences* (Glencoe, Ill.: Free Press and Falcon's Wing Press, 1957), and Karl Polanyi, Conrad Arensberg, and Harry Pearson, Eds., *Trade and Market in the Early Empires (ibid.,* 1957). Here also belongs Robert Redfield's qualification of the folk-urban dichotomy by his emphasis on the distinction between great and little traditions; see especially his *Peasant Society and Culture: An Anthropological Approach to Civilization* (Chicago: University of Chicago Press, 1956). This qualification appears to be particularly significant when the folk-urban dichotomy is seen alongside other civilizational and historical dichotomies in their attempts to come to terms with the emerging one world. A more specific correction of the outlook represented in them (according to which earlier or non-Western societies are characterized by sacredness, status, and ascription) is constituted by the discovery of the significance of kinship relations in societies characterized by secularization, contract, and achievement. Cf. Talcott Parsons, "The Kinship System of the Contemporary United States" (1943), Essays in *Sociological Theory, Pure and Applied* (Glencoe, Ill.: Free Press, 1949), Chapter XI [rev. ed. *(ibid.,* 1954), Chapter IX], Michael Young and Peter Willmott, *Family and Kinship in East London (ibid.,* 1957), and Leo A. Despres, "A Function of Bilateral Kinship Patterns in a New England Industry," *Human Organization,* **17,** 2 (Summer 1958), 15–22.

36. This dialectic between subjective and objective reason parallels Herbert Marcuse's between the performance (reality) principle and the pleasure principle: *Eros and Civilization: A Philosophical Inquiry into Freud* (Boston: Beacon, 1955). Space limitations forbid an examination of Marcuse's thesis.

37. This is a proposition more pointed to than explicitly made by some of the students of the most spontaneous, unconscious, varied part of culture, namely language. See especially the work of Dorothy D. Lee [particularly "Conceptual Implications of an Indian Language," *Philosophy of Science,* **5** (January 1938), 89–102; "A Primitive System of Values," *ibid.,* **7** (July 1940), 355–378;

"Lineal and Non-Lineal Codifications of Reality" (1950), *Explorations,* **7** (March 1957), 30–45, in which she says, "If reality itself were not absolute, then true communication of course would be impossible. My own position is that there is an absolute reality, and that communication is possible" (30)] and Benjamin Lee Whorf [particularly "A Linguistic Consideration of Thinking in Primitive Communities" (1936?), "Languages and Logic" (1941), and "Language, Mind, and Reality" (1941), all reprinted in *Language, Thought, and Reality: Selected Writings of Benjamin Lee Whorf,* edited and with an introduction by John B. Carroll (Cambridge, Mass., and New York: M.I.T. Press and Wiley, 1956)].

38. This distinction is developed by Child (*Categories*) and expounded in my "The Unique and the General: Toward a Philosophy of Sociology," *Philosophy and Science,* 15 (July 1948), 203-204 [Chapter 6], and more fully, *Inquiry,* 595-600 [Chapter 7].

39. Karl Mannheim, "The Problem of a Sociology of Knowledge (1925), Chapter IV, pp. 134–190, in *Essays on the Sociology of Knowledge, op. cit.,* pp. 136–144. [Reprinted in *From Karl Mannheim, op. cit.,* pp. 59–115.]

40. *Ibid.,* p. 136. Although the first, third, and fourth factors can be accounted for in terms of the immanent development of ideas, the second, the unmasking turn of mind, must be understood in terms of real, social developments which resulted in the rise of the oppositional science of sociology from Humanism and Enlightenment with their main task, the disintegration of the monarchy and the clergy (*ibid.,* pp. 139–140). Now that we are "increasingly aware of the fact that *all* thinking of a social group is determined by its existence, we find less and less room for the exercise of 'unmasking,' and the latter undergoes a process of sublimation which turns it into a mere operation of determining the functional role of any thought whatever" (*ibid.,* p. 144).

41. My attention to whom has been called by Professor Alfred Schutz, as I herewith gratefully acknowledge.

42. Cf. Wirth, *op. cit.,* pp. xiii, xvii, xxiii.

43. Mannheim, *op. cit.,* p. 139.

44. Merton, *Social Theory and Social Structure, op. cit.,* pp. 457, 458. See also H. Otto Dahlke, "The Sociology of Knowledge," in Harry Elmer Barnes, Howard Becker, and Frances Bennett Becker, Eds., *Contemporary Social Theory* (New York: Appleton-Century, 1940), pp. 64–65.

45. Wolff, *Inquiry* [Chapter 7 — the remainder of this section is a brief repetition].

46. In John Dewey's meaning, developed by Thelma Z. Lavine ["Naturalism and the Sociological Analysis of Knowledge," in Yervant H. Krikorian, Ed., *Naturalism and the Human Spirit* (New York: Columbia University Press, 1944), p. 184].

47. Wolff, *Inquiry,* 612 [Chapter 7].

48. Predominantly if (in addition to propositions) truth is also considered predicable of definitions. It can be so considered if a cognitive function of the

operational character of definitions is emphasized: in this case definition borders on hypothesis. It cannot be if a definition is considered an analytical proposition and nothing else: in this case it has no truth dimension; of course the *use* of the definition (in methodology or research) has, namely that of stipulative (hypothetical, propositional) truth.

49. On the concept of surrender see my "Before and After Sociology," *Transactions of the Third World Congress of Sociology*, Vol. VII, pp. 151-152, and more fully, *Loma Culture Change: An Introduction to the Study of Man* (Columbus, Ohio State University, 1952 [mimeographed]), "Introduction," pp. 22 ff. [Also see Chapter 8, n. 5.] It is a not irrelevant characterization of our time that one should be led to ask, in a footnote, whether the concern exhibited here with existential truth will not alienate professional colleagues or, hyperbolically, whether, in trying to save my life and the world, I am not risking the loss of my profession.

50. Paul Kecskemeti, "Introduction," Chapter I in Mannheim, *Essays on the Sociology of Knowledge, op. cit.*, pp. 15, 31. The difference between scientific and existential truth corresponds in a way that cannot be discussed here to that between mathematical and inner time (*durée*; on the latter see Alfred Schuetz "On Multiple Realities," *Philosophy and Phenomenological Research*, **5** (June 1945), 538–542; Pitirim A. Sorokin, *Sociocultural Causality, Space, Time* (Durham, N.C.: Duke Univesrity Press, 1943), Chapter IV; Igor Stravinsky, *Poetics of Music in the Form of Six Lessons* (1939–1940) (New York: Vintage, 1956), pp. 31–34.

51. Roscoe C. Hinkle, Jr., and Gisela J. Hinkle, *The Development of Modern Sociology: Its Nature and Growth in the United States* (Garden City, N.Y.: Doubleday, 1954), pp. vii, 73, 74.

52. Ernest Manheim, "Introduction" to Karl Mannheim, *Essays on the Sociology of Culture, op. cit.*, p. 5 (original italics).

53. [See the next chapter.] Cf. Grünwald, *op. cit.*, Chapter I. (This important work has not been adequately appreciated in this country. Aside from a few citations there is only, as far as I know, Child's analysis of Grünwald's own position [in several of Child's papers on the sociology of knowledge referred to in Chapter 7, n. 14] and a brief exposition of parts of it in Adler, "The Range of Sociology of Knowledge," *op. cit.*, pp. 412–413.) [Portions of Grünwald's book have since been translated by Rainer Koehne and published in James F. Curtis and John W. Petras, Eds., *The Sociology of Knowledge: A Reader* (New York: Praeger, 1970), pp. 187–243.] A more detailed presentation and critique of Grünwald's discussion of the psychological and historical theories, although relevant and highly interesting, exceeds the scope of this chapter. The central significance of his own position on the sociology of knowledge, however, must be registered. This position is what might be called "interpretational relativism": according to Grünwald, the sociology of knowledge is only one among many equally valid or invalid interpretations of intellectual phenomena. (It has also, and rightly, been designated as "postulational skepticism": Child, *Possibility*, p. 404; Wolff, *Inquiry*

[Chapter 28], 592–593, especially n. 21 [Chapter 10].) If we ask how it is possible that a number of interpretations can be entertained, that is, if we inquire into the basis of interpretational relativism, we find that interpreter and interpretandum emerge as relatively unanalyzable presuppositions or "givens." We find the dualism of reality to be relative and absolute—the same dualism we came on as a metaphysical premise of the sociology of knowledge. If this dualism is in turn posited in some sense as optional, the burden of proof rests on the exploration of this positing by which the continuity of analysis is made both possible and mandatory. This consideration vindicates the continuity of analysis (naturalism), the second metaphysical premise of the sociology of knowledge.

54. Merton, *Social Theory and Social Structure, op. cit.,* p. 449.

55. Many examples of such articulations are given and analyzed in Kahler, *op. cit.,* Chapters 4 and 5.

56. Wolff, *Inquiry,* 618 [Chapter 7].

57. Godfrey and Monica Wilson, *The Analysis of Social Change on the Basis of Observations in Central Africa* (Cambridge: University Press, 1945). For a convenient conspectus of many such dichotomies (and trichotomies) see Howard Becker, *Through Values to Social Interpretation* (Durham, N.C.: Duke University Press, 1950), pp. 258–261.

58. David Riesman, "Some Observations on the Study of American Character," *Psychiatry,* 15 (August 1952), 333.

59. Emile Durkheim, *The Division of Labor in Society* (1893), translated by George Simpson (Glencoe, Ill.: Free Press, 1947), preface to the second edition (1902), "Some Notes on Occupational Groups," and, particularly, *Professional Ethics and Civic Morals* (1890s), translated by Cornelia Brookfield (London: Routledge & Kegan Paul, 1957), Chapters I-III; Max Weber, "Science as a Vocation," *op. cit.,* p. 153; ". . . . the decisive state of affairs: the prophet . . . simply does not exist"; Karl Mannheim, *Essays on the Sociology of Culture, loc. cit.,* "The Problem of Ecstasy" [in "The Democratization of Culture" (1933)], the argument of which the translator, Paul Kecskemeti, characterizes (*ibid.,* p. 239, n. 1) as the "necessity to transcend the purely pragmatist and positivist approach"; Mannheim himself writes: "We inherited from our past another need: that of severing from time to time *all* connection with life and with the contingencies of our existence. We shall designate this ideal by the term 'ecstasy' " (*ibid.,* p. 240).

60. Related to these civilizational-historical dichotomies is that between culture and civilization, independently formulated by Alfred Weber and Robert M. MacIver [cf. Alfred Weber, "Der soziologische Kulturbegriff" (1912), *Ideen zur Staats- und Kultursoziologie* (Karlsruhe: Braun, 1927), pp. 31–47; *Kulturgeschichte als Kultursoziologie* (Leiden: Sijthoff, 1935), pp. 9–10, 421. MacIver has discussed the distinction in numerous places, from *Community* (London: Macmillan, 1917), pp. 179–180, to MacIver and Charles H. Page, *Society* (New York: Rinehart, 1949), pp. 446, 486–487, 498–506]. See also Robert

K. Merton, "Civilization and Culture," *Sociology and Social Research,* 21 (November-December, 1936), 103–113, and Howard Becker, *op. cit.,* pp. 165–168. In reference to the present chapter this distinction has a twofold significance: (1) It is a formulation of a dualism that parallels, within culture itself, that between what has been called here transcultural human nature and human culture. (2) It is an attempt at preserving historical continuity (through culture) and at the same time independence from it (civilization)—that is, at preserving both the absolute and the relative in man.

61. Its most dramatic expression is probably the confusion of Soviet communism with a historically more adequate version of liberalism and the shock, if not despair, on the realization of this confusion. See such works as Arthur Koestler, Ignazio Silone, Richard Wright, André Gide, Louis Fischer, and Stephen Spender, *The God That Failed* (New York: Bantam, 1952).

62. Reinhard Bendix, *Social Science and the Distrust of Reason* (Berkeley; University of California Press, 1951). See also Institut für Sozialforschung, *Soziologische Exurse, nach Vorträgen und Diskussionen* (Frankfurt am Main: Europäische Verlagsanstalt, 1956), Chapter XII, "Ideologie." Both this chapter and Bendix, *loc. cit.,* draw heavily on Hans Barth, *Wahrheit and Ideologie* (Zurich: Manesse, 1945). Chapter I of the Frankfurt volume ("Begriff der Soziologie") is an impressive description of the fate of social thought, beginning with Plato, in its shift toward sociology (Comte) and of the development of sociology itself to the present time. Among the various but rare critiques of modern sociology this and Bendix's are important. In this context special attention should also be called to C. Wright Mills, " 'The Power Elite': Comment on Criticism," *Dissent,* 4 (Winter 1957), 22–34.

63. Portrayed more in fiction than in social science, but see C. Wright Mills, *White Collar: The American Middle Classes* (New York: Oxford University Press, 1951), Part 3, and William H. Whyte, Jr., *The Organization Man* (New York: Simon and Schuster, 1956), Parts VI and VII.

64. See my "Before and After Sociology," *op. cit.,* p. 153, "Sociology and History; Theory and Practice" [Chapter 3], and John W. Bennett and Kurt H. Wolff, "Toward Communication between Sociology and Anthropology," William L. Thomas, Jr., Ed., *Yearbook of Anthropology—1955, op. cit.,* p. 330 [reprinted in William L. Thomas, Jr., Ed., *Current Anthropology: A Supplement to Anthropology Today* (Chicago: University of Chicago Press, 1956), same pagination].

65. This, on the surface of it, would appear to contradict Alfred Schuetz's characterization of the world of scientific theory (in his "On Multiple Realities," *op. cit.,* 563–575) but actually seems to be a consequence of affirming his proposition "that sociality and communication can be realized only within . . . the world of everyday life which is the paramount reality" *(ibid.,* 575). Space limitations make it impossible to enter into discussion of this important, if not crucial, question of the philosophy of science.

66. This meaning of substantive, in contrast to formalistic, is obviously different from H. Otto Dahlke's *(op. cit., passim, e.g.,* p. 86) or from Mannheim's

"empirical" (*Ideology and Utopia, op. cit.,* pp. 239 ff.), both of which contrast with epistemological.

67.   Compare Durkheim's *Rules of Sociological Method* (1895) or "The Determination of Moral Facts" (1906), Chapter II in *Sociology and Philosophy,* translated by D. F. Pocock, with an introduction by J. G. Peristiany (Glencoe, Ill.: Free Press, 1953), with his concern about anomie (cf. n. 59), or *Weber's Methodology of the Social Sciences, loc. cit.,* with his *Protestant Ethic,* and, on the discrepancy between Weber's methodological prescriptions for practice and his practice itself: Leo Strauss, *loc. cit.* [I am not acquainted with a corresponding analysis of Durkheim's work; see, however, some relevant observations in my "The Challenge of Durkheim and Simmel," *American Journal of Sociology,* 63 (May 1958), 590-596].

68.   In respect to American sociology, cf. the Hinkles' remark quoted above. On the unrivaled position of liberalism in American political and social thought, cf. Louis Hartz, *The Liberal Tradition in America: An Interpretation of American Political Thought Since the Revolution* (New York: Harcourt, Brace, 1955).

69.   Merton, *Social Theory and Social Structure,* Part III, "The Sociology of Knowledge and Mass Communications," *op. cit.,* pp. 439–455. The quotation is from p. 439.

70.   "Such dynamic categories, with little direct bearing on commercial interests, as 'false consciousness' . . . have as yet played little part in the description of audiences" (*ibid.,* pp. 451–452). Merton asks whether communications research may one day become "independent of its social origins," which question "is itself a problem of interest for the sociology of science," and whether the development of social science might not parallel that of the physical sciences in the seventeenth century, when the impetus came not so much from the universities as from the new scientific societies (*ibid.,* pp. 452–453).

71.   See n. 60.

72.   For divers items from such a list, see my "The Sociology of Knowledge: Emphasis on an Empirical Attitude," *Philosophy of Science,* 10 (April 1943), 122-123. [Chapter 5.] See also ns. 17-18.

73.   Alfred Schutz, "Concept and Theory Formation in the Social Sciences," *Journal of Philosophy,* 51 (April 29, 1954), 257–273, especially 271–272, and "Common-Sense and Scientific Interpretation of Human Action," *Philosophy and Phenomenological Research,* 14 (September 1953), 1–38, especially 26–37 [reprinted (abridged) in Lewis A. Coser and Bernard Rosenberg, Eds., *Sociological Theory: A Book of Readings* (New York: Macmillan, 1957), pp. 233–246, especially 240–246]. From Schutz's conception of social-scientific theory it is illuminating to go to scientific theory in general; see Morris R. Cohen and Ernest Nagel, *An Introduction to Logic and Scientific Method* (New York: Harcourt, Brace, 1934), pp. 397–399, and Philipp Frank, *Foundations of Physics* [Chicago: University of Chicago Press, 1946 (International Encyclopedia of Unified Science, Vol. 1, No. 7)], pp. 3–11.

74. Talcott Parsons, *The Structure of Social Action, op. cit.,* p. 24; Nicholas S. Timasheff, *Sociological Theory: Its Nature and Growth* (Garden City, N.Y.: Doubleday, 1955), pp. 9–10; Merton, *op. cit.,* rev. ed., pp. 96–97.

10

ERNST GRÜNWALD
AND THE SOCIOLOGY
OF KNOWLEDGE:
A Collective Venture in Interpretation. 1965

The *title* of this chapter suggests two themes. The first is Grünwald's own work in the sociology of knowledge; the second, an interpretation of it. This interpretation, in turn, proceeds in two steps, intrinsic and extrinsic. (The chapter thus falls into three parts.) The intrinsic refers, roughly, to an interpretation that is based only on the text to be interpreted; the extrinsic interprets this text from some "outside."

The *subtitle* tries to convey something not so much about the content of the paper as about the reader's hoped-for attitude toward it, about his relation to the writer. This relation is meant to be one between two parties to a common venture—precisely, that of interpreting Grünwald's sociology of knowledge. If successful, the reader will be drawn into it toward a perhaps unexpected climax.

GRÜNWALD'S SOCIOLOGY OF KNOWLEDGE

Ernst Grünwald, born in Vienna in 1912, had already given great promise as a contributor to the humanities and social sciences when, at the age of 21, he died in a mountain accident. A year before, he had completed a study posthumously edited as "The Problem of the Sociology of Knowledge: An Attempt at a Critical Exposition of the Theories of the Sociology of Knowledge" [1].

This book contains four chapters. The first and third, predominantly historical, deal, respectively, with the prehistory of the sociology of knowledge and its development. Chapters 2 and 4, predominantly systematic, present systematic analyses and discuss the relation between the sociology of knowledge and epistemology.

The two historical chapters justify Merton's calling Grünwald the first historian of the sociology of knowledge [2]. As far, at least, as the German contributions of the 1920s are concerned [3] (except for Scheler's and Mannheim's), he has hitherto remained the only one.

I limit myself to the two systematic chapters, which contain Grünwald's own conception, one, however, that flows from his understanding of the prehistory of the sociology of knowledge, that is, its roots and its problematics. Hence we began with a brief sketch of this prehistory.

The Prehistory of the Sociology of Knowledge. Grünwald discusses two roots, the psychologically oriented (literally, psychological) and the historically oriented (literally, historical). The psychologically oriented tradition claims to be empirical, grounded in actual experience. It is based on a theory of human nature, and its views of truth and error must be understood in reference to this theory. The historically oriented tradition, on the other hand, is based on a theory of history, in reference to which *its* views of truth and error must be understood. These two traditions delimit the whole possible field of themes of the sociology of knowledge; their relevance thus is not only historical but also "logico-systematic" (p. 49). In concluding his discussion, Grünwald writes:

The contrast between the psychological and the historical theory may be circumscribed schematically under the following heads:

1. Naturalism—objective idealism [4].
2. Empiricism: the criterion of truth is experience—antiempiricism: truth must be guaranteed metaphysically.
3. Epistemological optimism—counting on the possibility of an "impenetrable" "fraud."
4. Man's essence is found in nature—historicity is man's essence.
5. The world is meaningless—the world is meaning.
6. Psychological constants are the sphere of the absolute—history is the sphere of the absolute.
7. History in the proper sense, as understood by the historical theory, does not exist—nothing exists but history.

8. The aim of study is the formulation of general laws—
   [it is] the understanding of the unique, unrepeatable
   process.

9. "History" (as the psychological theory interprets it) is a
   chaotic pell-mell of blind forces of nature, the object of
   a *"logificatio post festum"*—history is the sphere of the
   realization of the spirit.

10. Man in his thinking and acting is caused by the totality
    of nature; he is a point of intersection of natural forces
    —man is the organ of the absolute.

11. The determination of thought occurs indirectly by way
    of the interests—determination occurs directly by the
    absolute.

12. The determination of thought proceeds across individual
    consciousness—determination is unconscious, *"a tergo."*

13. All cultural phenomena are a superstructure above the
    interests—all cultural phenomena are the manifestations
    of an all-pervasive principle.

14. Interests are the causes of error: [this assumes] causal
    relations—the thinking of the individual is the emana-
    tion of the absolute.

15. Only error, materially false consciousness, is linked to
    existence [*seinsverbunden*]—all consciousness is linked to
    existence.

16. The subject of imputation (as in naive [spontaneous,
    everyday] interpretation) is the thinking individual—
    the subject of imputation is a concretization of the abso-
    lute, such as class, nation, etc.

17. In principle, existentiality (*Seinsverbundenheit* [5]) can
    be eliminated; failure to remove the "personal equation"
    is an offense against intellectual honesty—in principle,
    existentiality [of one's thought] is unrecognizable.

18. Error is my [the individual's] fault—I cannot be held
    responsible for my false consciousness.

19. Experience is the Archimedean point which guarantees
    the truth of my thought and from which I can demon-
    strate the falsity of the thinking of others—the absolute
    itself must guarantee me the Archimedean point (pp.
    50–51).

Grünwald's own conception of the field is presented in seven brief sections.

Sociology of Knowledge and Sociology.   The sociology of knowledge is
the theory of "the connectedness of knowledge with social existence"

(p. 59). It can no more be considered part of *Gesellschaftssoziologie* ("sociology of society"—"(Vierkandt), a linguistically unbearable term, to be sure" [p. 60]) than can the sociology of religion, law, art, or music. These phenomena are rather the subject matter of *Kultursoziologie*, that is, of "the totality of the 'sociologies' of the various cultural phenomena, of the various 'manifestations of historical-societal reality' (Dilthey) . . . that have as their theme the connectedness of the various objectifications of culture with social existence" (p. 59).

The reasoning that leads Grünwald to this conclusion derives from his desire to find out in what sense the sociology of knowledge can be considered part of sociology at all. Among extant definitions of sociology, he examines Wilhelm Jerusalem's ("the science of the human group as a unit and its relations to the individual" [p. 56]) and Max Weber's well-known one ("a science that would understand social acting interpretively and thus explain it causally in its course and effects" [p. 57]). Both definitions leave no room for knowledge as the subject matter of sociology. Grünwald thus comes to the solution indicated.

Understanding in the Sociology of Knowledge. The sociology of knowledge is a *Geisteswissenschaft*, that is, one of the human studies [6]. Its method, therefore, is that of understanding. There are three kinds of understanding: first, the understanding of motives (psychological, motivational understanding); second, the immanent or intrinsic understanding of intellectual products, which aims at grasping their intended meaning; and third, and most characteristic of the sociology of knowledge, what Grünwald calls manifestational understanding or transcendent or extrinsic interpretation [7]; that is, knowledge (ideas, beliefs, and ideologies) is understood as the manifestation of society. It may, however, also be understood as the manifestation of other things and, indeed, has sometimes been. It is this plurality of transcendent interpretations, Grünwald insists, that invalidates each, for none can be scientifically demonstrated as true:

> Any other part of human existence—race, character type, national character, some depth strata of the soul, etc.—may be considered, with as much right as the social, to be the most real sphere allegedly manifesting itself in all others. . . . By means of manifestational understanding, knowledge, law, art, in brief, culture, may be interpreted as emanating from different strata that each time are posited as absolute (p. 64).

Being only one among other transcendent interpretations, the sociology of knowledge "is not a science whose propositions are unconditionally

valid for every thinking individual, but only a possible scheme of interpretation" (p. 66). [Cf. Chapter 28.]

Validity versus Manifestational Meaning. Every judgment, or proposition ("This is a chair," "The U. S. has a democratic government") has
two aspects, communication and validity. It communicates something
and it claims to be valid. We have seen that in Grünwald's view transcendent interpretation is interested in a proposition only as the manifestation of something else, namely, of the sphere posited as real. By
themselves propositions have no manifestational meaning; they are endowed with it when interpreted as manifesting this sphere. Nor can
such interpretation demonstrate the validity or invalidity of propositions.

*The Selective versus Constitutive Character of the Existentiality of
Knowledge.* Every object of knowledge, Grünwald maintains ("a chair,"
"beauty," "this house," "Smith's idea of God"), is the product of two
factors. The first is the object itself; the second is the social position of
the individual, or the standpoint, from which he experiences the object;
that is, the individual's standpoint *selects* aspects of the object. At the
same time the individual imparts some of his experience to the object
and thus coconstitutes it as an object of knowledge. In other words, the
existentiality of knowledge is both selective and constitutive. It is selective in that it singles out aspects of the object that the individual experiences—it is selective in respect to the object of experience; it is constitutive in respect to the object of knowledge, being coconstitutive of it.

*Elements of Knowledge Not Linked and Elements Linked to Its Existen-
tiality.* Drawing on Alfred Weber, Grünwald claims that the categories
of thought and the laws of formal logic are oriented exclusively toward
the object of knowledge. This means that they are *not* linked to the
existence of the thinker. In contrast to the categories of thought and the
laws of logic, however, metaphysical postulates and ultimate value decisions *are* so linked. A "glance at the history of metaphysical convictions
shows," Grünwald writes, "that these meta-empirical postulates are variable to the very greatest extent" (p. 87); and they vary, indeed, with the
thinker's existence, not with the object of knowledge, which presumably
is constant. Here, in other words, Grünwald appears to affirm, even if
indirectly, an actual impact of social existence on thought rather than
discussing thought as the manifestation of society. He continues:

> Atheoretical forces cannot without further proof be identified
> with influences of some existential sphere, even if there is a

high probability that some sphere of human existence is at work here—and yet, there appears to be no way in which these influences could be ascertained scientifically (p. 88).

Imputation. Because not all proletarians think alike (this is Grünwald's example) and some nonproletarians think like proletarians, the question is what do we mean by the proletariat to which a given thought is to be imputed. The answer is that class, as used in this instance and in the sociology of knowledge generally, does not mean what it means in general sociology—a number of people sharing certain characteristics. Rather class is a metaphysical entity, comparable to Hegel's world mind. As in Hegel's system the various folk minds are emanations of the world mind, the various classes are emanations of the social sphere. As to the process of imputation itself (the object of which is the class as a metaphysical entity), Grünwald follows Mannheim [8] in holding that a thought must be imputed to a world view, which in turn is to be imputed to a class (pp. 95-96). [Cf. Chapter 7.]

Sociologism, or Sociology of Knowledge and Epistemology. Whatever its variant, Grünwald argues, sociologism is based on two theses: (1) all knowledge is linked to existence and (2) the validity of knowledge is affected by this existentiality. Still, we can distinguish two types of sociologism: absolute and moderate. Absolute sociologism holds that existentiality destroys validity, but this is self-defeating for it also applies to itself and thus invalidates itself. Moderate sociologism, or (Mannheim's) relationism, holds that truth is relative to times and groups and that all knowledge is "perspectivistic." This is equally untenable, for the very thesis "that all that is given can be grasped only perspectivistically is meant to be valid not for one perspective only but absolutely" (p. 230). The self-contradictory nature of sociologism of both types, Grünwald observes, becomes understandable when we realize that it overlooks two facts. The first is, as we have seen, that the sociology of knowledge, like all transcendent interpretations, is concerned only with the manifestational meaning of propositions, not with their validity, about which it has nothing to say. The second is that the sociology of knowledge can establish only hypothetical, not real, relations between knowledge and the social sphere. Hence, because the sociology of knowledge cannot deal adequately with epistemological questions, Grünwald pleads that it not be concerned with them. "Sociologism," he writes in concluding his book,

is such an exaggeration of what the sociology of knowledge can reasonably be expected to accomplish that it can only end in complete failure and thus in the discrediting of the sociology of knowledge. The sociology of knowledge can become a science only if it abandons its pretension to be sociologism (p. 234).

AN INTRINSIC INTERPRETATION OF GRÜNWALD'S SOCIOLOGY OF KNOWLEDGE

The Prehistory of the Sociology of Knowledge. Many American sociologists *will recognize at least some of the 19 points under which Grünwald summarizes his extended discussion of the two traditions drawn on by the sociology of knowledge. They will recognize them as characteristics of familiar concepts, not only of the sociology of knowledge but of sociology and social science generally. Such concepts are distinguished from one another by the point of view, attitude, or perspective from which subject matter is viewed, hence the approach to it taken. Grünwald argues that basically there have been two such points of view and attendant approaches: human nature understood psychologically and analyzed natural-scientifically and history understood culturally or processually. He claims that to adopt these points of view entails ontological commitments. This means that the student who takes either of them posits the nature of reality, or at least of the reality that comes under his purview as his subject matter, to be such as he can adequately grasp only by taking the psychological or the historical approach.

The nature of Grünwald's undertaking is that of a systematic, not of a sociological or historical, analysis; that is to say, he does not inquire into the social or historical circumstances that might throw light on the fact that the views he summarizes have been held, defended, and fought. The execution of his assignment suggests that, between the two traditions he expounds, he himself more nearly belongs in the psychological, with its natural-science approach, than in the historical.

The Sociology of Knowledge and Sociology. Just as he raises no social or historical questions about the prehistory of the sociology of knowledge, so Grünwald does not ask why there should have been a controversy over the nature of *Gesellschaftssoziologie* and *Kultursoziologie*.

Understanding in the Sociology of Knowledge. To hold, as Grünwald does, that the sociology of knowledge is "not a science . . . but only a possible scheme of interpretation" means that science cannot choose among the various realities that are claimed to determine intellectual life. In another formulation, which from the point of view of science makes little difference, it means that there is one determining reality, which, however, cannot be scientifically known. It can only be posited by metaphysical fiat, which science cannot validate or invalidate. This view of Grünwald concerning the existentiality of knowledge is well designated as postulational skepticism (Arthur Child [9]); that is, Grünwald has not shown why a given thought may not be determined in a scientifically demonstrable sense by social circumstance, climate, or childhood experience; another, by body type, teaching, genetic structure; still another, by several of these or additional factors.

If under the first two heads—the prehistory of the sociology of knowledge and sociology of knowledge and sociology—Grünwald falls short on attention to history, here he falls short on science. He introduces his discussion of the scientific status of the sociology of knowledge by posing an ontological question and points out that if the sociology of knowledge makes ontological claims it ceases to be a science. He does not seriously consider the possibility that it need not make these claims and thus, on this score at least, can be a science.

Validity Versus Manifestational Meaning. This distinction is consistent with Grünwald's concept of manifestational understanding, and so should our comments be. Hence we must ask why a given proposition cannot be the result of one or more particular factors rather than their ontologically grounded manifestation. Indeed, to interpret a proposition as manifesting the real sphere has no bearing on the question of the validity of the proposition, but this observation, in turn, has no more than a remote bearing on the scientific question of the sociology of knowledge concerning the difference, and the relation, between the empirical genesis of a proposition and its validity.

The Selective versus Constitutive Character of the Existentiality of Knowledge. Grünwald's concept of this problem may be put briefly: the individual's selection of an object *for* knowledge coconstitutes it as an object *of* knowledge. He argues persuasively (p. 250, n. 59) that this concept [at which he arrives on analyzing the concept of "material of judgment" (pp. 82–83), here omitted] "actually grasps the intentions of the existing systems of the sociology of knowledge," notably Mannheim's but also Scheler's (as well as historicism). To have formulated it and to have identified it as the pervasive view of the existing sociology of knowledge is the result of an epistemological analysis, as he points out (pp. 83–84). Once more, however, as in respect to the prehistory of the sociology of knowledge and the relation of the latter to sociology, he does not ask whether and how the society and time in which this epistemological position is found may help to account for it.

Elements of Knowledge Not Linked and Elements Linked to Its Existentiality. We have seen that elements of knowledge discussed by Grünwald fall into two groups. The first, categories of thought and laws of formal logic, are not characterized by existentiality; the second, metaphysical postulates and ultimate value decisions, that is, the "subcategorial, meta-empirical sphere" (p. 87), are—as a look at the history of metaphysics shows. We also saw, however, that as soon as he had said this he insisted that the atheoretical forces he admitted to be at work in thought "cannot without further proof be identified with influences of some existential sphere" and that "there appears no way in which these influences could be ascertained scientifically." He thus falls back on his postulational skepticism. As in regard to his analyses of understanding and of validity versus manifestational meaning, here, too he stops short of investigating the possibility of scientific proof—this time of the existence of connections between social setting and thought. He merely proclaims his skepticism. He does not seem to see the relevance of Max Weber's discussion of this problem (to mention only the probably best known), whether in *The Protestant Ethic* or in several papers on methodology, especially his analysis of understanding and causal explanation. Once more Grünwald is short on scientific procedure [10].

Imputation. If class is indeed a metaphysical entity, imputation to it is a nonempirical, taxonomic, or logical process (which it is not, incidentally, in Mannheim, to whom Grünwald approvingly refers). Grünwald fails to face the scientific problem of imputation. He does not mention the possibility that class may be employed neither as a metaphysical unit nor in the sense of a collection of individuals with similar relevant social traits but instead as a self-conscious heuristic construct, proof to the verificatory claims of both ontologist and census taker. Thus Grünwald is not scientific beyond showing that imputation to a class as a metaphysical entity is not scientific. Nor does he consider any social unity other than class, however conceived, to which thought may be imputed. In this sense he is caught in the Marxist frame of reference of his time [11].

Sociologism or Sociology of Knowledge and Epistemology. This section, we saw, consists of a critique of the two varieties of sociologism and a plea that the sociology of knowledge give it up and thus become a science. Grünwald does show that it can become one merely by renouncing sociologism, which is not identical with the fundamental thesis of the sociology of knowledge, namely, "the connectedness of knowledge with social existence" or, more briefly, the existentiality of knowledge. We know Grünwald's conviction that this thesis is not scientifically demonstrable. He thus appears as apodictic (existentiality is undemonstrable) as is the sociology of knowledge or the sociologism (existentiality needs no demonstration) that he opposes, although substantively his position is different. As class is the only unit to which he considers thought imputable, validity is the only aspect of thought he considers in connection with existentiality. He does not fully face the problem whether existentiality might not be relevant to other aspects or elements of thought, such as empirical adequacy or objectivity, world view, attitudinal structure, and many more. Not "fully face": although Grünwald does discuss closely related matters (see, in particular, his analysis of elements of knowledge linked and not linked to existentiality), he suggests the possibility neither of a tentative conceptual scheme that might guide research designed to illuminate them nor of research itself (such as, among a few others, Mannheim engaged in [12]).

AN EXTRINSIC INTERPRETATION OF GRÜNWALD'S SOCIOLOGY OF KNOWLEDGE

What we have done so far is to read Grünwald carefully and to raise some questions that have come out of the reading. We have proceeded as have some other commentators on sociologists of knowledge—for instance, Child or Stark on Grünwald (and others) or Hinshaw on Mannheim [13]. Now, in an attempt to account for the characteristics we have found, we go outside his work into history. What this means will become clearer as we proceed.

Like other students of the sociology of knowledge, Grünwald thought of it as a "young discipline" (p. 1). One of the tasks he set himself was to survey it in order to clarify its place among the human studies. To judge from the tenor of his introductory pages he expected it to extend human inquiry to new areas and to enrich it by new points of view, but he hardly succeeded in defining these areas and in vindicating these points of view. He appears to have proceeded on the assumption that the sociology of knowledge is an addition to man's intellectual heritage and to have been guided by an image of orderly, cumulative progress characteristic of science, or its ideal, rather than by any image of history. Indeed, as we noted earlier, even his presentation of the prehistory of the sociology of knowledge is not historical but systematic, at least in intent: he presents ideas and their filiations, but the circumstance that these were formulated at particular times and places is irrelevant to his enterprise.

A historical, rather than a systematic or natural-scientific or scientific, approach characterizes the work of most sociologists of knowledge, notably Scheler and Mannheim. It may be asked, then, why Grünwald, who was so critical of it, should have taken its approach and *not* a systematic-scientific one. If he was short on history in his analysis of the prehistory of the sociology of knowledge, the place of the sociology of knowledge in respect to sociology, and his own epistemological position, we also saw that in his treatment of understanding, validity, existentiality, imputation, and sociologism he was short on science. Thus, if he failed in one way or the other on actually all eight counts of his presentation, why bother with him?

There may be readers of his work who will feel that he was a talented young man, confused by the authors he analyzed, yet capable one day of good social science, had it only been possible for him to receive training in scientific method. He might have learned it from the Vienna Circle or from American sociology, but he did not live long enough. Readers may find that he was ready for it to the extent of dissatisfaction with the sociology of knowledge of his time but that he was not yet sufficiently in command of it to transcend it. Had he been—and perhaps only his early death prevented him from developing toward this goal—he might have added his share to cumulative social science.

According to Grünwald's own scheme for the prehistory of the sociology of knowledge, such readers clearly stand in what he called the psychological tradition. For them the sociology of knowledge Grünwald examined, as well as his own, largely are deviations from scientific procedure or at best approximations of it—but perhaps their accounting for the characteristics and shortcomings of Grünwald's work is not exhaustive.

It is not exhaustive if, instead of taking a writer and his work literally, we take him as symptomatic, as I now propose to do. Rather than engaging in a theoretical analysis of the concept, I use "symptomatic" in the familiar practical, everyday way in which it is said that fever is symptomatic of pneumonia, upper-class juvenile delinquency of ennui, an editorial placing states' rights above civil rights of a decision for a restricted and against an expanded society. I wish to explore the symptomaticity of Grünwald's sociology of knowledge [14]. I submit that it is symptomatic of the meaninglessness of the human world that Grünwald, though not explicitly, proclaimed. I try to show this by reviewing some of the foci of his conception.

To introduce this review I call attention to one of the heads under which he summarized his discussion of the prehistory of the sociology of knowledge. For the psychologically oriented tradition, he says, "the world is meaningless," whereas for the historically oriented tradition, "the world is meaning" [15]. In this contrast there is, on one side, nature, with no place for history, "a chaotic pell-mell of blind forces of nature," and on the other, history, "the sphere of the realization of the spirit." Meaning being an exclusively human phenomenon is outside nature; in Grünwald's view and the historical tradition it is located in history. This contrast is at the base of the German division between the natural sciences and the human studies. It is reflected in Max Weber's distinction between what can be explained but is "devoid of subjective meaning" (Parsons' translation of *sinnfremd*) and what, because it is meaningful, can be understood—notably human acting [16]. Although for both the psychological and historical traditions and for Weber it is nonhuman nature that is meaningless, I now try to show that for Grünwald the human world is (or possibly is) too. I argue that his views on understanding, validity versus manifestational meaning, the selective versus the constitutive character of the existentiality of knowledge, elements of knowledge linked, and not, to existentiality, imputation, and sociologism (the last six of his eight foci) are facets of a view of the human world as meaningless.

Understanding. Grünwald does not question the possibility of understanding other people's motives and intended meanings (however difficult it may be), but the possibility of the third kind of understanding, manifestational, cannot be demonstrated. For Grünwald manifestational understanding is inseparable from the idea of an ultimate reality; but all we can know about such reality, the *ens realissimum* (*passim*), is what we posit as such; nor is there any way of deciding *what* we should posit.

In other words, Grünwald is convinced that it is impossible to know reality. This conviction is more than the optimistic and expectant contentment of the scientist with hypothetical truth; it rather recalls Max Weber's passionate conviction that it is impossible to know justice and values generally [17]. Both attest not so much to gaps accepted as to needs unfulfilled: Grünwald, to the need for a cosmology, Weber, to that for a normative order [18].

Validity Versus Manifestational Meaning. This distinction is the phrasing of the scientific distinction between validity and origin in ontological terms. What has been said about manifestational understanding, therefore, also applies here; that is, on the occasion of his analysis of the validity and meaning of propositions Grünwald indicates his lack of, but need for, knowledge of "reality" or a cosmology.

The Selective versus Constitutive Character of the Existentiality of Knowledge. The object of cognition is the product of the object itself and the experiencing subject. Like other writers on the sociology of knowledge [19], Grünwald does not raise the question of the theoretical possibility of a truth more objectively based than on a sharing of standpoints, in fact, of the theoretical possibility of standpoints being shared at all. If his analyses of manifestational understanding and validity versus manifestational meaning attest to his lack of a cosmology, his discussion of the selective and constitutive character of the existentiality of knowledge shows his lack of a truth that is independent of the knower's standpoint—universal truth.

Elements of Knowledge Not Linked and Elements Linked to Its Existentiality. Saying nothing to the contrary, Grünwald leaves the standpoints referred to under the preceding heading disconnected, discontinuous in time, and without order during the same time—once more like Weber's values. In the present context he seems to qualify his view of the object of cognition presented, for he now declares that certain objects of cognition are unaffected by the fact that all knowledge is knowledge from a standpoint, namely, those objects toward which the categories of thought and the laws of formal logic are oriented. If there are such objects, their existence guarantees the possibility of universal truth—a conclusion that Grünwald does not draw, nor does he draw the related conclusion that there are cognitive elements common to all men, as he could have from the possibility of understanding people's motives and intended meanings. He implied this possibility in his discussion of the first two kinds of understanding as well as in his observation that it is possible to understand the great variety of metaphysical convictions that a glance at their history displays. By failing to draw the first conclusion he denies the identity of objects or evinces an objectless world. By failing to draw the second he once more reveals his conviction that there is no common truth, nor does his remark about the history of metaphysical positions elicit in him any affirmation of history, hence a denial of the arbitrariness or disconnectedness of standpoints (metaphysical or other).

Imputation. This concept, too, is discussed in ontological terms: class, to which a thought is imputed, is a metaphysical entity. Grünwald does not consider the scientific treatment of imputation, the scientific investigability of social classes, the suitability of other social units for imputation, but although he considers manifestational understanding an act of arbitrary preference he does not similarly qualify imputation (we saw that he accepts Mannheim's method of it, without, however, granting its scientific status). Thus he must stand accused of arbitrarily subscribing to a scheme he considers ontologically grounded.

Sociologism or Sociology of Knowledge and Epistemology. Having shown his uneasy relation to science and to the sociology of knowledge as a science, his admonition that the sociology of knowledge can become a science only by abandoning epistemological claims sounds hollow. As suggested before, the discussion of the present topic is another occasion on which Grünwald shows his diffidence in regard to science.

Grünwald's Human World and We. Inspecting our results, we find that Grünwald wants—in the twofold sense of this term—a cosmology, universal truth, cognitive features common to all men, identical objects, points of view that could be understood with reference to an order of culture and history, and a science that can make testable claims about the origin of a given thought, about the relations between thought and social class, and about the existentiality of knowledge. His world is a world that exhibits these wants.

These wants are interdependent. Thus, if I cannot believe in the world as orderly (if I *want* an orderly world), I am bound to doubt such truth as I can even imagine all men to converge on; or, if I cannot believe in the universality of truth, I tend altogether to discard the notion of an orderly world—and similarly for relations among the other wants. This is not a world that turns meaningless by a subtraction, piecemeal or progressive, of items—cosmology, truth, objects, and so on—but rather the world of a man who has lost his continuity with history and with his fellow men with whom he is involved in a common history [20]. This man was not alone in this, nor is he (cf., among many other indications, the contemporary literature on alienation, and the mass society, etc.). Yet, being an individual, his particular meaningless world differs, of course, in some of its features and their configuration from that of others. It also differs in respect to the occasion on which he exhibited it, his inquiry into the sociology of knowledge, the "young discipline" whose promise he did not succeed in conveying.

Is there any validity in what I have said in the more explicitly interpretive parts of this paper, especially the last? How can I assert that Grünwald proclaimed a meaningless human world if we do not have his own word for it—which indeed, we have not? If we find grounds for assertion, what grounds can there possibly be for proof?

Let us go back to the imaginary but almost certainly existing reader of Grünwald's work who, we said, true to the psychological-natural-scientific tradition, would account for its characteristics in the way suggested [21]. We can characterize his procedure in a slightly different fashion by saying that this reader is interested only in the scientific or theoretical aspects of the work. He applies to it his generally characteristic interest in scientific or theoretical knowledge and truth; he examines writings that claim scientific status only with respect to that claim, that truth, that knowledge, but neither he nor Grünwald can refute the proposition that

> the type of knowledge conveyed by natural science differs fundamentally from historical knowledge—we should try to grasp the meaning and structure of historical understanding in its specificity, rather than reject it merely because it is not in conformity with the positivist truth-criteria sanctioned by natural science [22].

For present purposes historical knowledge may be grouped with practical or existential knowledge [23] and these varieties of one kind of knowledge contrasted with the scientific-theoretical. Knowledge concerning symptoms is a further variety of existential knowledge. The following passage from Mannheim's discussion of documentary interpretation also comes close to describing the procedure for arriving at truth concerning symptoms:

> This "documentary" interpretation of an *Ars poetica* or of an aesthetic theory put forward by the artist [or of any intellectual product whatever, such as Grünwald's book] does not consist, however, in merely treating these utterances as authentic reflections of the author's artistic personality. . . . *What we have to ask is not whether the theory is correct— nor what his proponent meant by it* [my italics]. Rather, we must go beyond this "immanent" interpretation [24] and treat the theoretical confession as confession: as documentary evidence of something extra-psychic, . . . just as a doctor will take the self-diagnosis of one of his patients as a symptom rather than as a correct identification of the latter's illness [25].

Why should one be interested in symptoms? The physician is, as a source of knowledge he needs the better to cure the patient. I suggested, however, that symptomatological knowledge is a variety of practical knowledge, the aim of which is broader than to cure, namely, to know how to act right. This, indeed, is the meaning of practical knowledge in everyday usage. In the extrinsic or historical interpretation of Grünwald's book (to the point we have gone with it) we have examined his concept of the sociology of knowledge with this meaning in mind. We have read his book to prepare ourselves for gaining knowledge on how to act right. To enable us to do so, our reading has been historical: we have asked who Grünwald (the "documentary Grünwald") was to learn better who *we* are as we compare ourselves with him. Is his world indeed as meaningless as we have come to hold it? Is ours? Practical knowledge or truth, unlike theoretical, is not "out there," but in ourselves: whoever wants to ask these questions seriously must ask them himself of himself.

Acknowledgment. This is a thorough revision of a paper presented at the 55th annual meeting of the American Sociological Association, New York, 30 August 1960. For criticisms and suggestions concerning the earlier draft I am deeply grateful to Arthur Child, to an anonymous, penetrating and critical reader, and to Michael Haber, Charles Levy, Young Ick Lew, Susan Sandler, and Dusky Lee Smith, students in a seminar on the sociology of knowledge at Brandeis University, Spring 1962.

NOTES

1. Ernst Grünwald, *Das Problem der Soziologie des Wissens, op. cit.* The information contained in this paragraph is taken from Walther Eckstein's "Vorwort." Eckstein also reports that at the time of his death Grünwald was engaged in a major work on the phenomenology of language. Page references in parentheses are to Grünwald's book. (For parts of Grünwald's book that have been made available in English since Chapter 10 was written see Chapter 9, n. 53.)

2. Robert K. Merton. "The Sociology of Knowledge," in Georges Gurvitch and Wilbert E. Moore, Eds., *Twentieth Century Sociology* (New York: Philosophical Library 1945), p. 367.

3. The only summary treatment of the latter in English [Franz Adler, "The Range of Sociology of Knowledge," in Howard Becker and Alvin Boskoff, Eds., *Modern Sociological Theory in Continuity and Change* (New York: Dryden, 1957), pp. 399–402]. is based mainly on the study by Ernst Grünwald.

4. That is, the "historical theory" postulates an objectively existing ideal realizing itself in the course of history.

5. *Seinsverbundenheit* is an untranslatable term, a key word in Mannheim's writings on the sociology of knowledge, perhaps coined by him; its use abounds in Grünwald and other writers on the subject as well. See Karl Mannheim, *Ideology and Utopia, op. cit.*, p. 239n, in which the English translation of the term as "social determination" is qualified as leaving the meaning of determi-

nation open; "existentiality" seems better (although not usable in adjectival form).

6. H. A. Hodges's rendition of the German term. See his *Wilhelm Dilthey: An Introduction* (New York: Oxford University Press, 1944), p. 157.

7. The articulation of the first kind of understanding, is, of course, Max Weber's. The distinction between the second and third, though not in Grünwald's specific sense, was made by Mannheim in his "Ideologische and soziologische Interpretation der geistigen Gebilde," *Jahrbuch für Soziologie,* **2** (1926), pp. 424–440, anticipated in his review of Georg Lukács' *Die Theorie des Romans* in *Logos,* 9 (1920–1921), 298–302 (both translated, with an introduction, by Kurt H. Wolff, *Studies on the Left,* 3 (Summer 1963), 45–66 [in *From Karl Mannheim*, pp. 116–131]. So far it has been most thoroughly dealt with by Arthur Child, *The Problems of the Sociology of Knowledge: A Critical and Philosophical Study,* University of California (unpublished Ph.D. dissertation), 1938, Chapter VII, "Immanent and Transcendent Interpretation"; Kurt H. Wolff, "A Preliminary Inquiry into the Sociology of Knowledge from the Standpoint of the Study of Man," *loc. cit.* [Chapter 7].

8. "On the Interpretation of *Weltanschauung*" (1921–1922), in *Essays on the Sociology of Knowledge,* Paul Kecskemeti, Ed. (London: Routledge and Kegan Paul, 1952), pp. 33-83 (henceforth *Weltanschauuang*). *(From Karl Mannheim,* pp. 8–58.)

9. Arthur Child, "The Theoretical Possibility of the Sociology of Knowledge," *Ethics,* **51** (July 1941), 404 (henceforth *Possibility*); see Wolff, *Inquiry,* pp. 592-593, n. 21 [Chapter 7].

10. The most cogent demonstration of the existentiality of thought I know is found in Child, *Possibility,* 413-415; cf. Wolff, *Inquiry,* 591-593 [Chapter 7].

11. On imputation cf. Arthur Child, "The Problem of Imputation in the Sociology of Knowledge," *Ethics,* **51** (January 1941), 200–219, "The Problem of Imputation Resolved," *Ethics,* **54** (January 1944), 96–109; Kurt H. Wolff, "On the Scientific Relevance of 'Imputation,' " *Ethics,* **61** (October 1950), 69–73 [Chapter 7]; Svend Ranulf, *Methods of Sociology* (Copenhagen: Ejnar Munksgaard, 1955), pp. 95–96.

12. Cf. notably "Historicism" (1924), in *Essays on the Sociology of Knowledge, op. cit.,* pp. 84–133, and "Conservative Thought" (1927), in *Essays on Sociology and Social Psychology,* Paul Kecskemeti, Ed. (New York: Oxford University Press, 1953), pp. 74–164 [the latter also in *From Karl Mannheim,* pp. 132–222].

13. Arthur Child, "The Problem of Imputation in the Sociology of Knowledge," 207–213; *Possibility,* 404–407; "The Existential Determination of Thought," *Ethics,* **52** (January 1942), 167–175; "The Problem of Truth in the Sociology of Knowledge," *Ethics,* **58** (October 1947), 21–22 (henceforth *Truth*); W. Stark, *The Sociology of Knowledge: An Essay in Aid of a Deeper Understanding of the History of Ideas* (Glencoe, Ill.: Free Press, 1958), pp. 194–196; Virgil G. Hinshaw, Jr., "The Epistemological Relevance of Mannheim's

Sociology of Knowledge," *loc. cit.*, "Epistemological Relativism and the Sociology of Knowledge," *loc. cit.*

14. Symptomaticity is related to documentary meaning as discussed by Mannheim, *Weltanschauung*, pp. 55–63.

15. *Welt ist sinnlos—Welt ist Sinn* (p. 50).

16. Max Weber, *The Theory of Social and Economic Organization*, translated by A. M. Henderson and Talcott Parsons, edited, with an introduction, by Talcott Parsons, *op. cit.*, pp. 88–93, including Parsons' footnotes on relevant German terms, and p. 93. On the problems of Weber's conception of sociology in the light of the *Gesellschafts-Kultursoziologie* dichotomy see Grünwald, p. 247, end of n. 28.

17. Max Weber, "The Meaning of 'Ethical Neutrality' in Sociology and Economics" (1913–1917), in *On the Methodology of the Social Sciences, op. cit.*, pp. 15–16; "Science as a Vocation," *op. cit.*, pp. 148, 150. For the outline of a socio-historical analysis of "value" see Hannah Arendt, *The Human Condition, op. cit.*, pp. 163-166; cf. [Chapter 4] (henceforth *Arendt*).

18. There still remains the question why Grünwald conceived of the understanding characteristic of the sociology of knowledge in ontological terms in the first place. The answer is perhaps quite simple: he found it conceived thus by the authors he examined and was caught by them.

19. See Child, *Truth*.

20. Cf. Kurt H. Wolff, "Surrender as a Response to Our Crisis," *Journal of Humanistic Psychology*, **2** (Fall 1962), 16–17, 27–29.

21. See the fourth and fifth paragraphs of this chapter.

22. Mannheim, *Weltschauung*, p. 61.

23. The question of the relation between practical, existential, and historical knowledge and truth may be left open; cf. Kurt H. Wolff, "The Sociology of Knowledge and Sociological Theory, in Llewellyn Gross, Ed., *Symposium on Sociological Theory* (Evanston, Ill.: Row, Peterson, 1959), "V. Scientific vs. Existential Truth," pp. 579-580 [Chapter 9]; "Sociology and History; Theory and Practice," *American Journal of Sociology*, **65** (July 1958), 36–37 [Chapter 3]; *Arendt*, 77-106 [Chapter 4].

24. Cf. n. 7 and the passage to which it refers.

25. Mannheim, *Weltanschauung*, p. 58. On "Symptoms of a Time and Reactions to It," illustrated by a brief discussion of action anthropology, the sociology of knowledge itself, and Max Weber's "ethics of principle" and of "responsibility"; cf. Kurt H. Wolff, *The Means-End Scheme in Contemporary Sociology and Its Relation to an Analysis of Nonviolence* (Oslo: Institute for Social Research, August 1959) (mimeographed), pp. 109–117.

This chapter is reprinted in modified form from *Journal of the History of the Behavioral Sciences,* **1** (1965), 152–164, by permission of the publisher. The essay has been edited and partially revised by the author.

III
SURRENDER

11

THE SOCIOLOGY OF KNOWLEDGE AND SURRENDER-AND-CATCH (1982)

I

From the beginning of its career — which by now is some sixty years old — the term "sociology of knowledge" has been a misnomer. In the first place, "sociology of knowledge" is a bad translation of the German *"Wissenssoziologie,"* the dictionary to the contrary notwithstanding: both terms are narrower in English than in German. "Sociology," at least at the time the term *"Wissenssoziologie"* was coined, was less far removed from philosophy than it is in the Anglo-Saxon world and has since become to some extent in German sociology as well; it is, or was, not so sharply distinguished from "social philosophy." But more important, and also more clearcut, is the difference between "knowledge" and *"Wissen."* For "knowledge" refers predominantly if not exclusively to positive or scientific knowledge, whereas the German term also covers such kinds of knowledge as philosophical, metaphysical, theological, artistic, or religious. The term "sociology of knowledge" thus means or connotes something other than its original.

But there is a second reason why "sociology of knowledge" is a misnomer: it is that in light of its practice, *"Wissenssoziologie"* itself is misleading. For speculations and analyses concerning it, and studies carried on in its name, have dealt, not so much with knowledge, even in its broader German sense, as with various related phenomena, all of which have to do with knowledge or contain it, but are not themselves knowledge—e.g., ideologies and uto-pias, concepts, such as freedom, conceptions, such as historicism, or—and these are hard to distinguish from topics of an even more general sociology of culture—forms of literature and the fine arts. In short, even the original term is too narrow, and a less confusing one would be something like "the sociol-ogy of intellectual life."

Indeed, it seems difficult to find theoretical grounds on which to argue the difference between the sociology of knowledge and the sociology of cul-ture; the grounds rather are historical. Here it must be enough to alert to a distinction once widely accepted in German sociology, that between *"Real-soziologie"* and *Kultursoziologie." "Kultursoziologie"* does mean "socio-logy of culture," but *"Realsoziologie"* does not mean "real sociology" or "sociology of reality" but, approximately, the sociology of the "real" world in the sense of what Max Scheler called *"Realfaktoren,"* by which he refer-red to biology, economy, and power; these for him were the conditions with-in the limits of which the *"Idealfaktoren,"* that is, spirit, mind, or culture, necessarily operate.

Far more than the sociology of culture, however, the sociology of know-ledge has a polemical character, which derives from one of its two historical sources—that is, two historical sources if we speak systematically; one, speaking historically. The two are Durkheim and Marx, and it takes little acquaintance with the matter to recognize that Marx is the decisive influ-ence and that Durkheim, though stimulating important studies carried on by anthropologists and sociologists like Marcel Mauss or Marcel Granet, hardly left any students who were in contact with the controversy over the sociology of knowledge which raged in Weimar Germany among discussants representing several varieties of Marxism and non- and anti-Marxism.[1] Above all, the controversy concerned the nature of ideology and of true as against pseudo-Marxism or Marxism betrayed. But fundamentally, in what-ever terms it was couched, it was a controversy over the power of mind as against material forces or, in terms used before, over the relative power of "ideal" and "real factors," hence of the relevance of *Kultur-* vs. *Realsoziologie.*

II

How did *Wissenssoziologie* come about? Karl Mannheim, one of its two founders—the other, Max Scheler, launching the enterprise just before him—raised this question and gave an answer to it. It is characteristic of him to have done so, as it would be uncharacteristic of Scheler with the ahistorical, partly systematizing, philosophical-anthropological conception of his undertaking. Mannheim's formulation of the problem reflects his particular though not explicated reading of modern Western history. In what along with the original *Ideologie and Utopie*[2] is his most searching analysis of the sociology of knowledge, he writes that there are four currents in Western intellectual history (Mannheim does not bother to specify the location of the history he is characterizing, but clearly means that of Western Europe): (1) the understanding of thought as relative to or in relation to something else; (2) the unmasking, or reductionist, style of such relativization; (3) the understanding of thought in relation to the "social sphere" (society, social structure); and (4) such relativization, not of a particular idea or thought, not of a certain conception or other part of a whole, but of all of the thought of an individual or an epoch — indeed of thought as such.[3]

The "self-relativization" of thought does not mean, Mannheim is eager to add in a footnote,

> epistemological 'relativism' but merely the opposite of 'autonomy'. One may very well assert [he continues] that thought is 'relative to being', 'dependent on being', 'non-autonomous', 'part of a whole reaching beyond it', without professing any 'relativism' concerning the truth value of its findings. At this point, it is, so to speak, still open [and here we are getting into the crux of Mannheim's epistemological dilemma for which so many critics, often with a feeling of superiority, have blamed him] whether the 'existential relativization' of thought is to be combined with epistemological relativism or not. [But now Mannheim's existential commitment comes to the fore:] In any case, however [he writes], we would like to go on record, at this point [which he never succeeded in going beyond[4]], that we cannot share the at present widespread fear of relativism. 'Relativism' has become a catchword which, it is believed, will instantly annihilate any adversary against whom it is used. But as to us, we definitely prefer a 'relativism' which accentuates the difficulty of its task by calling attention to all those moments which tend to make the propositions actually discoverable at any given time, partial and situationally conditioned — we prefer such a 'relativism' to an 'absolutism' which loudly proclaims, as a matter of principle, the absoluteness of its own position or of 'truth in itself', but is in fact no less partial than any of its adversaries — and, still worse, is utterly incapable of tackling with its epistemological apparatus the problem of the temporal and situational determination of any concrete process of thought, completely overlooking the way in which this situational conditioning enters into the structure and the evolution of knowledge (Mannheim, 1925, p. 62n.).

"At this point, it is, so to speak, still open whether the 'existential relativization' of thought is to be combined with epistemological relativism or not." What does this mean? Mannheim writes as if there were a choice and he doesn't yet know how to choose or what it is right to choose. But he fails to distinguish between two intrinsically heterogeneous matters, not sure whether they *are* intrinsically heterogeneous. The two are *understanding* and *validity*. It is one thing to understand something (whatever it be) in relation, or relative, to something else, including the social setting in which it is found; and the injunction so to understand it indeed is one meaning of relativism. It may be called methodological relativism and is the rule with which every scholar, including the social scientist, is familiar: it enjoins the understanding of whatever it be in its own context, not as it looks from the point of view of its student. A wholly separate issue is the question of the validity of that thought—not as it is understood by the thinker (the thinker's understanding of the validity of the thought is part of the demand of the student's contextual understanding), but by some other criterion, which may or may not be the thinker's own and must, even if it should coincide empirically, be distinguished analytically.

The passage repeated from Mannheim's long footnote may serve to illustrate the difference just presented. To repeat a second time: "At this point," Mannheim writes, "it is, so to speak, still open whether the 'existential relativization' of thought is to be combined with epistemological relativism or not"—whether, to use our words, methodological and epistemological relativism should or do go together; whether the requirement of contextual understanding brings with it or entails or leads to the relativization of validity; whether it means that there is no validity other than relative validity. (It is perhaps not necessary to point out that to validity in thought correspond such other objective features—and the meaning of "objective" will be discussed presently—as aesthetic satisfactoriness in works of art, logical correctness in reasoning, accuracy in observation, etc.) We may now apply our distinction to the sentence taken from Mannheim's passage. As a matter of fact, we have examined its validity or tenability and have wondered how it is that Mannheim could have failed to make the distinction we made, that is to say how he could write something invalid and, moreover, as was pointed out, how he could fail to discover and correct this invalidity. We thus raised a question of understanding—but have not answered it.

III

What would it mean to answer it? We could try an answer by reference to Mannheim's biography—in the sense of the way in which his personality was formed. This might be the approach taken by a psychologist. Or we could try an answer by reference to the times and places when and where he lived, the society or societies and their changes in which he participated; and this would be more nearly a sociologist's procedure. Both answers are what Mannheim himself called "transcendent interpretations," by which he simply meant interpretations relative to something outside the interpretandum, rather than in the interpretandum's own terms (Mannheim, 1926) — the latter he called "ideological interpretations." In order to use less loaded, as well as more telling terms, we will continue to speak of extrinsic and intrinsic interpretations. Among the former, the sociological, according to Mannheim, is among those that "proceed in terms of a totality"; and in its case, the totality is "existential." Like the "idealistic" extrinsic interpretation (whose most clearcut representative in modern Western history is presumably Hegel), the sociological takes "the entire ideological ["intellectual" or "mental" or "spiritual"] sphere, together with the social existence that lies behind it, as a unit," and thus these two extrinsic interpretations — the idealistic and the sociological — "represent the highest stage of total interpretation as such" (1926, pp. 129. 129-130). And Mannheim ends his paper on types of interpretations by pointing out that even his (eightfold) typology, listing, as he insists, only "the most important kinds,"

> shows the peculiarity of intellectual phenomena, which is that
> they can be approached from many different angles. It also shows
> that the kinds listed, of which the most modern is the sociological,
> cannot be fixed for all time. For they rise and change along with
> the historical development of consciousness and thus offer the
> possibility of an ever increasing and transforming penetration
> of the intellectual world (1926, pp. 130-131).

This passage gives us a new access to the problem of objectivity, and thus to a defensible meaning of "objective," the problem which has come up in the discussion of methodological and epistemological relativism and which we then said would be addressed presently. If, as Mannheim points out, intellectual phenomena "can be approached from many different angles" — and surely, this is something with which there can hardly be disagreement — one might ask, as Mannheim does not, how many the "many" are, whether their number is finite or infinite. If the number of ways an intellectual (or for that matter, any) phenomenon can be approached is finite, we need a method or a criterion by which to count them; but inasmuch as Mannheim does not seem to be worried about the meaning of "many," it is not surprising that he does not raise the question of such method or criterion — *if* their number is finite. On the other hand, it may be infinite. At first glance this may sound far more plausible. But if the ways in which something can be interpreted is really infinite, then the question is what is left of it once it has been interpreted in an infinite number of ways (which would, of course, take infinite time). To put it differently: what is the reality which is infinitely interpretable? What is there *objectively* which is appropriated subjectively in an infinite number of ways? (Or, finally, in phenomenological terms: what is the noematic nucleus on which the infinite number of noetic modifications, resulting in the infinite number of noematic modifications, is performed?)

One might be tempted to answer: the world *is* that which is infinitely interpreted or interpretable; this is what "world" means. Such an answer parallels the view that electricity is what the electric meter measures, or time what the clock measures, or length what the ruler measures, or weight what the scale measures. But such a view forgets that we first have to have something which we construct the electric meter or the clock or the ruler or the scale to measure.[5] It forgets that if we stick our fingers into an electrical outlet, something happens which makes us jerk and which, if we experience it for the first time, puzzles us. Just so, such a view forgets that it may be evening before we know it or that the train hasn't arrived *yet*; or that the other side of the table is too far for me to reach or the suitcase too heavy to carry. In other words, such a view forgets that there *is* an external or objective world — in which we have to live.

IV

Max Scheler does see the nature of reality in *resistance* — but this conception is not found in his outline of the sociology of knowledge. Instead, there are two passages in his work, *Erkenntnis und Arbeit*, a study, as its subtitle indicates, of "the value and the limits of the pragmatic motive," in which this conception is presented. In the first passage, it is couched in hypothetical terms:

> . . . if the investigation of this question [of the essence of "reality"] were to show that being real itself is given originally only in the resistance with which some inner and outer configurations of things assert themselves against [. . . our] impulses — then the pragmatically conditioned knowledge of nature would be securely founded in a primordial phenomenon of the world's ontic structure itself (Scheler, 1926, p. 281; italics omitted).

But in a later passage, he writes with certainty:

> Imagine the whole content of the natural world view [that is, of all that "is considered valid as unquestionably 'given' ": Scheler, 1924, p. 61] dismantled piece by piece; let all colors pale, all sounds fade away, the sphere of body consciousness disappear

with all its content, the form of space and time and all forms of being (categories) of things level off into an indeterminate existence [*Sosein*] — then there remains as that which cannot be dismantled a simple, no further analyzable impression of reality as such: the impression of something simply "resisting" . . . spontaneous activity. . . . To be real is not to be an object . . .; it rather is to be resistance to the primordially flowing spontaneity which is one and the same in willing and noticing of whatever kind (Scheler, 1926, p. 363; italics omitted).

Thus Scheler comes far closer than Mannheim to locating something like the objective nucleus of all interpreting. But he does not use the "resistance" of the external or objective world to conceptualize a transcendance of the relativism from which he suffered just as Mannheim did. For the failure to answer the question of the number and nature of approaches to the world or of the difference between the world interpreted and not interpreted means to be caught in relativism ("the world is the sum-total of its interpretations," that is to say, "the world is what I interpret it to be") even as does the failure to go beyond validity as relative validity only.

In his analysis of the sociology of knowledge, on the other hand, Scheler describes his effort to overcome relativism as follows: We escape relativism, he writes,

by hanging up, as it were, the sphere of absolute ideas and values, which corresponds to the essential idea of man, enormously [*ganz gewaltig*] much higher above all actual hitherto existing historical value systems . . . , preserving nothing but the idea of eternal, objective logos, to penetrate whose overwhelming mysteries . . . is not given to one nation, one culture area, one or all hitherto extant cultural epochs, but only to all of them together, including the future ones . . . (Scheler, 1924, p. 26; italics omitted; cf. Scheler, 1980, pp. 41-42).

But this does not appear to be a solution of the problem of relativism because it postpones the solution to the end of time when there is nobody left to undertake it. Scheler *hangs* the logos, and literally "violently much higher" (even though *"gewaltig,"* a term much used by Scheler, colloquially means no more than "very much" or "enormous" or "mighty" and no doubt is here so intended by him), thus saving it from relativization.[6] That is, Scheler preserves the spirit-in-itself, non-relativized, uninterpreted, by moving it out of reach — but the "hanging" and "violently much higher" suggest salvation by killing; which may shock us into associating his procedure with the "liberation" of a Vietnamese village by blasting it off the map.

In contrast, Mannheim admitted not to have found a solution to the problem of relativism. In what is probably his last statement on the issue, he wrote:

> . . . I want to break through the old epistemology radically but have not succeeded yet fully. But the latter is not one man's work. I think our whole generation will have to work on it as nothing is more obvious than that we transcended in every field the idea that man's mind is equal to an absolute Ratio in favour of a theory that we think on the basis of changing frames of reference, the elaboration of which is one of the most exciting tasks of the near future . . .[7]

In their very different ways, thus, the two founders of the sociology of knowledge confronted the problem of relativism (epistemological and what might be called axiological) and suffered from the incapacity to overcome it. It should be stressed that to confront this problem is a great deal more than to deny or ignore it, which is a judgment hardly found in most of the facile attacks on Mannheim. As not only the late letter shows, Mannheim was aware of his failure and suffered from it, whereas Scheler seems to have been less concerned or believed, perhaps, that he had solved the problem, possibly in the fashion here presented, which, however, is less a solution than something like a frantic disposal of it.

V

We asked earlier what it would mean to account for the fact that Mannheim could fail to recognize the difference between methodological and epistemological relativism. We mentioned two senses (there are more) in which an answer might be given, psychological and sociological. The sociological sense we now wish to consider is suggested by the observation that despite their intelligence and knowledge, Mannheim and Scheler failed to overcome the relativism into which their very intelligence and sensitivity had drawn them. For had they been more securely rooted in intellectual and moral tradition than they were—Scheler in particular espoused several traditions in the course of his relatively short and hectic life—they would not have had to face up to relativism in the first place, and shipwreck on it.

The sociologically interesting question thus suggested is not what *in their lives* drove them to confront and fail to resolve it but what current of the time in which they lived swept these talented men to their untenable positions. We cannot hope to give more than a tentative answer.

Its clue comes from the Marxian component in the origin of the sociology of knowledge or, to use a single and not quite unambiguous word, from
the unmasking element in its origin, which entered its conceptualization in
both Mannheim and Scheler, though in different ways. The discovery that
the autonomy of the mind was at least problematic can surely be shattering,
and it was a discovery made in two variants at about the same time—that
of sociological self-delusion (the sociology of knowledge, going back to Marx
and further to Hegel) and that of psychic self-delusion (Freud). One more
tradition or received idea, that of the autonomous mind, of autonomous
reason, had to be revised, and it was not clear how to revise it, whether, in
fact, it could be saved at all or had actually been destroyed beyond all
revisability, for what revisability there might beckon might be no more than
yet another illusion. It is against this intellectually and emotionally ominous
horizon that I suggest to consider the previously mentioned controversy over
the sociology of knowledge—practically, Mannheim's sociology of knowledge—that took place in Germany in the late 20s and early 30s.

VI

One way of reading the idea of "surrender-and-catch" is to take it as a response to relativism. The characteristic which connects it with several otherwise different conceptions of the world, including the sociology of knowledge,
is the demand to make conscious what has happened historically: the need
for revising received notions; and to meet this need by suspending, and
thus testing in the extreme situation of surrender, as many received notions
as is humanly possible—what "humanly possible" means depends on, is up
to, the individual human being. The "catch" is the yield, result, harvest
of the surrender.

The idea of surrender-and-catch flows from the *experience* of suspending
received notions. It builds on this experience, rather than fearing to be invalidated by it—and for the surrenderer to be destroyed by it. It takes the
problematic character of traditional orientations and their institutions seriously by realizing and affirming that the self alone is left as a source of
truth, theoretical and practical.

In such trust in the self, the idea of surrender-and-catch rediscovers the
received distinction between the empirical and the transcendental subject.
But it rediscovers it in the face of its own historical situation which is characterized not only by relativism and the failure to overcome it but also by
two most important unprecedented features which only *seem* unrelated to
the emergence and fate of relativism: the shrinkage and the endangerment
of the earth, our habitat. The idea of surrender-and-catch defines the human

being as that transcendental subject which can surrender and catch—which can catch that which is true, though changeable by a new catch. But such relativity to the catch does not mean relativism; it means the opposite. For the capacity to surrender-and-catch is universal among human beings; every catch therefore bears this mark of its universal provenience and thus can be translated into every other. The idea of surrender-and-catch comes up at this juncture in history as the *absolute* in the sense of the universal, namely, as that characteristic which is emerging as the feature among all features common to human beings which is to be entertained as historically relevant. At the same time and in the same process, the idea of surrender-and-catch also appears as the *access to the absolute*, that is, to that truth, theoretical and practical, which is universal because all its experiential modes are intersubjectively translatable.

VII

To make the view of the relation between the idea of surrender-and-catch and the sociology of knowledge which is here being articulated more intelligible, it helps to mention earlier phases of its development. That is, an autobiographical note must be inserted which concerns, however, the author not as a private or empirical person but only as the instrument of a developing conception, thus as a transcendental subject, to recall the distinction pointed to earlier.[8]

In the Foreword to this book, I comment, on several occasions, that instead of "sociology of knowledge" we might also say "surrender-and-catch."[9]

VIII

In Chapter 8, my last stocktaking of the relation between surrender and the sociology of knowledge before the present one, I end up (p. 196) with the sketch, certainly minimal and vague, of a vast area of research designed to lead to social change for the improvement of the human lot. The reading of the sociology of knowledge here presented, focusing on the problem of relativism, like the reading of the idea of surrender-and-catch, derives from a reading of our time. Two readings may be distinguished as two responses to this time. Surrender-and-catch is a protest against it and an attempt at remembrance of what a human being can be. The sociology of knowledge is a protest against its hypocrisy and against unexamined social influences. Like surrender, the sociology of knowledge does not fear but passionately seeks what is true and thus, like surrender, is a remembrance, proclamation, and celebration of the spirit. Both ideas, that of the sociology of knowledge and that of surrender, are critical, polemical, radical (Wolff, 1977; Ludes, 1977); so is the sociology of knowledge also in its practice, while in its practice surrender is cognitive love. Using a previously mentioned distinction developed by Mannheim, we may also say that the sociology of knowledge is an extrinsic interpretation of its time, our time; surrender, an intrinsic one: the former is, advocates, and practices such an extrinsic (sociological) interpretation but needs the latter to overcome the relativism it encounters in its practice by its remembrance, rediscovery, reinvention, the catch, of what is common to all human beings, what is universally human.

NOTES

1. The most important contributions centered on Karl Mannheim, especially (but not exclusively) his *Ideologie und Utopie* (1929). They have recently been collected by Volker Meja and Nico Stehr (1982); a shorter version in English is promised by Routledge & Kegan Paul.

2. Aside from the very useful preface by one of its two translators, Louis Wirth (Wirth, 1936), the English version also contains an introduction written by Mannheim for the occasion and a 1931 encyclopedia article on the sociology of knowledge, published originally two years after *Ideologie und Utopie*. Cf. Mannheim, 1936.

3. For somewhat more detail, see p. 208 above.

4. See Mannheim's 1946 letter, pp. 202-204 above. (This letter was written 21 years later, a few months before his death.)

5. Cf. Lundberg, 1936, pp. 708, criticized by MacIver (1942) 1964, pp. 157-158, n. 24.

6. My thanks to Rainer E. Koehne for calling my attention many years ago to this surely unintended pun of *"gewaltig."*

7. See pp. 203-205 above.

8. For a more detailed autobiographical presentation of the shaping of the relation between the sociology of knowledge and surrender, see the Foreword to this book above.

9. See esp. pp. iv-v, but also 195-196, above.

BIBLIOGRAPHY

Ludes, Peter, 1977, "The Radicalness of Surrender: Reflections on a Significant Concept." *Sociological Analysis*, 38:402-408.

Lundberg, George A., 1936, "The Thoughtways of Contemporary Sociology." *American Sociological Review*, 1: 703-723.

MacIver, Robert M. (1942), *Social Causation*. New York: Harper Torchbooks, 1964.

Mannheim, Karl, 1925, "The Problem of a Sociology of Knowledge." In Mannheim, 1971, pp. 59-115.

Mannheim, Karl, 1926, "The Ideological and the Sociological Interpretation of Intellectual Phenomena." In Mannheim, 1971, pp. 116-132.

Mannheim, Karl, 1929, *Ideologie und Utopie*. Bonn: Cohen.

Mannheim, Karl, 1936, *Ideology and Utopia*. Trans. Louis Wirth and Edward Shils. Preface by Louis Wirth. New York: Harcourt, Brace.

Mannheim, Karl, 1971, *From Karl Mannheim*. Ed. and with an introd. by Kurt H. Wolff. New York: Oxford University Press.

Meja, Volker, and Stehr, Nico, ed. and introd. 1982. *Der Streit um die Wissenssoziologie*. 2 vols. Frankfurt: Suhrkamp.

Scheler, Max, 1924, "Probleme einer Soziologie des Wissens." In *Die Wissensformen und die Gesellschaft, Gesammelte Werke, Band 8*, ed. Maria Scheler. Bern und Munchen: Francke, 1960.

Scheler, Max, 1926, "Erkenntnis und Arbeit." In *Die Wissensformen und die Gesellschaft, Gesammelte Werke, Band 8*, ed. Maria Scheler. Bern und Munchen: Francke, 1960.

Scheler, Max, 1980, *Problems of a Sociology of Knowledge*. Trans. Manfred S. Frings, ed. and with an introd. Kenneth W. Stikkers. London, etc.: Routledge & Kegan Paul.

Wirth, Louis, 1936, Preface. In Mannheim, 1936.

Wolff, Kurt H., 1977, "Toward Understanding the Radicalness of Surrender." *Sociological Analysis*, 38:397-401.

This chapter has not been published before.

INDEX*

*Foreword and notes have not been indexed.

48,966

© THE BAKER & TAYLOR CO.